The Faith that Works

The Relationship of Faith and Works in the Theology of Juan Luis Segundo, S.J.

Michael Hoy

University Press of America, Inc.
Lanham • New York • London

Copyright© 1995 by
University Press of America,® Inc.
4720 Boston Way
Lanham, Maryland 20706

3 Henrietta Street
London, WC2E 8LU England

Library of Congress Cataloging-in-Publication Data

Hoy, Michael, 1953-
The faith that works : the relationship of faith and works in the
theology of Juan Luis Segundo, S.J. / Michael Hoy.
p.   cm.
Includes bibliographical references and index.
1. Segundo, Juan Luis.   2. Faith--History of doctrines--20th
century. 3. Liberation theology. 4. Catholic Church--Doctrines-
History--20th century.   I. Title.
BT771 .2.H69   1995
230' .2 ' 092--dc20   94-40688 CIP

ISBN 0-8191-9814-5 (cloth: alk paper)

For

DAWN, MARTIN, PHILIP, *and* KATIE

who continue to liberate me

iii

Contents

Abbreviations   vii

Preface   ix

Acknowledgements   xiii

Introduction   xv

Faith that Works

Chapter 1   **Juan Luis Segundo's Theology of "Faith"**   1
                 and "Faith's Works"

Chapter 2   **Biblical Hermeneutics, Revelation,**   31
                 and Pauline Theology

v

The Faith that Works in Dispute

Chapter 3   Segundo's Theology in the Context of   73
             Contemporary Catholic and Protestant
             Theology

Chapter 4   Segundo and Luther on "Faith" and   113
             "Faith's Works"

Foundations for the Faith that Works

Chapter 5   The Inherent Problems in Segundo's   143
             Theological Presuppositions

Conclusion   Toward Dialogue on the Relationship   171
             Between "Faith" and "Faith's Works"

Appendix   The Life and Works of   175
             Juan Luis Segundo, S.J.
             (from 1925 to 1994)

Notes   181

Bibliography   237

Index   255

Abbreviations

All works cited here and in the notes without explicit reference to author are written by Juan Luis Segundo, S.J. For complete bibliographical data on all works, see the Bibliography. Abbreviations of most commonly used sources are listed below.

BoC	Tappert, ed., The Book of Concord.
Church	The Community Called Church.
ET	English translation.
Evolutionary Approach	An Evolutionary Approach to Jesus of Nazareth.
Fe e Ideología	El hombre de hoy ante Jesús de Nazarét, Tomo I, Fe e Ideología.
Función	Función de la Iglesia en la realidad rioplatense.
Gracia	Gracia y condición humana.
Grace	Grace and the Human Condition.
Hidden Motives	The Hidden Motives of Pastoral Action: Latin American Reflections.
Iglesia	Esa comunidad llamada Iglesia.
Las cristologías	El hombre de hoy ante Jesús de Nazarét, Tomo II/2, História y actualidad: Las cristologías en la espiritualidad.

Liberación	Liberación de la teología.
Liberation	The Liberation of Theology.
LW	Luther, Luther's Works.
Masas y minorías	Masas y minorías en la dialéctica divina de la liberación.
Paul	The Humanist Christology of Paul.
Sinópticos y Pablo	El hombre de hoy ante Jesús de Nazarét, Tomo II/1, Historía y acutalidad: Sinópticos y Pablo.
Theology and the Church	Theology and the Church: A Response to Cardinal Ratzinger and a Warning to the Whole Church.
WA	D. Martin Luthers Werke (Weimar, 1908).

Preface

This text is an analysis of the theology of Juan Luis Segundo, S.J., on the relationship of faith and works. It first appeared as my doctoral dissertation in 1990. My dissertation topic was sparked by an essay presented by my good friend and mentor of many years, Robert W. Bertram, at the "Liberation: Common Hope in a Complex Hemisphere" Conference in Seguin, Texas (February, 1984).[1] More than any other individual, Bertram has helped me to recognize the mutually affirming and radicalizing contributions that the theology of Luther and liberation theology bring to each other.

My doctoral advisor, Carl E. Braaten, encouraged me to pursue Segundo's theology as a subject worthy of further study, especially in the light of Lutheran confessional theology. I am grateful for his willingness to take me on as an advisee, for his guidance and direction, and for his friendly encouragement in the long and difficult process of writing my dissertation.

Since the completion of my dissertation, two additional texts have been published by Segundo. In The Liberation of Dogma, Segundo seeks to uphold the liberating dynamic of revelation and faith.[2] Signs of the Times is a collection of some of Segundo's most significant essays, many of which have never before been translated.[3] I have made an effort to incorporate some of these latest works by Segundo into this manuscript.

In mid-May, 1987, I wrote my first letter to Segundo. The letter was perhaps typical of a naive graduate student. I had written to request a complete copy of Segundo's bibliography, explaining my graduate project as an examination of his theology vis-à-vis the concept of "justification by faith." Segundo's response, dated August 4 of that year, was both humbling and encouraging. He regretted that he could not meet my request due to the *lack* of resources at his disposal--"*sin biblioteca, ni personal de secretaría.*" (It is to Segundo's enduring credit that he can be so prolific even while working under such limiting conditions!) Nevertheless, he thanked me for my interest in his thought and, as he phrased it, "*por uno de esos temas que siempre me han interesado: el de la justificación por la fe.*"

I regret that Segundo and I have not had the opportunity to meet face to face. I cherish the courtesy and friendship that Segundo has extended in our very occasional correspondence since 1987. As a North American (let alone a white male) who has studied liberation theology in depth, and Segundo's theology in particular, I cannot help but be repentant for the oppression of the poor in the southern hemisphere. To hear that call to repentance in the light of God's promising Gospel, it seems to me, is the basis for truly meaningful dialogue between those of us from different places, experiences, and traditions.

One final word is in order. It perhaps belongs equally well in the conclusion, but I state it here as a prefatory remark. Segundo offers a beautiful statement that places our feeble accomplishments in the service of the glory of God.

> The glory of God and the defense of the Absolute do not entail relativizing historical reality in order to make room for the irruption of God alone. The glory of God means seriously making human beings sharers in a joint construction project and giving them all they need to offer this cooperation, without which God will do nothing. The personal, creative stamp of each one of these human cooperators (*synergoi* in Greek) with God will be tested and verified in love, in "mutual service." Then it will be inserted in the definitive reality, in the only way that a finite freedom can do that: i.e., by hammering away, like a chisel of a sculptor, at the stubborn solidity of the resistant materials, but with the invisible hope that those materials will be overcome and to some extent turned into God's new heaven and humanity's new earth, the new creation as the joint work of Father and children.[4]

I affirm Segundo's emphasis that human beings are concrete cooperators in the kingdom of God. I am also sensitive to Segundo's contextual and polemical struggle in which this claim is made. This does not mean that we are in agreement on all points. Nevertheless,

I hope that my own chiseling efforts in this text have helped to enhance the dialogue for liberation and in that way the kingdom of God might better be served. So I affirm, and with all boldness: *soli Deo gloria!*

Michael Hoy
Capital University
September 29, 1994

Acknowledgements

I am extremely grateful for the supportive role of my readers, including Carl Braaten, Robert Bertram, Kurt Hendel, Wilhelm Linss, and José Davíd Rodriguez. These faculty at the Lutheran School of Theology at Chicago helped to provide an interdisciplinary theological reading of my work.

I wish to acknowledge the following persons and institutions for their assistance in tracking down several relatively inaccessible sources and articles by Juan Luis Segundo, either by pointing me in the right direction or by obtaining copies: Alfred T. Hennelly, Anthony J. Tambasco, Elvire Hilgert and the staff of the Jesuit-Kraus-McCormick library, Curt LeMay and the staff of the University of Wisconsin-Marathon Center library, the staff of Regenstein library at the University of Chicago, and the Marathon County Library, Wausau, Wisconsin.

I wish to thank Angie Williams, the primary editor of this manuscript, and the editors at University Press of America. I am deeply grateful for the valuable assistance of Doris Goodnough of Orbis Books. I also express profound thanks for the support of the faculty, staff and students at Capital University in seeing me through to the completion of this project.

I have sought to use existing English translations of original texts whenever possible. However, I accept responsibility for the translations that appear in this text.

Every effort has been made to secure proper copyright. Special acknowledgment is given here to the following publishers for permission to use copyrighted material:

xiv

Introduction

Liberating the Poor

"Liberation Theology" has to do with the liberation of those who have been oppressed sociologically, politically, economically, and theologically. It has three distinct forms today: the liberation of "minorities" (as evidenced especially in Black, or Afro-American, theology), the liberation of women, and the liberation of the so-called "third world."[5]

The Forms of Liberation Theology

The origins of black theology are traced to three principal events:

1. the civil rights movement of the 1950's-1960's, largely associated with Martin Luther King, Jr.; 2. the publication of Joseph Washington's Black Religion (1964); 3. the rise of the black power movement, strongly influenced by Malcolm X's philosophy of black nationalism.[6]

The liberation movement of Afro-Americans did not arise in the halls of academe, but "in the context of black people's struggle for racial justice."[7] Martin Luther King's efforts to bring the Christian gospel

to bear on that struggle for justice led to further investigation into the
roots of religious heritage that reached back well into the previous
century.[8] Joseph Washington's <u>Black Religion</u> was the first principal
text to contend for the religious values of black history and culture;
however, it was criticized by the black church for promoting the
philosophy "(1) that black religion is not Christian and thus has no
Christian theology; (2) that the Christian gospel has nothing to do with
the struggle for justice in society."[9] The "Black Power" movement,
under the leadership of Malcolm X, "consciously separated their
understanding of the gospel of Jesus from white Christianity and
identified it with the struggles of the black poor for justice."[10] The
early works by James H. Cone are considered the truly formative
writings of black liberation theology.[11] Since the early 1970's, black
theology has begun to discover its deeper relationship with other
liberation movements.   Black theologians recognize that they are
"partners in their identification of the gospel with the liberation of the
poor," and also affirm the rise of "black feminist theology."[12]

Feminist theology has its most distinctive origin in the late 1960's,
evidenced in the writings of K.E. Børrensen, Mary Daly, and
Rosemary Radford Ruether.[13]   Ruether, however, traces this
movement back as far as the pioneer efforts of Margaret Fell in a tract
entitled, <u>Women's Speaking Justified, Approved and Allowed of by the
Scriptures</u> (1667).[14] All feminist theologians affirm as their agenda
"the criticism of the masculinist bias of Christian theology."[15]
However, feminists are divided on their approach toward a second
agenda: "the discovery of alternative historical traditions supportive of
the full personhood of woman and her inclusion in leadership in church
and society."[16] Some, like Mary Daly, call for the abolition of the
Judeo-Christian tradition.   Others, including Ruether and Elisabeth
Schüssler Fiorenza, argue for the redefinition of the Judeo-Christian
tradition and its symbols to be inclusive of women.[17] In spite of these
internal differences, feminist theology is raising the consciousness of
women on a world-wide scale.[18]

Liberation theology has had a variety of distinctive expressions in
countries that are often classified (without seeking to be pejorative) as
the "third world"--Latin America, Asia and Africa.[19] "Third world"
liberation theology finds its distinctive point of origin in the mid-
1960's; but its roots are traceable to Bartolomé de Las Casas and his
efforts to liberate natives (1514).[20] The primary element of this form
of liberation theology is the "liberation of all forms of human

oppression: social, economic, political, racial, sexual, environmental, religious."[21] "Third world" liberation theology also insists "that theology be truly indigenous."[22] One can readily see how these elements would be inclusive of Afro-American and feminist liberation movements.

Latin American liberation theology is the most widely publicized of the "third world" movements. It received its initial impetus through the decrees of Vatican II, and "virtually exploded between the meetings of Latin America bishops at Medellín, Columbia, in 1968, and Puebla, Mexico, in 1979."[23] The groundbreaking text of Gustavo Gutiérrez, Teología de la liberación (1971; ET: 1973) is "hailed as the Magna Carta of liberation theology."[24] Other prominent Latin American theologians include Juan Luis Segundo, Rubem Alves, Leonardo Boff, Clodovis Boff, Hugo Assmann, José Porfirio Miranda, José Míguez Bonino, Jon Sobrino, José Comblin, Segundo Galilea, and Enrique Dussel. While most have been educated in European schools, their indigenous approach to the conditions that they experienced in Latin America has both "similarities and convergences."[25] Nevertheless, they are united in times of trial.[26]

Juan Luis Segundo, S.J., Liberation Theologian

The particular focus of this study is on the theology of Jesuit priest Juan Luis Segundo, one of the most prolific of the Latin American liberation theologians. Segundo was born on March 31, 1925, in Montevideo, Uruguay. He entered the Society of Jesus in 1941, and studied philosophy at the Jesuit seminary in San Miguel, Argentina. In 1951, he began his theological studies in Eegenhoven, Louvain, in Belgium. He was ordained a priest in 1955, and earned a licentiate in theology in 1956 and a doctorate of letter from the University of Paris in 1963. In 1965, he founded and directed the Peter Faber Center, and initiated the publication of Perspectivas de Diálogo in 1966. He continued to serve as director of the Peter Faber Center until it was closed by the Uruguayan government in 1975, the same year in which his ecclesiastical superiors suppressed the publication Perspectivas. He taught at several universities, including the Harvard Divinity School (1974) and the University of Chicago Divinity School (1978). Since 1959, he has been residing in Montevideo, Uruguay, where he carries on his pastoral and teaching duties.[27]

One noted scholar of Segundo's writings, Alfred T. Hennelly, has paid Segundo the compliment of being "the most profound and creative theologian now working in the Catholic Church--and arguably in the world."[28] Be that as it may, we must not understand "theologians" in any traditional, European sense. Segundo is "one of those 'spare-time theologians,' to borrow Gutiérrez's terminology, who have collaborated on the creation of Latin American theology."[29] Segundo defines "theologians" as those who are "involved in commitment, ours and others', who seek light from faith at the same time that we rethink faith from that commitment."[30]

For Segundo, theology is done for the purpose of liberating the poor. It is a theology that is "more interested in *being liberative* than in *talking about liberation*."[31] This conforms to Gutiérrez's understanding of liberation theology as that which "offers not so much a new theme for reflection as a *new way* to do theology," namely, "critical reflection on historical praxis."[32] Segundo regards "being sensitive to *our* oppression" as a helpful beginning point for theological reflection.[33] Through such sensitivity we can grow in our awareness of the sufferings of others who are oppressed. While Segundo's writings seek to address the oppression in his Latin American context, the valuable English translations of John Drury come as an appeal to North Americans to "understand the situation" in Latin America, and to "recognize how increasingly desperate it is."[34] Segundo's primary concern, as we will demonstrate, is a pastoral one for the poor of Latin America who need hope and promise in their lives. Therefore, it has been properly acknowledged that liberation theology "is *not* the voice of the poor. It is a bridge *to* the poor."[35]

The "Key" to Segundo's Theology

One of the difficulties in analyzing Segundo's theology is that it does not fit into a neat "systematic" package. Given Segundo's desire not only to do liberation theology, but to liberate theology as well, this should come as no surprise.[36] What is the best way to present Segundo's theology? If we may borrow a phrase from Segundo, what is his *hermeneutical "key"*?[37] There are at least three "keys" that have been offered and are worthy of examination here.

A common "key" that is used to interpret Latin American liberation theology as a whole is the concept of "Marxist praxis."[38] It is sometimes asserted that because of this influence of Marxist praxis, liberation theology must be rejected. Carl Braaten, for example, argues that Marxist praxis has made liberation theology "a mere ideology of the left just as the traditional dogmatic theology became, in the eyes of liberation theologians, the unselfconscious reflection of the ideology of the right."[39] Braaten considers this a "danger" to Christian theology, a "Trojan horse inside the walls."[40] Such an analytic interpretation of liberation theology, however, is a misrepresentation. Liberation theologians, of course, are not unfamiliar with Marx. All of them do (or at least did at one time) call for some form of socialism as the required socio-political option in the face of the injustice that capitalism has brought to Latin America.[41] Segundo, therefore, will claim that "the sensibility of the left is an intrinsic feature of an authentic theology."[42] It is important to understand what Segundo means here by "left." He understands the "right" as the "status quo"; and he defines the "left" very generally as "the conquest of that which is still without form, of that which is still unrealized, of that which is still in a state of utopia."[43] Segundo, however, states that the "most famous theologians in Latin America have nothing more than a polite relationship with Marxism."[44] The most extreme case of association with Marxism may perhaps be found in the writings of José Porfirio Miranda. But even Miranda is "not a Marxist ideologue, accepting without question the gospel of Karl Marx and Marx's self-proclaimed, latter-day disciples."[45] Even Michael Novak, who is no friend of liberation theology, states that "liberation theology forms a tapestry much broader than its Marxist part and is woven of many colors."[46]

A more accurate depiction of Segundo's "key" is the influence of Pierre Teilhard de Chardin. Craig Nessan has accurately reported that Segundo develops Teilhard's evolutionary categories in the interpretation of "Scripture, Christian doctrine, and history itself."[47] This Teilhardian influence is readily apparent in several of Segundo's works.[48] Nessan concludes: "It is this evolutionary understanding of history inspired by Teilhard which provides the hermeneutical key for understanding the praxis orientation of Segundo throughout his many writings."[49] However, Nessan fails to note that Teilhard is critically appropriated by Segundo. In other words, Nessan disregards the fact that Segundo is eclectic. Segundo incorporates other ideas into his analysis of "evolution," including those of "the British anthropologist and philosopher of science, Gregory Bateson."[50] Segundo is also keenly aware of the seriousness of Paul's concept of sin in Romans, which was a characteristic weakness in Teilhard's perspective.[51]

Furthermore, there are many elements that are interwoven in Segundo's
theology, including phenomenology, dialectical philosophy,
transcendental philosophy, and apophatic ontology (all from Nicholas
Berdyaev), French existentialism (Sartre, Camus), psychology (Freud,
Fromm), sociological analysis (Marx, Machoveč), as well as
evolutionary cosmology (Teilhard, Bateson).[52] The Teilhardian,
"evolutionary" perspective of history is only *part* of Segundo's
wonderful complexity as a thinker, but it is not the most essential part.

> It is more accurate . . . to say that he [Segundo] is primarily interested
> in carrying on a dialogue with all the major currents of contemporary
> thought, selecting ideas or illustrations from them for approving use,
> while at the same time summarily rejecting concepts or approaches with
> which he disagrees.[53]

In the final chapter of this text, we will see how Teilhard's
"evolutionary" concepts are intertwined with Segundo's theological
presuppositions, and how this poses inherent problems for Segundo's
central thesis.

Alfred T. Hennelly offers a third proposal for a hermeneutical
"key" to Segundo's theology. Hennelly suggests that we understand
Segundo's thought as an *"open" theology*. "By using this term, I mean
to stress the fact that in his approach methodological principles that
allow for constant growth and development take precedence over a
systematic organized body of theological content."[54] Hennelly,
therefore, explores a number of "themes" in Segundo's theology: faith,
ecclesiology, sacraments, biblical hermeneutics, ideology, spirituality,
and socialism.[55] Even here Hennelly alludes to the fact that later in
Segundo's career there might be the possibility of "a quite different
pattern of organization."[56] Hennelly is never quite specific about what
that "pattern of organization" may be, though he later implies the
"faith/ideology dialectic."[57] Hennelly is to be admired for his
tremendous sensitivity and insight into Segundo's theology. His
interpretation of Segundo may be the best to date, and it has been able
to commend itself favorably to Segundo.[58] Nevertheless, the
unresolved difficulty with Hennelly's interpretation is that it is not
explicit about how all these "themes" are held together.

The best answer to Segundo's "key" may come from Segundo
himself. At the Peter Faber Center, Segundo was responsible for
bringing a deepened theological education to laity. At a later time,

Segundo made this candid confession:

> I recall the time in Buenos Aires when I first proposed the idea of my
> five-volume series to my publisher and friend, Carlos Lohlé. I left it up
> to him to choose an overall title for the series, and he came up with
> Teología abierta para el laico adulto ("an open theology for the adult lay
> person"). When I first saw it, I must confess that I did not like it,
> though I did not say anything. After all, he was my friend and he was
> risking his money in the maddest venture to be found in today's world:
> publishing theology. But then, as time went on, I began to realize there
> was profound wisdom in his title. Perhaps, after all, those books were
> successfully managing to avoid being consumer theology precisely insofar
> as they were addressed *to lay people* rather than to theologians; insofar
> as they were trying to *open up paths* rather than provide systematic
> solutions; insofar as they offered a method more than a body of content;
> insofar as they did not prompt people to stop theologizing because *in
> them people could find valid answers to presumably general problems.*[59]

The concern for opening not just concepts but "paths" and "answers"
for the laity would be reflected again in the title of Segundo's three-
volume "christology": "The human being of today before Jesus of
Nazareth" (*El hombre de hoy ante Jesús de Nazarét*).[60] Regardless of
how successful Segundo was in bringing "Jesus of Nazareth" to bear on
the lives of contemporary men and women,[61] it is Segundo's *goal* here
that may well provide the best "key" to his thought. Segundo is
seeking to bring the consolation of the gospel to bear on the very
"faith-in-crisis" in Latin America.[62] The hermeneutic "key" to
Segundo's theology is, therefore, what Segundo himself regards as "the
most important task," namely, "*evangelization: getting faith to reach
people as 'good news.'*"[63]

"Evangelization" is so important to Segundo because people in
Latin America are not receiving the promising Word.

> The first and gravest defect that I see in evangelization is that it doesn't
> exist. It's confused with wanting Christianity to be accepted, but
> authentic evangelization doesn't take place. After establishing that it
> doesn't take place in Latin America, it would be interesting to ask why.
> One thing that shows there's no evangelization is that nobody identifies
> the gospel, the faith, and belonging to the church with good news, with
> great joy. And if Christianity isn't joy, it isn't Christianity, it isn't
> gospel.[64]

Segundo suspects that a "three-fold fearfulness" in the church's pastoral leadership is at the base of the problem.[65] First, "we are fearful for ourselves." Pastoral leaders are unable to risk the insecurity of making a bold witness, to move beyond the "material means of support."[66] Second, "we are fearful for the salvation of the masses." There is a greater attempt in the institutional pastoral praxis to protect the masses and avoid anything that would disturb the status quo.[67] Third, "we are fearful for the gospel." Church leadership tends to ally itself with the power bases of society, and to conform to the pressures of society in providing special services as the basis for the Church's existence, rather than seeing the gospel as power enough for the Church's life.[68]

The remedy of "evangelization" that Segundo offers follows Seumois' "three elements that go to make up authentic kerygma."[69] The first element is "communicating only the essentials of the Christian message." The central concern in this element is to "shift from exerting pressure on people to relying on the liberty of adults and respecting that liberty." Thus pastoral activity must approach the task of evangelization realistically, and get to the point more quickly.[70]

The second element is "communicating it as good news."[71] This involves "two practical consequences." The first practical consequence is an intentional "listening" in the form of "a friendly and thoroughgoing sharing of the life with the non-Christian. It must entail a shared historical sensitivity, shared commitments, and the recognition of the human values that the non-Christian holds and cultivates. This recognition, in turn, must be fleshed out in deeds."[72] The second practical consequence is to translate the good news into a language that the people can understand. In Segundo's situation, that means finding a message that brings consolation to people suffering from the "characteristic anxiety" of proffering their love in an effort that seems to be in vain.[73] Thus, Segundo suggests a new "formula": "No love is lost on this earth,"[74] or "love is worth the trouble" (*el amor vale la pena*).[75] "The Son of God (who is love) loved us to the end and died; but his love did not perish, and we express that belief by bearing witness to his resurrection."[76]

The third element in an authentic kerygma is "adding nothing further except at a pace that will allow the essential element to remain precisely that."[77] Patience is an evangelical virtue that allows people to have the necessary time to make the truth their own. "We must stop fearing the freedom of our listeners because only through the exercise of their freedom can the gospel message become a truly personal conviction giving direction to their whole life."[78]

Segundo seeks to bring "good news to the poor" (Luke 4:18). Hennelly, therefore, may have come closest in discerning Segundo's hermeneutical "key" when referring to "an *underlying pastoral orientation* that pervades most of his [Segundo's] published work."[79] But we want to be more explicit about the matter. Segundo sustains "sensitive hearts" by keeping them rooted in the promising Word: "your faith has saved you."[80] Because of that emphasis, Segundo may indeed be one of "the most profound and creative" theologians today.

Some Remarks on Method and Format

The analysis of Segundo's theology that follows utilizes largely an internal method. Liberation theology is a controversial subject. Our efforts here do not seek to diminish the "hard sayings and basic challenges" of liberation theology.[81] Segundo's theology is presented in the light of his own argument and sources; but he is also held accountable to his argument and sources. This method involves a dialogue between Segundo and his sources on the theological issues that he is raising.

The format of this analysis develops Segundo's central thesis in keeping with his evangelical concern. Segundo underscores the relationship of "faith" to "life with its commitments."[82] In short, Segundo is fostering a "faith that works." The first chapter highlights the distinctive features of Segundo's theological enterprise (ecclesiology and the "faith/ideology" dialectic) and demonstrates how they convey a central thesis: *"faith" and "faith's works" need to be distinguished, but they cannot be separated.* In chapter two, this central thesis is demonstrated to be continuous with Segundo's own understanding of the biblical tradition, especially St. Paul. Furthermore, an examination of exegetical sources validates Segundo's thesis.

Chapter three examines and confirms Segundo's critical appraisal of contemporary Catholic and Protestant theologies on the basis of his central thesis. Chapter four then turns to Segundo's critical appraisal of Luther's theology. This chapter notes that Segundo misunderstood the gospel-centered, Pauline emphasis in Luther's theology that makes Luther a radicalizing ally. Luther actually has more in common with Segundo's central thesis than Segundo himself realizes. The difference between Luther and Segundo is in their presuppositions. This leads to the considerations of the final chapter, where Segundo's theological foundations, or presuppositions, are examined. Ultimately, those presuppositions are demonstrated to be contradictory to the theology of Paul, and pose serious inherent difficulties for Segundo's own theology.

Chapter 1
Faith that Works: Part One

Juan Luis Segundo's Theology of "Faith" and "Faith's Works"

The two most predominant emphases in Segundo's theology are ecclesiology and the "faith/ideology" dialectic. The ecclesiological emphasis is dominant early in Segundo's thought. A number of facts may be cited to warrant this claim. Segundo's first major work in what could be considered Latin American theology was a text on ecclesiology, published in 1962.[83] Second, Segundo's two-volume doctoral dissertation under Paul Ricouer was an "analysis of the authentic meaning of the church in history."[84] Third, the first major series of texts put out by Segundo, in collaboration with the Peter Faber Center, was related to themes having to do with the valuable place of the church in history.[85] Furthermore, the first volume in this series is a work on ecclesiology.[86] Ecclesiology is also the central emphasis of a text published in the early 1970's.[87] It is no wonder that one noted scholar of Segundo's writings maintains that "ecclesiology is a central concern" in Segundo's theology--"perhaps the major one in all his writings."[88]

The "faith/ideology" dialectic was a later development in Segundo's thought, finding its first clear expression in the mid-1970's.

Evidence of a rudimentary expression of this dialectic appears in 1973.[89] Segundo's explicit use of "faith/ideology" dialectic, however, first appeared in 1974 in an article published in Perspectivas de Diálogo, the journal of the Peter Faber Center.[90] Segundo then expounded on the "faith/ideology" dialectic in the lectures that he delivered at Harvard Divinity School in 1974 and published in 1975.[91] Seven years later, Segundo released his three-volume work, El hombre de hoy ante Jesús de Nazarét (The Human Being of Today before Jesus of Nazareth).[92] This multi-volume work is often catalogued as Segundo's christology, but it really seeks to expand Segundo's understanding of the dialectic of "faith and ideologies" in the New Testament and church history, including the contemporary situation of the church.[93] Segundo's major strides in developing the "faith/ideology" dialectic have earned him the proper respect as "the most methodologically sophisticated of the liberation theologians."[94]

Given these two major emphases in Segundo's thought, the question may be posed: what is the point of relationship between ecclesiology and the "faith/ideology" dialectic? The answer to that question is the central focus for this chapter. We will contend that the "faith/ideology" dialectic is directly correlated with Segundo's ecclesiology and that the underlying basis for that correlation may be formulated as follows: *"faith" and "faith's works" need to be distinguished, but they cannot be separated.*

This chapter consists of three sections. The first section focuses on Segundo's understanding of the "faith/ideology" dialectic. The second section examines Segundo's understanding of the church. The third section elucidates concepts in Segundo's theology that help provide critical junctures for the correlation of these two emphases.

The title of this chapter indicates that this is the first part on the subject of "faith that works." The second chapter focuses on Segundo's analysis of biblical theology and especially the theology of Paul in Romans. That chapter will demonstrate that the operating thesis in Segundo's theology (*"faith" and "faith's works" need to be distinguished, but they cannot be separated*) is operative in Segundo's understanding of the biblical tradition.

I. The Dialectic of "Faith and Ideologies"

Even though the "faith/ideology" dialectic is a later development in Segundo's thought, it is examined here first because of Segundo's appeal to anthropological phenomenology. Since he does not think a definition adequately captures what he means by this dialectic, he builds his argument on examples from human experience.

The Fundamental Meaning of "Faith" as "Wager"

Segundo is critically suspicious of "a commonly held view" about human experience according to which "human beings are radically divided between those who have 'faith' and those who structure their lives around an 'ideology.'"[95] Segundo maintains that this dichotomizing is an inaccurate portrayal. Furthermore, he argues against the dichotomizing of "faith" in human experience. "Human beings are divided as such into those *without faith* and those *with faith*. I believe that the reality is more complex, or perhaps more simple. In any case, it is different."[96] Faith is a universal anthropological reality.

In presenting his position, Segundo uses the illustration of *Caligula* in the play by Albert Camus. Caligula is portrayed as a figure in deep turmoil.

The problem that torments Caligula is the difficulty that a human being seems to have in attaining *happiness*. Caligula, the Roman emperor, believes that at the end of their lives few human beings have the sensation of being happy; and he thinks this is due to the fact that in practice no one manages to reach the goal he or she has set out for themselves. The question, then, is: Why is this negative balance-sheet on the totality of an individual's existence such a general phenomenon? Caligula's conclusion is one with great logic to it. It is that human beings do not arrive at the goal they set for themselves; and they do not do so because they are distracted on route. They are not sufficiently serious and iron-willed in structuring what they do. Their actions, enticed by secondary aims and ends, are dispersed. The whole problem would be solved if human beings were logical in placing all in the service of the end or goal that they had chosen for their existence as a whole.[97]

With this goal in mind, and with all power at his command, Caligula sets out on a quest to make himself "a universal example of that logic, and to give the gift of happiness to human beings by showing them the path toward the goal."[98] Caligula regards "emotions" as the primary obstacle to the "logic" of happiness, and therefore he sets out on a preliminary venture to be *free*--to rid himself of anything to which he has emotional attachment. "Rights, loyalty, friendship, love: all are sacrificed to that pitiless logic of becoming truly free."[99] But the sad conclusion of Caligula's life is that he does not find happiness, and his life-goal is a dismal failure.

> In destroying his affectivity, Caligula has also destroyed the source of the values that could give meaning to that this freedom. His freedom is now prepared to choose with complete logic, but it no longer has anything to choose; and death comes as an additional sign of this *impasse*. With this iron logic the road to happiness seems more tightly closed than it was before. Caligula has not taken even a single step towards it.[100]

Segundo draws two conclusions from this example. The first, or "direct," conclusion is that life involves choices in the exercise of human freedom. All choices nullify the possibility of other competing choices.[101] However, it is really the second, "indirect" conclusion that Segundo regards as more relevant to the meaning of "faith": "every human being must *risk* existence, or *take a chance* on life. . . . It is not possible for us to go to the end of life in order to see whether it is worth the trouble [*vale la pena*] to realize it, and then, with that certitude [*certidumbre*], return to the beginning in order to attempt such a realization."[102] Faith presupposes the "wager" (*apuesta*) that one's life is worthwhile, that life is worth risking.[103] This is the first, fundamental meaning of "faith."

"Faith" Needs the Verification of Witnesses

In addition to the fundamental meaning of faith as the wager that one's life is worthwhile, faith also requires some kind of verification (*verificación*). In order for someone to claim that life is worthwhile, there is some need for verifying that there is some *value* in life. But where does that value originate? Segundo contends that such values originate from values which others have experienced.

> Experiences of effectively realized values are conveyed to us by our fellow human beings. Before we have these experiences ourselves, we perceive their value and their possibilities for satisfaction in and through the experiences of others. Thus, faced with the necessary limitedness of our lives, we are all dependent on each other.[104]

These "*referential witnesses*," as Segundo calls them, help shape the values that people have.[105] Values cannot exist without them. For example, Segundo points out that when Caligula eliminated all the possible witnesses from his life, he was faced with the ultimate dilemma of a life without value, without meaning.[106]

Segundo develops this concept of "referential witnesses" through an examination of three developmental stages in human life--the young child, the adolescent, and the adult. A young child develops values through the witness of its "parents or educators." The young child may not understand everything about those values, but

> normally it has "faith" in what it perceives. This is the stage when such people as parents or teachers seem to the child to have satisfactory answers for all the problems of life. Their assumed omniscience deserves the tribute of "faith": i.e., of subordinating one's conduct to canons which are no longer decreed by simple, immediate satisfaction but rather by the comprehension of a certain system of means and ends (however limited it may be at the child's age).[107]

Children may learn, therefore, to identify their faith in abstract form with "the name which adults give to their structure of values."[108] "It is not surprising, then, that a small child will call itself a Christian, a Buddhist, an atheist, a liberal, or a Marxist. For that is the label which those in whom it has 'faith' apply to themselves. . . ."[109]

The adolescent searches for "identity in a structure of meaning or values" by trying to emulate "the ideal."[110] Critical of the younger-child "faith" rooted in the values of parents and educators, the adolescent

> discovers that they [parents and educators] are far from being omniscient; that they have problems as everyone else does, and no solutions for many of these problems; and that as referential witnesses of meanings and values, they are puny figures when compared to the great personages of past or present history.[111]

Nevertheless, while this is a rebellious (though never total) departure from the past world of values, the adolescent is still confronted with the need to find "a new 'faith,' one that will be his own."[112]

The adult "faith" is past the point of the "fluidity" noticeable in the adolescent. The value system at the adult stage is pretty much established. Even at this stage of development, however, people will objectively seek to "re-examine their 'faith' to certify--and often force-- its compatibility with the price they have had to pay in the face of resistance to the values which are presented by nature or society."[113]

"Faith and Ideology": Value and Efficacy

"Faith" is that which "teaches us which value is the one to which we can 'entrust' our whole lives." "Ideology" is concerned "with effectiveness in using available means" toward the end of absolute value.[114] "Ideology" is defined by Segundo as "the system of goals and means that serves as the necessary backdrop for any human option or line of action."[115] Segundo uses the example of driving a nail into a wall in order to illustrate the meaning of "ideology." In this example, one must make a "choice of instruments"--that is, one must "pay attention to the objective difference of efficacy that, in view of the goal, seems appropriate--for example, whether to use a hammer or some pliers."[116]

Having established this concept of "ideology," Segundo turns to an analysis of the experience of "failure." Failure could be perceived as an indication of a problem in one's "faith" (that is, one's "meaning or value"). But failure might also be perceived as an indication of a problem in the method one has chosen for "efficacy" (that is, the method chosen for the "implementation of one's faith").

> Analysis of my failure in terms of effectiveness presumes that I, without changing my system of values, could possibly have chosen a more effective method to obtain what I was seeking. Analysis of my failure in terms of meaning is more subtle, but equally universal. It involves asking myself whether there is not some value in the very fact of failure when one holds my particular scale of values: or, to put it another way, it means asking whether failure itself was not a price worth paying in order to achieve a higher end, and in the end this would come down to saying that it was not such a failure after all.[117]

Segundo upholds the importance of the distinction here between "value" and "efficacy." Neglecting the distinction can lead to a misreading of the experience of "failure."

> If someone considers failure solely from the viewpoint of efficacy, that person will end up paying any price (in value) to obtain whatever is desired. If someone considers failure solely from the viewpoint of their

possible value, in the end that will turn every inept, ignorant, or lazy person into a hero or martyr: ineffectiveness will be canonized.[118]

Segundo uses the concepts of "value" and "meaning" to describe "faith" *in order to distinguish* these from "means" and "efficacy," the equivalents of "ideology." This point is confirmed by Segundo's distinction between "ideology" and "faith".

We recognize an ideology in the fact that it has *no pretensions* to an *objectively* absolute value. In other words, an ideology is worth as much as the reasons or arguments which support it. . . . Faith, on the other hand, is recognized by its *pretensions* to an *objectively* absolute value. In other words, in his faith a person supposedly comes in contact with an objective source of total truth.[119]

On the other hand, while "faith" and "ideology" are to be distinguished, they cannot exist apart from each other.

Faith and ideologies are not to be identified, but they cannot be separated. Faith has a greater relation to the goal; ideologies serve as the instrument. No one can live without these two. They are poles of human existence through which it is necessary to resolve the problems which are set before human beings. They are separable only in explication. In a moment one can ask me why it was not more efficacious; in another, if it had been all in vain. But both matters have to answered, because in substance they are inseparable. Efficacy and signification are to be distinguished, but they are inseparably involved, and mutually influence each other in the search for the realization of humanity.[120]

"Inseparability" is synonymous with "complementarity." "Meaning and efficacy are two *different but complementary human dimensions*."[121] *Both* poles, though distinct, do not exist without each other.

To illustrate this point, we may again return to Segundo's example of the maturation process. The young child does not clearly distinguish between "faith" and "ideology." His actions and reactions are largely "instinctive." Thus, the child models both the "faith" and the "ideology" of his parents or educators. In adolescence, however, the distinction between "methods" and "values" becomes more pronounced.

The adolescent is introduced into a different world: that of objective technique; that of knowing how to do things. Before, those techniques were only inculcated in an impersonal manner. . . . The adolescent discovers that the values and methods belong to two different worlds. In due time, the disappearance of rewards and punishments help to make this fundamental distinction, since his task as a human being consists precisely in making both worlds *complementary.*[122]

In the adult experience, "the reflection turns less and less to that issue [of faith], and more and more to the problems of method."[123] Through "experience" (i.e., "systematized knowledge of methods and techniques"), an adult "possesses greater, and frequently a more complex and profound, awareness of the objective conditioning elements to which the search for values is subjected."[124]

Segundo's claim that "faith" and "ideologies" are distinct but inseparable elements in human experience is established. Segundo's willingness to exchange the concepts of "faith" and "ideologies" for "other synonymous or equivalent" concepts is also helpful.[125] However, this begs the question: how does Segundo's reading of human experience through the lens of "faith" and "ideologies" compare with other efforts to understand human experience? A comparison between Segundo's concepts of "faith" and "ideology" and the concepts by other contemporary thinkers is therefore in order.

A Comparison of "Faith" and "Ideology" with Other Concepts in Defining Human Experience

Segundo likens his concept of "faith" to Wolfhart Pannenberg's concept of "fundamental trust," and David Tracy's concept of "religion," noting in each case the similarities and differences. Segundo quotes Pannenberg's definition of "fundamental trust":

Actually, *faith as a vital act is synonymous with trust, a trust that has to do with the fundamental and basic moments in any human life.* Like any such moment in life, this trust extends beyond the boundaries of any Christian avowal. . . . The trust we need to live does not extend solely to specific circumstances, things, and persons; going beyond them, it leads us to trust in the undetermined. . . . So we can say that above and beyond any circumstances, things, and persons among which our life moves, there is a deeper, unconditioned trust by which we live. But even this unconditioned trust, for all its openness and unconditionality, is a trust in something where any human being is concerned. It is always concentrated in a person or thing. In the first stages of infancy, this pristine trust is bound up with father and mother. Later it must be freed from them, but it still remains the basic condition for the formation of a healthy personality. Under normal circumstances, most human beings reflect little on the foundation of this fundamental trust which constitutes the bulwark or support of their lives. Normally we do not consider the object of our fundamental trust. The latter is not shaken or even called into question. . . . Where do we place the ultimate concern of our hearts? What do we trust in ultimately? This is the most serious question that a human being can ask himself or herself. "The faith and trust of the heart make. . . both God and idols." This is one of Luther's enduring statements.[126]

Segundo affirms the similarity of Pannenberg's concept of "fundamental trust" with his own concept of "faith," contending that "Pannenberg is talking about an anthropological dimension rather than a specifically religious act."[127] Nevertheless, Segundo also contends that

Lack of "faith" [Segundo's term] would disorient a human being; lack of "trust" [Pannenberg's term] would paralyze him or her. Or, to put it another way, lack of "faith" would paralyze a person through disorientation whereas lack of "trust" would paralyze a person with timidity and atony--two very different things.[128]

Despite this difference with Pannenberg, it is interesting to note that Segundo affirms (correctly) the similarity of his own position with Luther's position.

It is worth noting that the phrase of Luther cited by Pannenberg does not, strictly speaking, apply to what Pannenberg calls "fundamental trust." It really applies to the anthropological faith that I am talking about, the faith whereby we concretely choose the value (God) or antivalue (some idol) to which we are going to dedicate our lives.[129]

Segundo also compares his concept of "faith" with David Tracy's concept of "religion," described in limit-language.

Employed in our common discourse, "religion" usually means a perspective which expresses a dominating interest in certain universal and elemental features of human existence as those features bear on the human desire for liberation and authentic existence. Such features can be analyzed as both expressive of certain "limits-to" our ordinary

experience (e.g., finitude, contingency, or radical transience) and disclosive of certain fundamental structures of our existence beyond (or, alternatively, grounding to) that ordinary experience (e.g., our fundamental trust in the worthwhileness of existence, our basic belief in order and value).
We can often both experience and articulate the "limits-to" aspect of the religious perspective. On such occasions, we may also find the ability occasionally to speak, more often to "show" or "disclose" the horizon, ground, or "limits-of" such language and experience. In either case, we need to reflect upon both *the explicit limits-to our ordinary experience (the everyday and the scientific, the moral, aesthetic, and political) and the implicitly disclosed dimension which functions as limit-of or ground to (e.g., fundamental faith or trust) our more ordinary ways of being-in-the-world.*[130]

Segundo affirms the idea, evident in Tracy's limit-language, "that every human being must face up to our limited supplies of energy" and "make an 'imaginary' trip to the limits of his or her existence in order to give it meaning."[131]   Nevertheless, Segundo's principal difference with Tracy, much more forcefully pronounced than his difference with Pannenberg, is that the term "religion" is misleading.

First of all, this divinizing terminology tends to minimize the all-too-human components that enter into our conception of the "god" which religion handles so explicitly and so vaguely. . . .   Secondly, this approach situates religion on the plane of fundamental values. . . [and] thus loses sight of the fact that the most common and perhaps primitive function of explicit and recordable religions has been "ideological" in my sense of the term: *instruments* for any and every class of values.[132]

This leads Segundo into a further examination of Jesus' polemic against "religion."   In Jesus' time, "religion" was used to conceal the "bad faith" or hypocrisy of the so-called "religious."[133]   However, Segundo returns to a more positive appraisal of "religion" when he discusses the dimension of "religious faith."   This dimension will be discussed in greater detail in this chapter when we look at the correlation between human experience and the community called Church.
    Segundo recognizes two major obstacles to an appreciation of his own term "ideology" when compared to other uses of this term.   The first obstacle is that "faith and science" or "faith and reason" are often

seen as *opposed* alternatives, and not as *complementary*.[134]   To illustrate this point, Segundo examines the insights of Milan Machoveč and Gregory Bateson, respective representatives of "science" and "reason." Segundo begins with Machoveč's own summation of the goal of Karl Marx's philosophy:

> There can be no doubt that *Marx wanted to* organize all progressive people oriented towards the future, *through a strict and objective scientific analysis* of the central problems of his historical period. At the same time, he wanted to lay the foundations for a more human society, and hence for a more free and mature human individuality.[135]

Segundo highlights from the above text what Machoveč may not have realized. There is an emphasis on *intention* ("Marx wanted to") and an emphasis on *mediation* ("through a strict and objective scientific analysis").[136]   Segundo directly correlates these two emphases with the two poles of "faith" and "ideology." "In short, Machoveč has just been telling us that not enough attention has been paid to the complementarity between 'faith' and 'ideology' in Marxist thought when embodied in political reality. The only difference is that he uses the term 'scientific method' where I use the term 'ideology.'"[137]

Segundo then examines the post-positivist epistemology of Gregory Bateson. Segundo quotes Bateson: "The living man is thus bound within a net of epistemological and ontological premises which--regardless of ultimate truth or falsity--become partially self-validating for him."[138]   Segundo notes that the premises, whether epistemological or ontological, are self-validating because they suggest the values of the reasoner. "I believe that it should now be clear that Bateson, in talking about ontological and epistemological 'premises,' is referring to the very same anthropological dimension I have been calling 'faith.'"[139]   However, this need not negate the validity of another understanding of reason that "studies real possibilities in order to implement one's values." This conforms to Segundo's concept of "ideology." Segundo contends that Bateson is arguing for that latter understanding of reason and that Bateson has developed "a complementarity between a-rational *premises* ["faith"] and the use of *reason* ["ideology"]."[140]

The second major obstacle Segundo perceives is that his term "ideology" may be confused with two of the more current Marxist uses of the term. One of the current uses is "neutral" and "goes back to

Marx himself"; the other use is "negative" and is "derived from Marx rather than actually present in his own work."[141] Segundo cites from Marx's The German Ideology:

> Morality, religion, metaphysics, *all the rest of ideology* and their corresponding forms of consciousness, thus no longer retain the semblance of independence. They have no history, no development; but men, developing their material production and their material intercourse, alter, along with this their real existence, *their thinking and the products of their thinking.*[142]

Segundo sees "ideology" (as in the phrase, "all the rest of ideology") as a "neutral" reality from the standpoint of value. According to Segundo, this is synonymous with "the consciousness of a culture." "Depending on circumstances, in other words, laws, political structures, arts, and (?) religions might be good or bad, better or worse."[143] But there is perhaps a more dominant sense in Marx's thought in which "ideology" has a "negative" connotation. Such negativity is implied when people believe it is necessary to "alter their thinking and its products when they alter their material production."[144] Segundo elaborates:

> It should be noted that this negative use of the term has been a major landmark in the growth of the sociology of knowledge. Even non-Marxist thinkers and scholars (e.g., Karl Mannheim) have acknowledged that fact. The ideological superstructure, after all, is situated in the lofty region of thought and is easily dissociated from the realm of material production; indeed, it tends to evade and hide the latter realm. So it is only logical to assume that ideology is not fortuitous but "interested." In other words, whether they believe in the ideology or not, those who profit from the existing mode of production are the authors and defenders of that ideology.[145]

To summarize, Segundo claims that the "more *neutral* sense refers to everything that lies outside the precision of the sciences, to the suprascientific or the superstructural realm," while the *negative* sense "refers to all the cognitive mechanisms which disguise, excuse, and even sacralize the existing mode of production, thus benefiting those who profit from that mode of production."[146]

Even after making this distinction between the two more common uses of "ideology," Segundo concludes that neither of them are proximate to his use of the term "ideology."[147] These other uses are actually closer to Segundo's understanding of "faith." They reflect values, whether lofty ideals or distorting interests. The problem with Marxist scientific theory is that it *confuses* "faith" and "ideology." However, Segundo believes that a proper discernment can rescue the helpful elements in Marxist thought for a proper use of the term "ideology." Segundo concludes with a word of caution:

> Any science is obliged to theorize if it wishes to study such a complex and evasive form of concreteness. And once it begins to theorize, science itself enters the realm of *ideology* and must be analyzed from that standpoint; otherwise science will become dehumanized, serving as a pretext for new forms of disguised exploitation of real human beings and their labor. "Ideological" naivete is always fatal, no matter how scientific it may be.[148]

We may conclude from this investigation that Segundo's use of the term "ideology" is unique. Whatever value judgment we may wish to make of his usage, the key point here is that Segundo is novel in his distinguishing and combining the two elements of "faith" and "ideology" in his analysis of human experience. Segundo is aware that this "anthropological dualism" underlying his terminology "is hard for people to accept."[149] Nevertheless, Segundo regards this dualism as an essential dimension of human experience.

> From what has been said here, it should be clear that these dimensions of efficacy and of meaning are intimately related, but not to be confused. One who is preoccupied with meaning at the exclusion of efficacy (the temptation of the childish Christian) or one who is preoccupied with efficacy while failing to attend to meaning (the temptation of technicians, politicians, or others), they can lose an essential human dimension. It is not easy to keep both [dimensions] together, among other reasons, because both dimensions have different rules of the game even in the use of language. A human being must be capable of speaking *two* languages. Moreover, he ought to be able to connect them without confusing them, and without distorting either of them. Here we face one of the greatest challenges of our technological or, as some prefer, post-industrial culture.[150]

II. The Community Called Church: "Faith and Love"

Ecclesiology plays a major role in Latin American liberation
theology. The "primary embodiment of liberation theology" may be
found in the "church base communities" (*comunidades eclesiales de
base*).[151] It is not surprising, therefore, that Segundo's first major
effort in what can properly be called liberation theology was a text on
ecclesiology.[152]

Two Understandings of the Church's Mission

In his early ecclesiological work, Segundo focuses his attention on
the problem of two divergent understandings on the mission of the
Church in the countries separated by the River Plate--*viz.*, Argentina
and Uruguay.

> For some, the function of the Church and its problems are the unique
> ones which have absolute value in our national reality. For others, that
> function and those problems have limited the Church's sector: the
> religious realm is only one of the aspects and one of the problems of
> national reality.[153]

The "first" position regards the Church's function and problems as
unique and absolute. This is the position of the established Church.
This position also enjoys a more established theological tradition. The
strength of this position is that is makes a strong case for the very
existence of the Church: "In other words, would the institution by
Christ of the visible Church and the declaration of its absolute necessity
make any sense if people were saved outside the Church as well as
within it?"[154] The weakness of this position is that it does not express
a strong concern for human history. Human history is relativized and
reduced in significance by the understanding of "salvation" inherent to
this position, characterized by Segundo as follows: "At the end of the
journey of life, the one who is saved knows, and he who is not saved
does not know anything."[155]

The "second" position is described by Segundo as having a more
"apostolic spirit" of "Christian activism."[156] It does not enjoy the
same richness of an established theological tradition as the first
position. "Clearly, it appeals to the evangelical texts which deal with
charity, and certainly material charity, which the Christian ought to

have with his neighbor. . . . It appeals to the dogma of the incarnation, of the insertion of God and of his Church into human history."[157]   Segundo affirms this position for its critique of the "duplicity" evident in the first position. From the vantage point of the second position, the position of ecclesiastical absoluteness is like a doctor operating on a patient only to save the patient's soul. There is more at stake in the ecclesiological mission. Hence the phrase of Jean Giano echoes prominently in the second position: "I do not wish to be that man who crosses a battlefield with a flower in his hand."[158]   The principal weakness of this second position is that it is "intuitive and sentimental," unorganized in the practical implementation of its vision.[159]

To help illustrate the differences in the two positions, Segundo remarks on how their values and means clash in the three sectors of parish life, socio-economic concerns, and political concerns. At the level of parish life, particularly in urban centers, the first position fears the decline in membership, and seeks to turn the focus of the church inward. The second position is more interested in going out into the world, with less interest in declining membership.[160] In the sector of socio-economic concerns, the first position emphasizes private funding for the established Church and its programs, cashing in on consumerism. The second position reflects a greater ignorance or at least a lack of interest in Church funding and is more sensitive to the issue of economic dependency.[161]   Finally, at the political level, the first position seeks to secure alliances with political leaders and tries to get political advantages for the Church. The second position is more interested in working for change, with or without the assistance of political leaders.[162]

Segundo notes the dilemma that these "alternative" positions present for Christian life, quoting from Teilhard de Chardin's The Divine Way:

> Either the Christian, inhibiting his taste for the tangible, is strengthened in not being interested in more than the purely religious objects and, therefore, tries to live in a divinized world through the exclusion of the greatest possible number of terrestrial objects; or, wearied by the interior opposition which bridles him, he sends to the devil the evangelical counsels and decides to carry on that which seems to him to be a human and authentic life; or--and this is the most frequent case--he refuses to understand: never totally emptied toward God, never completely

overturned in the matters, imperfect in his own eyes, insincere before the judgment of man, he resigns himself to carry on a double life.[163]

New Testament Soteriologies

Segundo's goal is to try to develop an ecclesiology that can reconcile these two positions. To accomplish his goal, Segundo regards it essential to "consult what is, for the Church, the source of its true mission: the truth revealed by its founder, Jesus Christ."[164] Segundo regards "salvation" as the reason that Jesus Christ came into the world. The message of salvation, therefore, is the *raison d'être* of the Church's mission.[165] However, when Segundo examines the New Testament, he notes a "double line of thought" on the theme of salvation.

> On the one hand, salvation is attributed formally and clearly to entrance into the Church through faith and sacraments. In a text of chief importance, since the Evangelist gives it as a kind of testimony to the risen Christ, "the last time" Jesus spoke to his disciples before ascending to the Father, he told them on what the mission of the Church will be founded: "Go into the whole world preaching to all people the Gospel." And in order to give that task the weight and the value which it deserves, Jesus adds: "He who believes and is baptized will be saved. He who does not believe, will be condemned" (Mark 16:15-16).[166]

Segundo cites the texts of John 3:14-18 and Acts 16:30-33 as further examples of this theme. He then continues:

> Nevertheless, with equal clarity, there appears in the writings of the New Testament another line of thought about salvation; and we find it in a place as central as the previous position. Before going to his suffering and death, Jesus gave his last sermon, which is also the sermon about the last things, about the end of time in which God will cast his view in judgment over what has been accomplished in history, seeking what is of lasting, decisive value. In that judgment, before which "all human beings" will appear, what will decide the eternal destiny? Answer: The religious attitude, as it could be no less; that is, the attitude which human beings have had with respect to the Christ of God. And that religious attitude before Christ, will it be adoration, faith, belonging to the true Church? No. The Gospel says to us that the Judge will ask if they have given food when he was hungry, a drink of water when he was thirsty, help, consolation, companionship. . . .[167]

Segundo then paraphrases the judgment scene in Matthew 25:

> And all the multitude of people, from the prehistoric man to the Soviet astronaut of the twentieth century, will say [to the Judge]: "But how can you judge all people on earth by what they did for you during the thirty years in which you traversed our human history?" And the Judge will answer: "Even though you could not see me, even you, Neanderthal men, who could not know me; even you, distinguished people of Argentina and Uruguay of 1961, who knew me as evil that it could almost be worth more for you to pretend that you did not know me, whenever you gave someone bread when they were hungry, or a drink of water when they were thirsty, so spontaneously, without pretension, simply because the other was thirsty, 'you did it for me,' and the reward is eternal salvation (Matthew 25:31-40).[168]

Segundo also cites James 2:14-16 as a further example of biblical support for this understanding of salvation. He then concludes: "of these two lines of thought, there is one which has a direct, intimate, essential relationship with the totality of the New Testament."[169]

Segundo looks to the First Epistle of John as the source for defining that "direct, intimate, essential relationship." Specifically, Segundo notes there the repeated phrase, "God is love" (I John 4:8, 16). But what is "love"? Segundo confesses that "love" is a word which has been degraded, not because it has lost much of its content since the time of the epistle, but because "real life" has degraded it.[170] "Love" is "*agape*", "charity", meaning

> to give of our own substance, to give that limited measure of what we are, to extract from our being and from our flesh what we can offer to a beloved being; in other words, self-giving. But it is also to receive, to receive something gratuitously, what we could not in any way get from ourselves, something which, nevertheless, completes us and affects us to the greatest depths of our being. And to live as one who loves is to live dependent, suffering with the suffering of the alienated, and feeling the joys of the alienated, being eminently accessible and vulnerable.[171]

The picture that Greek philosophy paints of an immutable and impassible deity is an inaccurate picture of the Johannine message, "God is love." Segundo claims, "God can be hurt, because God is love."[172] And that message is shared by our participation in the sufferings of the world.

God is essentially and intimately love. And God puts in our limited and poor being that marvelous capacity of self-giving which is all authentic love over the earth. That gift which God gives to us, so superior to biological life, opens to us horizons of a new existence, but no less an existence which is palpable, tangible, historical, such that St. John says, "We know (experientially) that we have been transferred from death to life because we are able to love one another" (I John 3:14).[173]

From there, it is an easy step to demonstrate the relationship of love to the identity and mission of the Church.

That love, *old as the world*, that love which has been a fortress for all sacrifices, all the loyalties, all the silent charities, all the simple, constant, and pure events of togetherness which have existed in human beings, the Christian message says that such love has a *divine origin*, that it is a supernatural possibility *placed in our souls by Another who gave his life for us.* . . . But not only does the divine character of all authentic love appear in its origin, according to the revelation of Christ. The divine character also appears in its object, and this will be very important in studying next what the mission of the Church concretely means in our historical reality.[174]

In examining the "double commandment" (to love God and to love the neighbor) in Matthew 22:39 and in the text of I John 4:20, Segundo concludes that love for "the neighbor, the one closest to us, the visible human being who is beside us in history" is at the heart of Christianity.[175]

Somehow Christianity has missed out on this central message. The "religion" of Christianity has been restricted to "the domain of the sacred and its sector; the rest is profane, temporal, human."[176] What is needed, therefore, is a "religious revolution" which can "*radically abolish that distinction.*"[177] Segundo argues:

How can we call profane or temporal the bread which satisfies the hunger of God? How can we call profane the technology which serves for curing God? Or the structures which offer or do not offer to God in our brothers a life with meaning and dignity, in place of an animal existence? The great religious revolution of Christianity has been the abolition of the profane. And that, not on behalf of the religious, as the first conception [of the Church] wishes, but on behalf of the absolute religious value of that same thing we call the profane. This was precisely the first step of our pathway toward understanding the mission of the Church in Argentina and Uruguay today.[178]

The "love of Christ" becomes the basis by which the first and second positions on the understanding of the mission of the Church are reconciled. "Faith" needs to be "active in love." The first position, in Segundo's estimation, has neglected this religious dimension in its effort to uphold the "unique absolute value" of Christianity. "But its conception of the religious ignores an essential data, the most revolutionary of the Christian revelation."[179] Segundo points out how the gospel has failed to bring meaning to Catholics in their daily life. The result has been "a massive dechristianization" in Argentina and Uruguay.[180]

But what about the "second" ecclesiological position? It is clear that Segundo views this position more favorably because it is moving toward a "religious revolution." Nevertheless, Segundo argues that the Church cannot exist apart from its function in "faith and sacraments," as the first ecclesiological position contends.

The Essence and Necessity of the Church

Segundo believes that the Church serves an *essential* role as the custodian of the "faith and sacraments." The Church is the "community of believers, that is, of those who have faith in what God has revealed."[181] In possessing revelation, the Church "possesses the secret of what is happening in human history, knows its warp and woof, and understands the stakes that are being played out"[182] Furthermore, this revelation is what makes the Christian unique. "The Christian is *he who already knows.* This, undoubtedly, is what distinguishes and defines him."[183]

What is the *necessity* of this unique revelation? In answering that question, Segundo draws upon an illustration from Karl Rahner.

The whole process can be compared to the life shared in common by two lovers. Everything they do is sustained and transformed by this love and is its--very discreet, almost imperceptible--expression, even the insignificant, ordinary things which seem to have quite a different meaning and purpose from love and which would have to be done even if there were no love between two persons. And yet, sometimes, and even often, they must tell each other openly, in words and by gestures which are nothing but the expression of love--of a love which was

already finding expression in everything they do. It is as if the hidden
law of the whole of their two lives united together must continually bring
forth new formal, outward expressions (*Gesaltwerdungen*) of their love,
in which this love, which after all is always there, realizes itself ever
more fully and in ever new forms. These are only gestures, not love
itself--gestures "which do not really seem to matter" compared with the
proving of one's love in deed and in truth; and yet *love lives by them.*
Love would die if it were not for these expressions which are not love at
all and which those not in love consider superfluous "formalities." . . .
But the everyday course of love will always go on concentrating itself in
such gestures and love itself will always draw new life from them.[184]

A similar example may be found in friendship. No one would claim
that a handshake between friends is "of little importance, that the
substantial reality [of friendship] remains the same" even without this
sign or symbol.[185] In the same way, Segundo queries, what is it
about "faith and sacraments" that people can not seemingly live
without?

Would it not seem equally logical to deny any decisive importance to the
proclamation of the faith. . . which, in the final analysis, is nothing more
than an ensemble of sounds which symbolize a reality infinitely more
solid, and that, one might suppose, remains the same with or without the
ensemble of sounds? Why the madness, then, that human beings will let
themselves be killed for that little ensemble of sounds which is a "yes"
or "no," or for that little collection of pen strokes which is a personal
signature?[186]

Segundo then answers his own question: *"The Church, the visible
community with its formulas of faith and its sacraments, is to the
cosmic community of God's people what the aforementioned signs are
to the reality they signify and convey."*[187]

In this correlation, we have the clearest indication of the absolutely
essential dimension of faith. *Love*, in order to truly live, needs *faith*,
as much as the *world*, in order to live, needs the *Church*. Without
faith and the Church, love and the world die. The rationale with which
Segundo is operating points us back to Christ. Christ is "the Heart of
the world" (*el Corazón del mundo*).[188] This is the "secret"
(*mysterion*) of the Church. The preaching of the gospel and the
administration of the sacraments "gives full consciousness [faith] to
what before was only spontaneous [love]."[189] The question could be

raised whether or not faith, in fact, *creates* that spontaneity. For now, it suffices to recognize that the overarching thesis--that "faith" and "faith's work" need to be distinguished, but they cannot be separated--is evidenced in the Church in the distinction-without-separation of "faith" and "love."

A "Minority" Church in a "Mass" World

We cannot leave our discussion of the ecclesiological dimension without taking note of a central concept in Segundo's theology: *masses and minorities*. Their conceptual emergence is traceable to the socio-political sphere with the rise of Marxism. But Segundo implements them for his own purposes and finds multiple usages. Hence, the discussion of "masses and minorities" is not limited to Segundo's ecclesiology, even though it plays a major role in that understanding.

A more significant, overarching use of "masses and minorities" is evident in Segundo's use of the evolutionary categories of Teilhard de Chardin. Segundo connects, by way of analogy, "minorities and masses" to Teilhard's concepts of "entropy" (the conservation of energy) and "negentropy" (the degradation of energy).[190] Segundo quotes approvingly Teilhard's own ecclesiological definition: "The church is the reflectively Christified portion of the world; the church is the principal focus of inter-human affinities for super-charity; the church is the central axis of universal convergence and the precise emergent point of encounter between the Universe and the Omega Point."[191] Teilhard's understanding of history moving towards an "Omega Point" is also affirmed by Segundo, even though Segundo prefers the New Testament term, "recapitulation": "the path by which all human beings of the universe, guided by the grace of Christ, in accordance with his function, his place in the cosmos, move toward an end in which the whole of history will reveal Christ's mystery."[192]

The concept of "masses and minorities" plays a prominent role in the discussion of ecclesiology because Segundo sees the contemporary situation as ripe for the emergence of a "minority" Church in a "mass" world. A "minority" Church is a heroic community that orients itself toward the "essential . . . Christian message: *the cross*."[193] It is that community that dares to live out the promise of the gospel in the real-life context where "faith's work" (love) needs to be happening. Hence, in one of the few cases where Segundo quotes Joseph Ratzinger with approval, we find these words:

> Essential to the one and only salvation plan of God is a correlation
> between "the little flock" and "the multitude." The two terms exist *for
> each other.* This correlation is one aspect of the way in which God saves
> the world; it does not represent a *failure* of the divine will. . . . It is
> quite clear from Scripture that God divides humanity into two groups,
> one being "the little flock" and the other being the vast "multitude." The
> point is made repeatedly in the Scriptures: "The gate that leads to life
> is small and the road is narrow, and those who find it are *few*" (Matt.
> 7:14); "labourers are *scarce*" (Matt. 9:37); "For though many are
> invited, *few* are chosen" (Matt. 22:14); "Have no fear, *little flock*" (Luke
> 12:32). And Jesus himself gives up his life as a ransom for "many"
> (Mark 10:45).[194]

"Masses", on the other hand, are more critically described as those who "follow the crowd, assimilate propaganda, allow themselves to be led by those psychological and sociological mechanisms that manage what is precisely called 'mass behavior.'"[195] The two basic characteristics of "masses" are "simplification" (simple values are chosen in all situations, however complex) and "immediacy" (immediate ends are sought at the expense of long-range goals and ends).[196] Hence, common-places such as "mass media" or "mass communication" come into play as "means intended to organize masses, to direct masses, and to manipulate masses."[197]

Segundo is not calling for the abolition of "masses." In fact, he argues that "mass means" are essential for the development of human community.[198] Segundo is also quite sensitive to the charge of "elitism" and does not believe his position is elitist.[199] But he does argue that values are daily absorbed by the "masses" in the "mutilation of the mind" via means that are already controlled by the value-interests of others.[200] In the midst of this situation, the Church can provide a "sign-bearing function," not in order to control others, but in order to set others free from the mechanisms that enslave them. The Church, therefore, has a mission to those outside her walls: "*leaven* in the dough, *salt* in the meal, and *light* for all those who dwell in the human household."[201]

The greater difficulty Segundo recognizes is that the established Church continues to cling to the out-dated models of Christendom. Assailed by fear and insecure of what may happen to the Church if she moves too closely to minoritarian visions, the Church makes its primary appeal to the "masses" by seeking to incorporate as many as possible. The maxim of the established Church is: "Make the minimum of demands, so as to keep the maximum of people."[202] The result is that the established Church has sought to make it "easy and beneficial to adhere to an ideal which was, in itself, the most difficult and complex in the world."[203] But the times are such that "from now on, Catholicism will have to be proven to each person, by having recourse to that which is the most profound, the most personal, and the most heroic [elements within the Christian faith], and in a free fight with all other systems which claim to explain and orient human life."[204] Who, then, is going to perform this minoritarian task and exercise the freedom of faith in the work of love for the world? Segundo answers that such a task may well be left to the courageous efforts of the "grassroots Christian communities (*comunidades de base*)."[205]

III.   Toward a Correlation of Human Experience and the Community Called Church

Segundo's analysis of human experience and ecclesiology confirms the overarching thesis that "faith" cannot be separated from "faith's works" (whether those works are understood as "ideologies" or "love"), even though "faith" can and needs to be distinguished from those works. There are elements in Segundo's theology that serve to correlate human experience in general and the Christian community in particular. In this section, we will demonstrate that correlation by examining two additional concepts in Segundo's theology: "religious faith" and "preparation for the gospel."

"Religious Faith"

Earlier, we noted that Segundo cannot accept Tracy's concept of "religion" because it is not concrete enough to the human experience nor does it help to disclose "bad faith" or hypocrisy. However, Segundo does think there is an appropriate use of the "religious" that conforms to his own concept of "anthropological faith"--*viz.*, "religious faith."[206]

"Religious faith," according to Segundo, is something that is both continuous and discontinuous with "anthropological faith." "Religious faith" consists of two elements: "transcendent data" and "a tradition composed of witnesses." "Transcendent data" is continuous with "anthropological faith" because there is a *value*, perhaps even a "utopic" value, that one "wagers." However, it is discontinuous because the value is enhanced in such a way by some new *data* that "transcends all concrete [human] experience."[207] For example, Segundo claims that Jesus' coming and proclaiming the "kingdom of God" was a "transcendent data" that appealed to his hearers who were waiting for just such a kingdom (continuous), but changed or altered or re-prioritized that value to include *new depths of promising meaning* that his hearers could not possibly have understood (discontinuous). Thus, "'good news' and 'conversion' are not incompatible."[208]

By way of summary, Segundo highlights four central points that characterize the meaning of "transcendent data":

The first point is that on the human level values are not chosen or preferred unless some nonistrumental conception is part of that decision. In this case the conception has to do with the ultimate possibilities (or limits) of the universe and the human being. In that sense every values-structure contains at least one transcendent data.

The second point is that no scientific reasons exist for or against those limit-possibilities. By their very nature they escape experimental verification. . . .

The third point is that, despite the above, language not only can but must use some such expression as "data"; otherwise an area that is decisive for values-structures would lack adequate means of expression and communication. . . .

The fourth point is that the faith which embraces those transcendent data does not in any way belie the primacy of the human valuational criteria preexisting in the person who believes. Anthropological faith is not displaced. Only by building on the latter can we develop faith in the transcendent data. Thus it still remains irrelevant whether this faith is accepted explicitly or not, whether we consciously cross this overall limit of experience. Much more decisive is the matter of determining what values of what meaning-structure those transcendent data support, correct, develop, or deepen. What matters is their potential contribution to basic anthropological faith.[209]

The second element of "religious faith"--"a tradition composed of witnesses"--corresponds to, or is at least continuous with, the element of "referential witnesses" in "anthropological faith." However, the unique difference or discontinuity is that these witnesses testify to a specific "tradition": "living experiences that teach people how to learn."[210]   For Christians, that tradition includes the entire Judeo-Christian history, and it is a tradition that continues to grow.   Thus, "dogmas," which "represent the transcendent data recognized by that tradition," are intended to be "symbols of a world of values, of a world that is clearly in movement, of a world engaged in learning."[211]   In summary, therefore, "religious faith" is succinctly defined by Segundo as follows:

> a faith which defines values, not because those values are suddenly revealed to human beings who have been without them up to that point, but because this faith constitutes a system of learning-apprenticeship transmitted by historical witnesses which enables people to recognize and discern genuine transcendent data; and those data, in turn, become defining factors of people's meaning-structures.[212]

We should note that Segundo upholds a continuous-yet-discontinuous relationship between anthropological faith and religious faith in order to correlate human experience and the community called Church. He is also clearly giving greater weight to human experience. How successful he is in this correlation is another question. Segundo might be criticized here on whether his position really allows for discontinuity. In response, we might offer that his understanding of the all-pervasive "love of Christ," particularly as it was evidenced in our analysis of Segundo's ecclesiology, may have more than a little to do with Segundo's heavy accent on continuity. Nevertheless, this ought not take away from the fact that Segundo has made a consistent and cohesive argument which demonstrates the connection between human experience in general and the community called Church.

"Preparation for the Gospel"

Segundo's use of the concept of "preparation for the gospel" provides a second approach that helps to correlate human experience and the community called Church.   The origin of the concept is traceable to <u>Lumen Gentium</u>, the Dogmatic Constitution of the Church of Vatican II, where it states:

> Those who, through no fault of their own, do not know the Gospel of

Christ or his Church, but who nevertheless seek God with a sincere heart, and, moved by grace, try in their actions to do his will as they know it through the dictates of their conscience--those too may achieve eternal salvation.   Nor shall divine providence deny the assistance necessary for salvation to those who, without any fault of theirs, have not yet arrived at an explicit knowledge of God, and who, not without grace, strive to lead a good life.   Whatever good or truth is found amongst them is considered by the Church to be a *preparation for the gospel* and given by him who enlightens all men that they may at length have life.[213]

Segundo traces the history of the concept back to the early church disputes with the Pelagian and semi-Pelagian heresies.   At the Council of Orange (529 C.E.), in an attempt to resolve the dispute once and for all, "it was declared that the Church saw man's whole journey under the guidance of conscience as the *start of faith*, presupposing an already present attraction toward full knowledge of the divine message; hence it had to be regarded as supernatural, even as faith itself is."[214] Segundo then elaborates:

the relationship between the man of good will and the Christian who was working for the betterment of the world--the one divine vocation of all men--did not simply mean that they were collaborating from their different levels of knowledge: one having anonymous, implicit, spontaneous knowledge and the other having precise, explicit, and reflected knowledge.   It also meant that this work was the start of faith for the man of good will.   It was a journey toward an encounter, the preparation for a dialogue, the gradual formulation of a question that sought, with the ever-growing intensity of love itself, the good news that the Christian had to give.[215]

Segundo concludes, "if love is a faith that is beginning, *this faith is made to dialogue with the full faith.*"[216]

Segundo then proceeds to demonstrate exactly how this dialogue between *beginning faith* and *full faith* takes place.   The first point that Segundo makes is that "all authentic love is a beginning of faith."[217] Love begins in enthusiasm and instinctive attraction.   But one discovers that loving is "truly a gift of oneself, and that to give oneself is the most serious, the most demanding, the most unpredictable, and the most irreversible adventure that can happen to a human being."[218] When this is realized, a basic, essential, and haunting question begins to emerge: "Is love worth the trouble [¿*vale la pena amar?*]?"[219]

To love means to lose our autonomy and to become dependent on another. And this dependence may end up one day as disillusionment and heartbreak, leaving us empty inside. All love is a gamble [*lotería*], wherein we risk the best and deepest part of ourself.

There are no guarantees in this world to cover the risk [*riesga*]. We either accept or reject love. For this very reason every act of love is more than an act of good will: it is an act of trust [*confianza*], and act of faith. It is an act of faith launched into the air, without any precise name or clear content. One "has to value the trouble [*valer la pena*]" in spite of fate and in spite of the blind indifference of life which does not seem to notice the terrible gravity which it has for each one's being and deliverance.[220]

We would note that this is an almost identical parallel to the phenomenological analysis with which we began this chapter. But Segundo seeks to advance his argument here in such a way that a correlation can be perceived between human experience and ecclesiology.

We then, *we* [Christians] know that such trust is well placed. We know that it is placed in good hands; that is, that there is Someone who has responded with a "yes," and that such gesture is not lost in the void. As St. John has said, we are precisely "those who have believed in love [*creído en el amor*]" because we know the name of Him who is the origin and object of all love.[221]

In yet another text, Segundo provides this moving description of Christian faith as a daring, but promising venture in the midst of life's challenges:

It is as if Jesus had said something like this: "Through my resurrection and the sending of the Spirit, I have replaced proclamation with reality. Henceforth I shall never calm the storm again as I once did. But my Spirit will calm the storm when you have mastered the technique of constructing ships strong enough to ride out its waves. I shall never again return to feed a multitude in the desert, but I shall do it when my creative Spirit in you has led them to improve the earth's soil and distribute its fruit better. And if you suffer in these love-inspired tasks, I cannot help it. Because now I am no longer 'in your midst' and rather 'within you': as the source of the love, the creativity, and the persistence that leads men to love each other more effectively and fraternally. Indeed it is I in each of you that suffers from the stormy sea, the arid soil, the misery of poverty and alienation. Like you and with you I suffer too. I have not shipped you off on a voyage without knowing whether the port of arrival is worth the trip. The great guarantee, the only guarantee, that I can give you is that I have shipped out with you in a committed and definitive way."[222]

The second point that Segundo makes about the dialogue between beginning faith and full faith is that "beginning faith must pose questions and encounter the corresponding answer that can only come from full-fledged faith."[223] There are two questions that beginning faith poses. The first question has to do with the "hope [*esperanza*]" of love: "Is love worth the trouble in light of the possibilities of the failure of love?"[224] Such questions are prevalent when there is a "crisis of hope" (evidenced, for example, in experimental marriages and the fear of nuclear annihilation). Segundo sees such times of questioning, however, as occasions in which "God's grace is preparing a dialogue with the faith which springs from the revelation of God."[225] It is a time for the community called Church to recognize that it has something to offer.

Do we not know that no love is ever lost? We know from our faith that what love constructs is not destroyed by any obstacle, even though it may seem so. Authentic love builds the new earth in some unseen way. And in that new world we will be astonished to see standing the things that we thought had been destroyed over and over again. This does not give us concrete solutions. But it does mean that the solutions which we must seek out with the rest of humanity bear the stamp of certainty [*certidumbre*] which springs from our faith.[226]

The second question has to do with the "scope" or "extent [*amplitud*]" of love: "Is love worth the trouble beyond the restricted circle of family, of those who think the same way, of those who are of the same class, the same race, the same religion, or the same nation?"[227] The concern for security is prominent in such a question, leading to the temptation "to put controls on love and not let it have free play."[228] The Christian may not have a precise response; but again, there is something that full faith may contribute to the question of beginning faith: "the least of human beings has an absolute value and hence an absolute right to be loved, whatever the price may be: 'Anything you did for one of my brothers, however humble, you did for me' (Matt. 25:40)."[229] Segundo calls Christians "to recognize the 'signs of the times,' that is, to have the capacity to analyze contemporary happenings in relation to the divine plan that paves the way for this saving dialogue."[230]

Segundo's masterful endeavor to prepare a dialogue between beginning faith and full faith helps demonstrate a useful correlation between human experience and the community called Church. In some respects, the dialogue Segundo presents resembles Paul Tillich's recognition of a dialogue between "justification and doubt."[231] However, the question might be raised: what if the promising "signs of the times" are not present? What if there is no sign of the serious practitioner of love (or, in Tillich's case, no serious doubter)? What implications might this have for the dialogue between a beginning faith and full-fledged faith? Segundo might respond that such questions are merely hypothetical. At root, however, such questions might pose some interesting challenges to Segundo's anthropological and ecclesiastical understandings. For the moment, however, our concern is only to see the intricate consistency of Segundo's theological position on how the relationship of "faith" to "faith's works" is one of distinction-without-separation.

Chapter 2
Faith that Works: Part Two

Biblical Hermeneutics, Revelation, and Pauline Theology

In the previous chapter, we examined the two predominant emphases of Segundo's theology: the "faith/ideology" dialectic and ecclesiology. We noted, furthermore, that Segundo has correlated these two emphases in such a way that a central thesis emerges from his theology: *"faith" and "faith's works" need to be distinguished, but they cannot be separated.*

What we need to examine in this chapter is how this thesis is in continuity with what Segundo himself calls the "fountainhead of our faith, that is, the Scripture."[232] In the first part of this chapter, we will demonstrate how this thesis is in continuity with Segundo's understanding of biblical hermeneutics and revelation as an "educational process." Then we will consider, in the second part, the specific focus of Segundo's analysis of Pauline theology, especially in Romans. The choice of Pauline theology is not arbitrary. Within the context of Segundo's own biblical theology, Paul plays a prominent role.[233] Segundo has also dedicated an entire text to Paul's theology in Romans.[234] Here, we are particularly interested in demonstrating that the central thesis we have noted in Segundo's theology is consistent with Pauline theology. The third section of this chapter, we will determine whether or not Segundo enjoys an exegetical consensus to support the central thesis vis-à-vis Pauline theology.

I. Biblical Hermeneutics and Revelation

Segundo regards the Scriptures as the common source of all Christian theology. "Christianity is a biblical religion, that is, the religion of a book or of various books, for that is precisely what the word 'Bible' means."[235] Hence, there is no distinction between liberation theology and academic theology on the use of the Scriptures per se. All theology "must keep going back to its book and reinterpreting it."[236] Furthermore, both liberation theology and academic theology avail themselves to the critical sciences that help to unlock the past: "general history, the study of ancient languages and cultures, the history of biblical forms, and the history of biblical redaction."[237] The "fundamental difference" between these theologies, according to Segundo, is that liberation theology seeks to "combine the disciplines that open up the past with the disciplines that help to explain the present" precisely because the understanding of the theological task is "to interpret the word of God as it is addressed to us here and now."[238] "Without this connection between past and present there is no theology of liberation in the long run."[239] Hence, the biblical interpreter must not only examine what the text is saying, but she must also be aware of the factors that influence her present understanding of the text and the present ideologies to which the text must speak.

The Hermeneutic Circle

We could debate how accurate Segundo is in his critical assessment of "academic theology." But the key thing we want to recognize here is that the distinction he is drawing is the basis for his definition of a key methodological concept in his theology, the *hermeneutic circle*, defined as "the continuing change in our interpretation of the Bible, which is dictated by the continuing changes in our present-day reality, both individual and societal."[240] It takes as its impetus the recognition that "each new reality obliges us to interpret the word of God afresh, to change reality accordingly, and then to go back and reinterpret the word of God again, and so on."[241]

The concept of the "hermeneutic circle" presupposes two conditions: First of all, there must be something about reality that gives rise to change in interpretation. "The questions rising out of the present must be rich enough, general enough, and basic enough to force us to change our customary conceptions of life, death, knowledge, society, politics, and the world in general."[242]   The second condition is that the new understandings of the Scriptures can address the questions that reality poses.   "Moreover, if the interpretation the Scripture does not change with the problems, then these problems will go unanswered, or what is worse, receive answers [that are] old, unserviceable, and conservative."[243]

Keeping these two conditions in mind, Segundo outlines the four principal and operational factors of the hermeneutic circle.

> *Firstly* there is our way of experiencing reality, which leads us to ideological suspicion. *Secondly* there is the application of our ideological suspicion to the whole ideological superstructure in general and to theology in particular. *Thirdly* there comes a new way of experiencing theological reality that leads us to exegetical suspicion, that is, to the suspicion that the prevailing interpretation of the Bible has not taken important pieces of data into account. *Fourthly* we have our new hermeneutic, that is, our new way of interpreting the fountainhead of our faith (i.e., Scripture) with the new elements at our disposal.[244]

We note that the use of the term "hermeneutic circle" is derived from Bultmann,[245] and the use of the term "suspicion" is derived from Paul Ricouer.[246]   All derivations aside, Segundo is using the terms in his own way to capture a complete hermeneutic approach to the Scriptures: one that takes cognizance of past and present reality and finds ways to use the Scriptures as an instrument for liberation in the present.   Alfred Hennelly describes Segundo's method as "*deideologizing,*" which makes it "far more comprehensive and profound in its implications for all humanity than the demythologizing [and existentially individualistic] project of Bultmann and the theologians who have followed him in this century."[247]

The "faith/ideology" dialectic described in the previous chapter is very much recognizable in this hermeneutical method. The "ideology" of a particular moment in history may well constitute an expression of "faith."   But the times may be such that new *expressions* of "faith" (new *ideologies*) may be required precisely to express the "faith" in that new era, together with its new problems and challenges.   This recognition of the "faith/ideology" dialectic within the hermeneutical method leads us into a consideration of Segundo's concept of "revelation." On the basis of that consideration, we will then see how the central thesis is particularly prominent in Segundo's biblical theology.

Revelation as "Educational Process"

Segundo is critical of many ways in which biblical revelation has been appropriated. At the heart of his criticism is that most approaches are too "static" in their concept of revelation. They take a particular text or a particular insight from Scripture, and then they insert that text or insight into the contemporary situation as the "word of God" for our time.[248]

Many of Segundo's compatriots in liberation theology do not escape the scalpel of his argument on this point. Segundo points out that much of liberation theology shows a decisive preference for "the Old Testament in general, and for the Exodus event in particular."[249] The rationale for that preference is understandable, given the Latin American situation of oppression and the suitable biblical emphasis on "God the liberator and the political process of liberation which leads the people of Israel from bondage in Egypt to the promised land."[250] But in Segundo's estimation, such a preference is too simplistic because it oblivious to the fact that, in the New Testament, the liberation Jesus brings and Paul advocates has little to do with any "liberation vis-à-vis political oppression."[251] Furthermore, Segundo regards as "forced" the argument of some European and Latin American scholars that Jesus was aligned with the Zealots of Israel.[252] The real oppression, Segundo emphasizes, was coming from the Jewish theocracy, controlling the lives of the people through the Mosaic Law. Jesus' theological opposition to the Law "was such a political threat that the authorities of Israel made use of Rome's authority to eliminate this dangerous *political* adversary."[253]

This argument does not negate Segundo's firm affirmation of the biblical focus in liberation theology. However, it does call for a more profound reading of the Scriptures. The Old Testament, as a history of the people of Israel, is a history in process, an *educational process*. Throughout its history, the Hebrew community encountered unique problems that required new and more promising answers. "Only in connection with the problems that are embodied in the questions of the community can we comprehend who exactly this responding God is.

If we fail to understand the situation and problems of the community, we cannot possibly come to know that God."[254]

Segundo believes that this kind of ongoing educational process carries on into the New Testament. This becomes evident in Segundo's response to the question: "What is the exact relationship between. . . the revelation of Jesus in the New Testament and the revelation of God in the Old Testament?"[255]

Segundo thinks that most answers to that question tend to move in opposite directions. On the one hand, there is the theory of *continuation*: "Jesus constitutes one more link in a chain of revelation, the revelation itself being one basically and all of it being true."[256] Segundo cites Matthew 5:17-18 ("Do not think that I have come to abolish the law or the prophets [i.e., the Scriptures]. . . .") as evidence to support this position, and concludes that

> Jesus, with these words, seems to be presenting his message as one more element in a direct and positive continuity with the past revelation. The implication seems to be that the Scriptures are not a body of law in the modern sense of the term. Instead, they embody a divine plan of long-term duration. Jesus did not come to alter this plan, but to bring it to its fulfillment and completion. And if we consider that plan as an educational one, then we are forced to conclude that Jesus is making himself a part of that plan rather than upsetting it.[257]

In contrast to the theory of continuation, there is the theory of *correction*, which claims that there is "a break in continuity, a qualitative leap (difficult to describe precisely) in Jesus' revelation beyond the older divine teaching."[258] Here, Matthew 7:28-29 ("Jesus . . . taught them *as one who has authority*") is cited as textual support for his corrective stance vis-à-vis the Mosaic Law. Also cited are "Jesus' authoritative statements on gratuitous love" that call for the loving of enemies (Luke 6:27-36; Romans 12:17-21) and are in direct contrast to the holy war invectives of Deuteronomy 7:14 ff.[259]

Catholic theology has postulated a theory of *sensus plenior*, the "fuller sense" of Scripture, as an attempt to reconcile the conflicting theories of "continuation" and "correction." According to this "fuller sense,"

> Jesus' revelation allegedly pointed up the true sense of older revelation, a sense that had not been appreciated even by those who wrote down

God's revelation. With his revelation, in other words, Jesus provided
people with new light for understanding the real import of persons,
doctrines, and events in the Old Testament.[260]

Segundo, however, explicitly rejects this mediating approach, together
with the theory of "correction," because he believes that both distort
the "unity of faith." But this does not mean that Segundo embraces the
theory of "continuation." There is no easy reconciliation of conflicting
texts between the Old and New Testaments.[261]

In an effort to propose his own solution, Segundo suggests that
there is something continuous as well as something discontinuous in
each stage of revelation. Here the "faith/ideology" dialectic comes into
full prominence. "One element is permanent and unique [hence,
continuous]: *faith*. The other is changing and bound up with different
historical circumstances [hence, discontinuous]: *ideologies*."[262] In
this framework, Segundo is able to look at the whole of Scripture as a
book of faith that remains an ever-continuous and liberating process
throughout history, but it is expressed in various ideologies that change
to meet the needs of the times. There is always one faith, but there are
many ideologies, many expressions. Segundo calls for "a *clear
distinction* between [these] two elements."[263]

The deeper ramifications of that conception is that it extends into
the ongoing revelation of God through the tradition of the church and
into the present time. Segundo opts for an approach that seeks

> to invent an ideology that we might regard as the one which be
> constructed by a gospel message contemporary with us. What would the
> Christ of the Gospels say if he were confronting out problems today? If
> the faith is one amid the diversity of history, then there must be some
> ideology that can build a bridge between the faith and our present-day
> situation even as there were such ideologies in the past.[264]

How does one go about determining "what Christ would say"?
Segundo suggests that one needs to see revelation for the present time
in a process of "learning to learn" or "deutero-learning" from previous
expressions that are present in Scripture.[265] "Faith. . . is the total
process to which man submits, a process of learning in and through
ideologies how to create the ideologies needed to handle new and
unforeseen situations in history."[266] Segundo contends that it is in the
context of this faith-process that the Spirit of Christ is active.[267]

The obvious implication of this perpetual construction of ideologies by faith is that *the two cannot be separated*. Segundo says as much:

> From what we have said so far it seems clear that is makes no Christian sense at all to try to separate ideologies from faith in order to safeguard and preserve the latter. Without ideologies faith is as dead as a doornail, and for the same reason that James offers in his epistle: it is totally impracticable (James 2:17).[268]

It is interesting that at this point Segundo offers four brief and condensed remarks about Paul's hermeneutic of "Christian moral obligations in light of the revelation of Jesus." Even though the next section of this chapter will explore Segundo's understanding of Paul's theology, the four points are worth citing here for our consideration of Paul in the larger spectrum of biblical revelation.

> a) Only concrete love gives meaning and value to any kind of law existing in the universe (Rom. 13:8-10).
>
> b) Any and every type of law represents a decisive element for Christian conduct insofar as it points up more or less constant relationships between things and persons. But such laws are not decisive as moral laws (Rom. 14:14). They are decisive as constants in the service of the love-based plans and projects of human beings (1 Cor. 6:12 ff.; 10:23 ff.), since they furnish these projects with criteria for judging what is or is not *expedient* in carrying them out (1 Cor. 10:23-29; Rom. 14:7-9).
>
> c) Since this desacralizes the law as a static inventory of questions concerning the intrinsic morality of a given line of conduct, the conduct of the Christian must undergo a basic change. *Faith* rather than the law must serve as the springboard for launching into a new adventure. One's destiny will depend on this venture, but it possesses no *a priori* criteria established in advance. The Christian must accept the riskiness of projects that remain provisional and will often go astray (Gal. 5:6 and *passim*; Rom. 14:1 ff.).
>
> d) Therefore this faith does not consist in intellectual adherence to a certain body of revealed content as the definitive solution to theoretical or practical problems. Nor does it consist in having confidence in one's own salvation, thanks to the merits of Christ. Instead it entails the freedom to accept an educational process that comes to maturity and abandons its teacher to launch out into the provisional and relative depths of history (Gal. 4:1 ff.; Rom. 8:19-23; 1 Cor. 3:11-15).[269]

"Faith," concludes Segundo, is "maturity by way of ideologies, the possibility of fully and conscientiously carrying out the ideological task on which the real-life liberation of human beings depends."[270]

All of this tends to conform to the central thesis that Segundo claims: a distinct, but inseparable, relationship between "faith" and "faith's work" (ideologies). "While faith is not an ideology, it only has meaning as a foundation for ideologies."[271]   Faith is a *"freedom for history, a taste for the future, an openness for the provisional and relative."*[272]   Faith is "ever in the service of historical solutions to human problems--even though the latter solutions will always be provisional and incomplete. Faith, then, is a liberative process. It is converted into freedom for history, which means freedom *for ideologies.*"[273]   Faith is, therefore, neither "a plane of eternal certitudes which are destined to be professed" nor is it some phenomena which is to be simply "translated into actions."[274] "Christians cannot evade the necessity of inserting something to fill the void between their faith and their options in history. In short, they cannot avoid the risk of ideologies."[275]

II. Pauline Theology

Segundo's theological enterprise, including his approach to biblical hermeneutics and revelation, is consistent and consonant with the central thesis regarding the relationship between "faith" and "faith's work." In this section, we will focus more closely and explicitly on Segundo's understanding of Pauline theology. At the outset, there is a need for a disclaimer, or at least a qualification. Our purpose *here* is not to engage in a critical evaluation of Segundo's understanding of Paul. That will be addressed further in the final chapter. Our purpose here is to demonstrate the *consistency* of Segundo's thought by demonstrating that the central thesis (*"faith" and "faith's work need to be distinguished, but they cannot be separated*) is evident in Segundo's understanding of Pauline theology.

One might think that Segundo, especially in an effort to uphold the proximity of faith and works, might be more inclined to give larger place to the Epistle of James than to the epistles of Paul. Nevertheless, when Segundo marshals his evidence on how "the earliest Christian communities were aware of the problem stemming from the necessary complementarity of faith and ideologies," he looks first to Paul.[276] Segundo contends that Paul and James are continuous, and not antithetical, in their perspectives.

> "Faith" (in Paul's sense) is necessary in order to liberate human beings from their obsession with their own safety and security. With such "faith" they are freed from "religious" inhibitions as they immerse themselves in a relative and changing history and go to "work" (in James's sense) in accordance with the values-structure implied by their faith and demanded by reality.[277]

One may perceive Segundo's affinity for Paul from his earliest writings onward. When Segundo seeks to define the meaning of "orthopraxis" ("Christian conduct in accordance with the Gospel"), his primary source is Paul.[278] Segundo claims that it was Paul who first called for a Christian morality that was creatively free, that was progressive in bringing that freedom to bear on humanity's needs in each epoch through love, that was thoroughly social in outlook, and that was significative in the world through ongoing dialogue.[279] When Segundo describes the biblical understanding of the length, height, breadth, and depth of God's grace, he supports his description by appealing to Paul.[280] When Segundo develops his concept of "masses and minorities," he turns first to the New Testament theology of Paul.[281] Much of Segundo's earlier analysis of the theology of Paul culminates in his commentary on the theology of Paul in <u>Romans</u>.

Introduction to The Gospel of Paul

If "faith" brings promising answers to the problematic questions of every age through varying "ideologies," then it would seem logical that the same understanding applies to Paul's role in the "educational process" of revelation. Segundo's analysis of Paul's Epistle to the Romans is within the larger framework of his expansive treatment of the "faith/ideology" dialectic. <u>El hombre de hoy ante Jesús de Nazarét</u> is organized in such a way that the first volume lays the foundation for the "faith/ideology" dialectic. The second volume carries that foundational understanding into the New Testament (specifically, the Synoptic Gospels and Paul's Epistle to the Romans) and into examples from later Christian spirituality (specifically, Ignatius and Segundo's own contemporary evolutionary approach). In the "General Introduction" to the second volume, Segundo begins with a long quotation from Leonardo Boff's <u>Pasión de Cristo</u>.[282] This quotation is intended to convey the important and necessary task of developing a contemporary expression of *gospel* (good news). That task outweighs the need for a scientific christology. A christology, according to Segundo, is designed for the purpose of making the faith something that can be intellectually grasped. "A gospel, by contrast, is preached or proclaimed. In it the faith is offered to people. They are summoned to let themselves be captured by its allure and to structure their world of meaning and values accordingly."[283] Segundo, therefore, prefers to call his approach an "*antichristology*," that is, "an effort to talk about Jesus in such a way that it may open people up to seeing him as a witness to a more humane and liberated human life."[284] Segundo clarifies further:

> I am not proposing a *logy* about the Anti-christ. Instead I am trying to offer an anti-logy about Christ. I am trying to free him from all the false pretensions of human beings, of Christians certainly, to grab hold of him, box him in universal categories, and thus strip him and his cross of their bite and scandal.[285]

The question of Augustine becomes "the respectful but unavoidable human question we must put to Jesus: *Why are you talking to me?*"[286] It calls for a promising answer that the person of each age can understand, one that does not wander from the construction of "a valid bridge between christology and soteriology."[287]

Essentially, therefore, Segundo is arguing for "the ongoing task of creating gospels that are truly goods news for our contemporaries, while still continuing to verify their *coherence* with the gospel that was preached in history by Jesus of Nazareth."[288] "Jesus of Nazareth should be able to speak very different languages. The manifold meaningfulness of his life and message for humanity should be clear and free to operate."[289] In light of this evangelical understanding, Segundo turns to Paul's Epistle to the Romans in order to "interpret Paul, and through him, Jesus."[290]

Segundo regards an "anthropological" key as the most appropriate hermeneutic for Romans (thus, "The *Humanist* Christology of Paul"). Segundo contends that Paul perceived the existential life of *every human being* caught in a battle ground between contending forces: Flesh and Spirit, Sin and Faith, Death and Life. Paul "personifies *the forces that intervene significantly in every human life*, the forces that any human being will detect when it looks into the depths of its own existence, regardless of outer circumstances or religious background."[291] At the heart of the Pauline gospel is the claim that "God, moved to compassion by the sacrifice, merits, and justice of Christ, declares just someone who continues to be impious."[292] The key ingredient of this gospel is "Faith," by which the impious receive Christ's justification. "Only faith. . . is capable of leading the human being, enslaved to Sin, to a declaration of justice and hence reconciliation with God."[293]

Segundo's analysis of Romans is divided into eight chapters, each corresponding to the following pericopes: 1:16-32; 2:1-28; 3:1-31; 4:1-25; 5:1-20; 6:1-7:13; 7:14-25; and 8:1-39.[294] With the exception of the sixth and seventh chapters, therefore, each chapter of Segundo's text corresponds to a chapter of Romans. For the purposes of our analysis here, however, we will make four thematic divisions of Segundo's material: (1) Sin's Enslavement of Humanity (Romans 1:18-3:20); (2) "Declared Just" by Faith (Romans 3:21-4:25); (3) The Reconciliation in Christ (Romans 5); and (4) Faith at Work in Liberation (Romans 6-8).

(1) Sin's Enslavement of Humanity (Romans 1:18-3:20)

In Segundo's analysis of Romans, "Sin" is the enslaving force of both pagans and Jews, that is, all of humanity as conceived in Paul's historical framework. Segundo maintains, however, that Paul treated paganism in one section (1:18-32) and Judaism in another (2:1-3:20) because the *mechanism* of Sin is different for each group. By "mechanism," Segundo is referring to the "means" that Sin uses as its force to enslave the human being.[295]

In his provocative commentary on Romans 1:18, Segundo contends that the mechanism of Sin for the pagan is "injustice."

> There are two parts to the verse in which Paul sums up pagan enslavement to Sin: "The wrath of God is being revealed from heaven against every type of *impiety* and *injustice* of human beings who are holding truth fettered in *injustice*" (1:18). In the first part Paul cites two possible types of sins that can be committed and undoubtedly are: sins vis-à-vis God (*impiety*) and sins vis-à-vis human beings (*injustice*). In the second part, however, Paul drops any mention of impiety. Injustice alone is left as the mechanism of enslavement to Sin. And so we get to the curious opposition that becomes central in Romans 1: *truth/injustice*.

. . . It is *injustice*, and injustice alone, that subjects the human being to Sin.[296]

While Segundo regards "injustice" as the mechanism that Sin employs, he also notes that human beings are already highly susceptible to its influence in their "*desire or craving* for injustice."[297] "Paul attests to this pre-existing element when he tells us three times that God '*hands over*' the human being to itself or to something inside it."[298] Toward the conclusion of his second chapter, Segundo offers a definition of this "pre-existing element":

> The word used here [in Greek it is *epithumia*, which means "strong or passionate desires", "cravings"] is translated as "concupiscences" [*concupiscentias*, in Latin Vulgate]. It introduces a new character in Paul's anthropological analysis: *the Flesh*. That character plays a major role in the behavior of the Galatians and the Corinthians, as we have noted. In Paul's system, the Flesh is the seat and source of the strong, root desires of the human body, its cravings, which are really akin to what Freud calls "instincts" in his psychology.[299]

In an earlier source, Segundo indicates that he is following Karl Rahner's understanding of "concupiscence."[300] Rahner describes "concupiscence" as the "basic nature" inherent in human beings in tension with the "person" of free decision (which is God's gracious gift to *all* human beings). "Concupiscence" weighs down the "person," the core of one's free being, keeping it from ever fulfilling itself. Thus people cannot recognize their actions as their own.

> Concupiscence consists essentially in the fact that man in this regime does not overcome even by his free decision the dualism between what he is as nature prior to his existential decision and what he becomes as person by this decision, not even in the measure in which it would absolutely speaking be conceivable for a finite spirit to overcome it. Man never becomes wholly absorbed either in good or in evil.[301]

Segundo clearly exercises this understanding of concupiscence in the first part of his schematic reading of the mechanism of Sin that enslaves (pagan) humanity:

> [First, there is the] *desire or craving for injustice*, [secondly,] self-justifying and self-deceiving reasonings, [thirdly,] creation of an

infrahuman idol that justifies injustice and, finally, the fall into infrahuman mutual relations. *There would be no enslavement, you see, if the human being were master of its actions, no matter how bad those actions might be.* But by stopping their ears to the truth that disturbs them, human beings become enslaved beings, beings driven by an alien power. Their works serve the purposes of another; and that other in Sin, which is the negation of God's project.[302]

It would be erroneous to conclude that Segundo does not recognize sin as a serious problem. All human beings ar truly enslaved and plagued by Sin throughout their historical existence. But Segundo is more intent on demonstrating concrete human sin as the "*result*" of human inability to withstand the mechanism of Sin. In other words, Segundo understands *sin as something that enters between the "spontaneous intention" and "concrete performance" of human actions.*[303] This is consistent with Segundo's earliest position on the subject of sin:

> While it is certain that there exists in every human being a personal principle of liberty, a desire and an exigency to determine for oneself what one aspires to be rather than to be handed this ready-made, it is no less certain that the natural order of the universe seems to be unaware of this principle of liberty and treats man as just another cog in its mechanism. . . . All of us human beings possess an incipient liberty that seeks fulfillment. But in the power of nature that invades us and dwells within us, *our incipient liberty encounters something which belongs to us and conditions all our executions even though it is indeed alien to the innermost core of our own ego.*[304]

Note that sin is not is an *inheritance* affecting the very core of our being, with the direct consequence of "punishment or vengeance" on God's part.[305] As it will become clear later on, the victory over Sin comes in the *ability to connect* the two elements of "spontaneous intention" and "concrete performance."

Before leaving this section on Sin's enslavement of humanity, however, we need to examine the mechanism of Sin that is effective in Judaism (Romans 2:1-3:20). Romans 2:8 ("indocile to the *truth* but docile to *injustice*" [Segundo's translation]) regards the mechanism of Sin in Judaism as similar to the mechanism of Sin in paganism. The result is the same: "a dehumanization of human relationships."[306] Segundo's comparative list of sinful conduct among Jews and pagans in Romans is most illuminating:

> "There is no one who is just, no one who has sense," parallels "replete
> with every injustice . . . senseless" (3:10-11 and 1:29.31). "No one who
> seeks God" parallels "haters of God" (3:11 and 1:30). "All have gone
> astray, all together have become useless" parallels "to do the unsuitable"
> (3:12 and 1:28). "There is no one who does good, not even one"
> parallels "replete with every . . . wickedness" (3:12 and 1:29). "An
> open grave is their throat, with their tongues they are in the habit of
> deceiving, snake poison is under their lips" parallels "full of . . . deceit,
> malice, gossipers" (3:13 and 1:29). "Their mouth is full of curses and
> bitterness" parallels "slanderers . . . insolent, haughty, boastful" and
> "full of . . . murder, quarreling" (3:15 and 1:29). "Destruction and
> misery pile up along their ways and they have not known the way of
> peace" parallels "replete with every . . . wickedness, outrage . . .
> inventive in wickedness . . . pitiless" (3:16-17 and 1:29-31).[307]

But Judaism is significantly different from paganism in that it has been
entrusted with the "normative revelation" of God's Law. Their
"dehumanizing cravings or desires" and their unique mechanism of Sin
is, therefore, in their sense of *privilege* as bearers of the Law.

> Sin enslaves by *shackling* that revealed and normative truth. To do that,
> it must darken the heart of the Jews and cause them to become entangled
> in their own reasonings. . . . Sin accomplishes this by turning Jewish
> attention from the *fulfillment* of the Law to the *privilege* they enjoy by
> virtue of having the Law. This means that the Law ceases to provide the
> disturbing knowledge of Sin and at the same time enables the Jews to
> justify their dehumanized relationships with people of other religions and
> non-Jews in general.[308]

In effect, the same schematic pattern that was noted in Segundo's
analysis of the Sin of paganism is apparent in the Sin of Judaism; but
the mechanism is different: (1) craving of injustice (via special
privilege in the Law); (2) self-deception an self-justification; (3)
idolatry of the Law; (4) dehumanized relationships.

> Here, then, is the great paradox. The Jews, making use of God's own
> normative revelation, commit the very same sin of idolatry that pagans
> do, and for the very same reasons: i.e., to set free their cravings and
> dehumanize their relationships with other human beings. Deceiving
> themselves, they end up entangled in their own self-deception and

enslaved to the power that wields self-deception against God, i.e., Sin.[309]

(2) "Declared Just" by Faith (Romans 3:21-4:25)

Segundo notes correctly that beginning with Romans 3:21, Paul begins to establish the theological solution to the enslavement of humanity under Sin: "God sets up *a counterweight to both Jewish and pagan enslavement to Sin*: namely, *Faith*.[310] One is "declared just," or "saved," by faith.[311]

Segundo postulates that Paul has divided God's saving plan in human history into three stages. The first is the stage of *universality*, beginning with Adam. This stage is characterized by the universal criterion of salvation based on one's works--whether the works are "good or evil." The ambiguity of this stage gives rise to the second stage of *particularity*. This stage begins with Moses and the giving of the Law to Israel as a "mediator" of the necessary "moral *discernment*." But even this particularity becomes a problem with the emergence of a sense of sacred privilege. This leads to the final stage.

> The final stage must combine the positive elements of the first two stages: the universality of the first stage with the moral level of the second stage. And it must do away with the unsuitable aspects of the first two stages: the moral confusion of those depending solely on subjective conscience and the moral conceitedness of those who regard their objective, sacred particularity as a privilege vis-à-vis God. So this dialectical process will culminate in the third stage, the Christian one.[312]

Later in his analysis, Segundo will elaborate on this thematic of the "three stages." He will refer to it in the dialectical categories of thesis-antithesis-synthesis, respectively.

> As Paul sees it, then, the plan of God is to lead human beings "from faith to faith" (1:17) to justice. That is a bird's-eye view of the whole process, which starts with a universal "thesis", proceeds to a particular "antithesis", and then reaches its "synthesis" in the recovery of universality that is embodied in the *singularity* of Jesus Christ.[313]

The similarity of this framework to the categories of Hegel is obvious to the reader, and Segundo is aware of this fact. Nevertheless, he insists that "dialectical thinking is much older than Hegel, and that it is in fact a normal human way of envisioning processes."[314] In fact, Segundo challenges "any exegete to present a non-dialectical explanation of the role played in Romans by God's granting of the Law and the stage that begins and ends with it."[315]

What is apparent in the so-called "third stage" of God's plan in human history, according to Segundo, is that God judges humanity with "a new criterion: *Faith*. All human beings are and remain sinners, but God declares just those who believe in Jesus."[316]

Segundo follows the consensus of exegetes who maintain that *dikaioō* means "to *declare* just." God does not "first *make* a human being just and then *declare* him or her to be so."[317] Segundo's point is that God exercises a "*judicial*" justification upon sinners while they are still "unjust." Justification is not something to be earned. Indeed, the justification Faith brings cannot be earned, but is received as a gift of God's new judgment. "By being *declared just* in this judgment, human beings obtain *redemption* (3:24) and expiation of all 'earlier sins' (3:25). They are then at peace with God (5:1) and saved (5:9), because those who are in Christ Jesus will not be condemned (8:1)."[318] "Faith" is juxtaposed to "works of the Law" (3:28), "works" (3:27), and "Law" (3:21).[319] This sets "faith" in opposition to "glorying" and "boasting" in one's keeping the Law.[320]

However, Segundo affirms a very important point here: *while "faith" and "works of the Law" are antithetical, "faith" and "working good" (Romans 2:10) are not contradictory.* Segundo calls our attention to Paul's use of the terms "works" (plural) and "work" (singular). "*Works*" refers to a sinful system of self-justification. "*Work*" refers to the product of "faith."[321] This might help explain why Segundo opens his discussion of Romans 3 by returning to a detailed exposition of Romans 2:6-11, where "*working* good or evil [is] the criterion of universal judgment."[322] Segundo does not abandon the concept of a universal judgment. We have already seen in Segundo's earliest and formative writings that the Matthean judgment scene (Matthew 25), with its emphasis on "salvation by love," holds a key role in Segundo's understanding of that judgment. This seems to be in contradiction to Segundo's assertion (via Paul) that we are "saved by faith." Segundo's resolution of that contradiction may be present already in his claim that "in Paul's view salvation does come from faith alone, but only because faith enables a person *to act*, to go to work, in a certain way."[323]   Thus, "faith" and "faith's work" are very much related in the reality of salvation, especially given the understanding of Sin with which Segundo is operating.   "Sin and Faith seem to measure *the gap or distance* that is always there between what the human being *intends* and what he or she *actually performs or accomplishes.*"[324]

Turning to Romans 4, Paul cites Abraham as the example *par excellence* of what it means to be "declared just by faith" (3:21-31). Segundo is quick to note, however, that Abraham "could not possibly have had faith *in Jesus.*"[325]   For Paul, Abraham also constitutes "biblical proof" of God's new judgment based on "faith" and not on any kind of "works". The proof is based on three points: the text of Genesis 15:6 which reads that "Abraham *had faith* in God, and *it was credited to him* as justice"; the place of that text "*before* the account of Abraham's circumcision" in Genesis 17; and the fact that "Abraham was 'credited' with justice before God tested his fidelity with a concrete *order*" or command (Genesis 22).[326]

Segundo acknowledges that Abraham is a greatly admired personage in Israel's history. Paul's contention that Abraham was in fact a "sinner" and an example of God's "declaring just the impious" (Romans 4:5) would seem to negate that tradition.[327]   However, Paul's admiration of Abraham is based on a different criterion: the fact that Abraham lived and acted in faith, which sets him above the "infantile" pursuits of those who seek to earn God's favor through obedience to the Law.

> Abraham, by contrast, has an *adult* filial relationship with God, who makes him a father in turn. Abraham is free to resolve moral cases in terms of the suitability of a course of action, as Paul would have the adult Christian do (see 1 Cor. 6:12; 10:23). There is no doubt that Paul displays a nostalgic longing for Abraham's sort of situation, the most *Christian* one before Christ. In Paul's eyes, the transition from that magnificent situation of mature freedom, based on confidence in God, to the observance of commandments is a kind of death (see 7:9).[328]

In Segundo's three-stage depiction of human history, Abraham obviously belongs to the first stage of universality. Nevertheless, Abraham is seen as "a moment of promised synthesis or *pre-synthesis* embodied in a *pre-Christ.*"[329]   It is Abraham's *faith* that makes him such a momentous character. Segundo adds that this "mini-faith" already present in Abraham "should find its maximum development in

Christians because in their case something becomes clear, universal, and certain, that was only a vague, particular, crazy wager [*apuesta*] in the case of Abraham."[330]

What is it that Abraham believed in? Segundo says that Abraham had a "faith *in God*," or more specifically, "the victory of life over death that God makes possible and promises."[331] Segundo bases this on what he refers to as Paul's "creed" in Romans 4:16-17: "[Abraham is] the father of us all . . . in the eyes of God, in whom he had faith as a God *who gives life to the dead* and who calls into being what does not have being."[332] Such a "victory of life over death" includes the evangelical hope which so inspired Abraham "that he could seek the blessing of all human beings and that justification would be given him as well. And what he believed, God turned into reality for him--faith collaborating with his works."[333]

This description of the "minimum content" of Abraham's faith (a faith "in God" and in the "victory of life over death") leads Segundo to make a distinction between "faith in the vaguest sense" (Abraham's faith "*in God*") and "faith in the strictest sense" (Christian faith "*in Jesus*").[334] This distinction is important for Segundo to establish his concept of the universality of faith. There are two points that Segundo highlights from the biblical example of Abraham in this regard. First, Abraham represents universal humanity *in process*.

> [Even] though Abraham is the first *biblical* character who is said to have been declared just by reason of his faith and hence declared *the father* of all, was no one before Abraham able to have that sort of faith, in the first stage of existence? . . . It is hard to imagine that he [Paul] pictures Abraham as a unique and miraculous figure preceded and followed by an enormous void.[335]

Second, when Abraham was declared just by faith, he was still *uncircumcised*. "The Jews divided humanity into the circumcised and the uncircumcised. . . . The term 'pagan' or 'Gentile', synonymous with 'uncircumcised', is applied to the justified Abraham by Paul in accordance with the Bible itself."[336] Segundo then postulates a venturesome conclusion from this analysis:

> Who then shares the faith of Abraham in Paul's view? Without much risk of error we can say: anyone whose actions or works imply that there exists in the universe a power that can give life to the dead and call

into being what does not exist. *Who is a child of Abraham, "the man of faith"? Every atheist, pagan, Jew, or Christian who refuses to have a contractual relationship with the Absolute, who trusts in the promise inscribed in the human values offered by existence and fights for them as if death did not render that struggle futile.*[337]

According to Segundo, Abraham's "faithful" progeny includes many more than those who are normally considered as belonging to the people of God. "*Faith must be an attitude accessible to every human being always, just as enslavement to Sin is accessible to them (to say the least).*"[338] The theological core of this conclusion is evidenced in Segundo's analysis of Romans 5.

(3) The Reconciliation in Christ (Romans 5)

The theme of Romans 5 is "the *great reconciliation* [that] takes place with the death of Jesus Christ."[339] Segundo divides Romans 5 into two parts: the "*moment* and *function* of reconciliation" (Romans 5:1-11) and the "*extent* of reconciliation" (5:12-20).[340] Regarding the *moment of reconciliation*, Segundo writes:

> When God reconciled the human being with God, the situation of that being was *the worst* it could possibly be. It was when we were without power, sinners, enemies of God (5:6.8.10). It was then that God "proved his love for us . . . by the death of his Son" (5:8.10), the greatest and most precious thing God could give us.[341]

Because this "total gift" of reconciliation takes place at the "worst" of all possible moments, Segundo establishes three points about the *function of reconciliation*. The first point is that "Jesus dies *before we can have faith in him.* . . . Faith could not have been a precondition for the gift. It was a consequence of the gift, included in it."[342] In this regard Segundo demonstrates continuity with his earlier writings by taking the side of Karl Barth who limits the role of faith so that it does not become a "restrictive condition" for the "total victory of Christ over Adam."[343] Segundo's second point about the function of reconciliation is that faith was *not* a "consequence" of reconciliation, not even "a secondary or *contingent* consequence that comes *after* human beings have been reconciled and *only now and then*, thus differing a group among the reconciled who are going to receive a

declaration of justice."[344] As evidence, Segundo notes the parallel
contrast between Paul's assertion in Romans 5:1 ("We have been
declared just *by faith*") and Romans 5:9 ("We have been declared just
by his [Jesus'] blood").[345] Given that faith cannot be either a
precondition or a contingent consequence of the reconciliation, Segundo
concludes his analysis of the function of reconciliation by saying
exactly what *is* faith's role in the reconciliation event: "faith can only
be *the reconciled being's whole way of being and acting, freed from
fear and calculation.*"[346] This is especially evident in the example of
Abraham. Abraham was not declared just because God was somehow
obligated to do so when Abraham demonstrated his faithfulness. That
would make "faith" a "wage" to be earned. On the other hand, God
could not renounce his verdict of justice upon Abraham when Abraham
carried out God's command, because "this would invalidate the
principle" of faith.[347]

> The only possible hypothesis is that faith was an *attitude* [*actitud*] which
> did in fact make Abraham a just person, an attitude of walking with God
> as a reconciled person. And this was so because faith was a general
> attitude towards his whole life, dovetailing in its primitive way with the
> type of humanity demonstrated and endorsed by the message, life, death,
> and resurrection of Jesus of Nazareth.[348]

The one who lives in faith's freedom, therefore, lives as a reconciled
being. But faith's liberated function is precisely to work in love.

> To sum up: As we move from the abstract principle enunciated in the
> latter part of Romans 3 to the concrete exemplifications of it in Romans
> 4 and the first part of Romans 5, we discover that in Paul's thought *faith*
> does not replace working (or doing) in God's judgment. On the
> contrary, faith enters into the process of working, transforms it, makes
> it human and mature, and *thereby* receives God's approval in the form
> of a declaration of justice. And the justice is real, even though it may
> be imperfect and compatible with many sins.[349]

The ramifications of this line of thinking become more explicit
when we consider Segundo's analysis of the *extent of reconciliation* in
Romans 5:12-21. Because Christ's victory over Adam is complete and
full, the event of reconciliation must have some value for "*all the
children of Adam*, i.e., the whole of humanity."[350] But how is that
value to be understood? Does this mean that "faith" is given to "all the

children of Adam"?   Segundo's answer is an unequivocal "*yes.*"   It
may not be that *particular* kind of "faith" known as *Christian faith*, but
everyone will have some kind of faith, some kind of "beginning faith"
perhaps, that is "a life-attitude that bets on the immortality and
infallibility of love--not because that attitude precedes reconciliation but
rather because it is *part and parcel of reconciliation itself.*"[351]   It is
here that Segundo is unabashed in his depiction of the universality of
faith and the extent of reconciliation.

> In how many human beings will God find or place the wager [*apuesta*]
> that love is *worthwhile* [*vale la pena*], the hoping in love against all
> hope?   Once again, as if the first part of Romans 5 did not suffice, the
> second part replies: *in all the children of Adam.*   That is what Paul
> thinks, however strange it may seem to us after all the speculation on the
> quantification of eternal rewards and punishments.[352]

Segundo will later claim that all humanity shares this one common
transcendent datum of "faith": that "*loving is worthwhile*, whatever it
may cost in self-giving and even death. . . . It is a 'hope against all
hope', wagering on a future that verifiable existence seems to
belie."[353]   Segundo puts forward three further assertions to elaborate
on this understanding of the extent of reconciliation.   First, Segundo
understands Paul to be saying in Romans 5:20 that Christ's victory over
Sin is universal, reaching back retroactively to the earliest stages of
human history.   "We know find that Sin, which reigned in the first two
stages (Adam to Moses; Moses to Jesus), has been conquered in the
third stage, at least insofar as its enslaving power is concerned."[354]
Secondly, Christ's victory is not only universal but it is also "superior"
to the Sin of Adam.   "There is a 'much more' in the case of Jesus.   He
is a 'superwinner', and he makes superwinners of those whom he loved
(8:37)."[355]   The saving victory of Christ is primarily to be understood
as a "qualitative" victory in the lives of human beings.

> Only one verse clearly indicates the reason for Christ's superiority,
> which lies in the "results".   Grace (Jesus) achieves its result, "following
> the many offenses" (5:16).   The disproportion, then, is *qualitative*.   Sin
> cannot end in Death after one single Grace, one single Love, whereas
> Grace can end in Life and a declaration of justice after all the
> offenses.[356]

But Segundo also concludes that Christ's reconciliation is *necessarily* universal, regardless of whether or not people "accept" the offer of that reconciliation. To assume otherwise "would throw the parallelism of Adam and Christ out of line, at least insofar as results were concerned, with Adam emerging the clear favorite."[357]   "Hence those 'predestined' to be declared just are, *quantitatively, all the children of Adam.*"[358]   Segundo explicitly rejects "the idea that God in divine foreknowledge predetermines those who will and will not accept the redemption and salvation offered to all."[359]   While Segundo considers this divine predestination a "more logical and sensible" conclusion, he maintains that Paul ventured "to predict the use that humans will make of their liberty in responding to God's gift."[360]   That is, *all* human beings, at least sometime in their lives, will exercise their "faith" by which they have already been "declared just."   And "if the freedom of the human being is capable of carrying out what it chooses and, thanks be to God, chooses the good, *one single performance of the good means more than all the abhorrent 'alien' stuff* that has accumulated in the human life."[361]

> Only one hypothesis seems logical on the basis of such a prediction. Human beings will make unforeseeable use of their freedom, to be sure; but there is a *qualitative disproportion* in the *necessary mixture* of their works, which are simultaneously influenced by both Sin and Grace. This disproportion, inherent in the work itself, is what permits Paul to foresee the victory *in all.*[362]

Segundo's third, and final, assertion about the extent of reconciliation is that "Paul's antithetical parallelism spells out what Adam gave to humanity in inaugurating the reign of Sin, and what Christ gave to humanity in inaugurating the reign of Grace."[363] Through Adam, we have received "sin, death, condemnation;" but through Christ, we have received the "declaration of justice, life, justice."[364]   The contrast has to do with the "results" of Sin and Grace, respectively.   Sin is belittled by Grace, because the worst that Sin do is bring the "result" of Death; but Death is overcome by the "result" of Life, "*the Resurrection of all the dead.*"[365]   This emphasis on "results" is intended to replace what Segundo regards as the more "infantile" views of "punishment" (for Sin in Death) and "reward" (for Grace in Life).[366]   More significantly, it clearly understands Life as greater than Death, and "Faith" as greater than "Sin."

[The] enslavement of Sin is a life without hope or meaning for any human course of action guided by some overall purpose. In short, it is a sort of "death in life", a death to purpose and meaningfulness even while physically life persists. Physical death is merely the logical culmination of the whole situation. Hence Paul offers the contrary argument about the Life, or *Vitality* if you will, of human beings of *faith* such as Abraham. These are the people who seek "incorruption" and live trustingly in a Promise. They act gratuitously, motivated by values that they seek and hope to achieve.[367]

Segundo concludes with a vivid description of how "Faith" is able to conquer Sin by bridging the gap or distance between "spontaneous intention" and "concrete performance."

The enslaved human being lives and works as an alienated being. It can be said to *live* a life of its own only if it and all it has done are liberated from their master, even if that be only at the end. Confronted with that Life, the gift of Jesus, Death will have to let go of its prey. The release takes place first invisibly in the interior of the human being, so that it can act *as if* it were child and master. Then the same sort of release must take place exteriorly. The human being must be given back its work and its own physical life, though the latter will not be superior and incorruptible.[368]

(4) Faith at Work in Liberation (Romans 6-8)

Segundo's analysis of Romans has been strictly toward the development of Paul's "humanist christology," especially in the opening chapters. Romans 1:18-3:20 is concerned with the enslavement of all humanity under Sin. Romans 3:21-5:21 develops Paul's understanding of the justification and reconciliation of all humanity by Faith (understood in its most universal, anthropological sense).

With Romans 6, the focus shifts to a very specific consideration of the particular "faith" of those "baptized in the name of Jesus"--i.e., the "Christian" faith.[369] However, this shift does not connote a sense of particular "advantage" for Christians. The salvation that comes from God is based on the criterion of "faith," whether the faith of humanity in general or the faith of Christians in particular.[370] If there is a difference, it is that Christians have a distinctive clarity or knowledge about God's plan that others do not.

The greater significance of this shift, according to Segundo, is for the purpose of a distinctive discussion of the theme of the liberation "faith" brings. Segundo's outline is as follows: Romans 6 addresses the theme of "liberation from Sin" to converted pagans. Romans 7:1-13 addresses the theme of "liberation from the Law" to converted Jews.[371] In Romans 7:14-25, according to Segundo, Paul returns to the anthropological focus and "analyzes the mechanisms that induce *human beings* to become slaves of Sin whether they be pagans, Jews, or Christians."[372]   Romans 8 is Paul's return to "the theme of authentic liberation."[373]

Segundo begins his analysis of Romans 6 with an explanation of the "new instrument specific to the Christian community: *Baptism*, the rite of initiation into membership in that community."[374] "Paul makes clear that this Baptism aims at liberation from Sin. To put it more exactly, he says that Baptism signifies a 'death' that liberates from Sin and the Law."[375] For the churches of Paul's time, Baptism

> served as a suitable sign of the great happening and the distinctive transcendent datum of Christian faith: Jesus put to death and then resurrected by God to a new and higher life (6:4). In Baptism catechumens embraced that happening, grounded their own lives in it, and "assimilated" themselves to its two aspects: death and resurrection (6:5).[376]

The result of this baptismal assimilation into the death and resurrection of Jesus is a "transformation," in which the human being enslaved to Sin dies and the "new human being" is raised to new life as one "declared just of Sin (6:7)."[377]

With this transformation, therefore, it is inconceivable that one continue to be enslaved to Sin.[378] "The new life would consist in not obeying those cravings [of Sin], something which should be possible."[379] Paul, therefore, asserts in Romans 6 that the faith of the baptized Christian affirms "*a new way of behaving that was not possible before but is now.*"[380] Baptism brings "*the possibility of snatching human instrumentality from the service of injustice and putting it in the service of truth*, of the *just* intentions of the human being (6:13-19)."[381] Death has long reigned as the consequence of Sin. Segundo understands Death as the "empty life" that comes through shame and "*alienation*": "the attitude of attempting to disown what one has done so that others will take responsibility. In other words, one puts *distance* between the free 'I' and the work performed."[382]   In

Baptism, Sin and all its consequences (Death) is conquered.

For Jews, Baptism symbolizes a liberation from the Law as an occasion for the Flesh (Romans 7:1-13). Segundo understands Flesh as an attempt "to use the religious realm in a desperate effort to secure for oneself, in a calculable and certain manner, the divine benefits."[383]   The fear of insecurity leads to a "specific craving for security" in the Law.[384]

Baptism sets the Christian free from these "legal commitments."[385]   Christians are free to live in the new life that comes through the Spirit, "the power that God gives human beings to overcome fleshy fear by faith and discover the true purport of the Law."[386]   Faith frees the human being "from the obsession of bargaining with God to obtain salvation through 'works' based on the letter of the Law. Faith frees human beings to be their own masters in their activities rather than continuing to be slaves."[387]   The liberation that faith brings prompts one to do the "suitable" thing that fulfills the *spirit* (rather than the *letter*) of the Law: engaging in "mutual love" (Romans 13:8-10). "Here we have the basis of the attitude of *faith* whose *work* is love (Gal. 5:6)."[388]

But the fact remains that Christians are still "in the flesh" and are besieged by the forces of Sin, Death, and the Law.[389]   The "same mechanisms are still around, capable of enslaving even those who have accompanied Jesus in his death and resurrection."[390]   The reality is that the "*human condition* [of the Christian] is such that it tends to fall into enslavement, hence Death, with or without Law."[391]

The recognition that "the Christian, like any other human being, *is a divided being*" is the focus of Romans 7:14-25.[392]   Here, Paul seems to exercise "his own peculiar pessimism."[393]

Paul clearly equates the "I" with the innermost center of the human being, its authentic, inner humanity endowed with freedom (7:22). But in moving into action and accomplishing work, the human being must travel from inside to outside itself. And in this process, says Paul, impersonal forces take control of human action. So we have a divided human being, described summarily by Paul in these terms: "I know that the good does not dwell in me . . . since *wanting* it is within my capacity but *accomplishing* it is not" (7:18).[394]

In other words, Sin continues to hold sway by putting "distance . . . between intention and performance," depriving the human being of his freedom "to carry out or accomplish what one has chosen."[395]

There is no unambiguous resolution of this conflict between intention and performance by the end of Romans 7. Nevertheless, Segundo maintains that "Paul's existential analysis coincides with a reflection on the significance of the resurrected Jesus. And the resurrection of Jesus, first-fruit and guarantee of the resurrection of all human beings at the end of history, was an *eschatological experience.*"[396] Segundo expands on this point with what he regards as five "distinctive features" of Pauline eschatology:

(1). We must assume that new reflections about the meaning of Jesus' resurrection led Paul to a gradual but thoroughgoing transformation of his earlier conception of eschatology [i.e., Thessalonians]. . . .

(2). We must assume that the resurrection of Jesus does not mean that the kingdom has finally arrived, or that it is about to arrive at any moment. . . . The point, you see, is that it is not simply a matter of knowing what God alone did or did not do. The kingdom of God, or whatever term Paul might use as its equivalent, is a common work of Jesus *and* his disciples, or God *and* God's collaborators (*synergoi*). Its dependence on the work of such collaborators must form a part of eschatology. . . .

(3). Following the same thread, we must also assume certain things about Jesus of Nazareth, the model or "standard of teaching" for his co-workers. Despite his resurrection, he visibly left his kingdom at the mercy of the powers that corrupt human projects, *as if* his, too, had been a "flesh of Sin". . . .

(4). We must assume that only those projects that face up to this resistance to love and overcome it *as effectively as possible* will constitute a definitive service to the plan of God, even though they may seem to be buried under the weight of reality and statistics. . . .

(5). We must assume that there is a *qualitative* disproportion or imbalance, associated with the power of the kingdom, that enables us to determine where the real, definitive victory lies. . . . Only love is constructive, and constructive forever.[397]

This eschatological awareness leads to the hypothesis that the conflict is "*simultaneously a victory and a defeat, but on different levels.*"[398] Romans 8 establishes the validity of that hypothesis by exploring "the relationship between the (historically) visible and the eschatological, between what can be ascertained by analysis and what *will be manifested* in the end (8:17-18.18-21). Paul explicitly emphasizes the difference between what is *seen* and what is *hoped for* (8:24-25)."[399]   From the vantage point of the "historically visible," all that can be seen is a *"mixture* of Sin and Grace in every human action, the combination of egotism and love, self-determined intention and alienated result."[400]   The idea of *dualism* is not unique to Paul; but "Paul is the only New Testament writer to suggest a vision of divine judgment that takes into account the *mixed nature of human action.*"[401]   Segundo offers an example of this Pauline tendency, citing the text of 1 Corinthians 3:10-15.

> Let everyone be careful how they build. . . . For no one can lay any other foundation than . . . Jesus Christ himself. And whether one builds on it with gold or silver or precious stones, or with wood or hay or straw, the work of each one will be made manifest. The day will make it manifest, appearing with fire, and fire will test the quality of each person's work. If a person's work, built on the foundation, stands the test, the person will receive recompense. But the person whose work is burned up will suffer the loss. Nevertheless, that person will be saved, but as one passing through fire.[402]

From this brief passage, Segundo notes the following points. First, Paul makes an "explicit reference to God's universal, eschatological judgment."[403]   Second, "the criterion of judgment is applied to the totality of a human being's activity," that is, one's "work" (singular).[404]   Third, the "suitable" human activity is that which edifies others (1 Cor. 10:23-24; Romans 14:19-20).

> Love consists in collaborating with God in the work of building or constructing a human existence for human beings. Hence the importance of this *work*: it is--partially and secondarily, to be sure--the work of God himself (14:20) on behalf of humanity, and we are cooperators and joint workers (*synergoi*; see 1 Cor. 3:9) in it.[405]

Fourth, there is a crucial difference between "human *work* in the singular, as opposed to human *works* in the plural." The former is based on *"faith;"* the latter is based on *"the Flesh* and its fear-ridden, dickering mentality."[406]

> By *work* in the singular Paul means the free prolongation of the human being in reality through the one and only project that is truly free: i.e., that which unites the human being with God in real, effective love of

brother and sister humans. *Faith* is necessary for us to forget self, our natural fears as creatures, and our sterile accounting approach to our salvation. By faith we put our trust in the gracious gift of the promise. Giving up self-preoccupation, which makes us an easy prey for natural and societal mechanisms, we concentrate all our energies on the project we hold in our hands. In short, as we have already seen in the case of Abraham, *faith* is not opposed to *work*. On the contrary, *only faith makes possible human work*: i.e., free work that bears the stamp of the human being and defies death.[407]

This point is most likely the *norma normans* for our understanding of other statements by Segundo that would otherwise seem reckless: "*Love, faith working in love*, or simply *faith* constitute . . . radically synonymous terms designating the unique criteria by which God will exercise divine judgment over all humanity in all three stages of human history, according to the gospel of Paul."[408] "[For] three centuries after Paul, no one thought of opposing *faith* to *works* and giving faith the decisive role in the face of God's judgment."[409] Finally, the fifth point is that human work is "*a mixture of materials of diverse quality and resistance.*"[410] What "does not proceed from *faith* is Sin" (Romans 14:23) and will not withstand the divine judgment; but God will value and uphold "that dose of 'faith working through love' (Gal. 5:6)."[411]

Segundo then carries this development into his analysis of Romans 8. To be sure, the human being is "divided between its projects and its actual accomplishments" (Romans 7:14-25).[412] Nevertheless, on occasion and perhaps "imperceptibly, the distance between intention and performance in a project of love will almost disappear."[413] Even human history will show signs of this ambiguity.

Analyzing history, we see that progress turns on and against humanity. Even the most humanitarian and promising revolutions go astray. Social consensus, the pledge and jewelpiece of any democracy, has buried within it a crushing mass force. The ideologies of liberty, brotherhood, and love become sclerotic and bureaucratic. The martyrs are lost in the mists of incomprehension and forgetfulness. The sacrifices, in the long run, are made in vain.[414]

The ultimate promise that Segundo holds before his readers is that death and resurrection of Jesus shares in and reshapes the destiny of all human beings.

Only the *unverifiable and eschatological* aspect of the paschal experiences makes clear that God "condemned Sin in the Flesh" (8:3), not to reward Jesus with individual power but to provide his project of the kingdom with the power needed to turn it into a reality. The real victory of Jesus does not change the "appearance" of defeat of a verifiable level. It operates on a deeper level, in which we must believe as we believe in his resurrection, the first-fruit and pledge of our own resurrection and that of all human beings.[415]

Jesus' resurrection victory is "a *transcendent datum* concerning what we can hope for with respect to our existence (8:24-25)."[416] *Faith* in Jesus' resurrection is "the crucial human quality . . . capable of directing all the energies of the human being into the creative project of *love*."[417]   Through faith, the Spirit is at work, snatching from Death's reign "not only Jesus but also his and God's project of full humanization for the human being."[418]   Indeed, the "resurrection of the body" means the resurrection of "human life with all its relationships and projects."[419]

Segundo postulates that Paul puts forward two further transcendent data.   In addition to the resurrection victory of Jesus, there are "the datum of *adoption as children of God* and the datum of *brotherhood and sisterhood* in relation to Jesus."[420]   "In both of them *Faith* will surface implicitly once again as the crucial attitude."[421]

According to Segundo, Paul translates these data into the concrete reality of daily life.   Hence, the "adoption as children of God" means that God is not only Father but also "*creator*" who invites his children to cooperate in the free and creative task of liberating the whole creation which is held "*hostage*" to Sin.[422]   "Being 'heir' does not mean inheriting something already acquired.   It means inheriting something immensely worthwhile *to do*.   And we know that creation remains something to be done because we know that all creation is groaning in the pains of labor up to now (8:22)."[423]

The "universal brotherhood and sisterhood" datum finds its concrete expression in the task of making "human beings *real* brothers and sisters of Jesus."[424]   "It entails the abolition of all more or less religious criteria that give some human beings an excuse to place themselves above other human beings."[425]   The acceptance of this task "depends on *Faith* and the renunciation of security and privilege."[426]   *All humanity* in bondage to alienation constitutes the "second *hostage*" of Sin.[427]   Nevertheless, faith is able to respond to that crisis.

> All the objects of our fear, which detour us into the byways of security
> and the easy way out, have been defeated at their very roots. And this
> is true no matter how much we may try to hallow them religiously by
> placing them above human beings and giving them high-sounding names
> and superhuman attributes: death, life, angels, principalities, present,
> future, powers, height, depth . . . (8:38-39).[428]

Segundo considers this liberation to be "specifically but not
exclusively" a task for Christians.[429]   The Christian is not
independent from humanity's destiny. Nevertheless, Christians are
those for whom "God's plan *is revealed*. . . . Knowing God's plan
should help to enlighten them, and make it easier for them to carry on
the humanization of humanity in history."[430]

Conclusion: Summary of Segundo's Analysis and Proposal

Segundo's summarizes his analysis of Paul's Epistle to the Romans
with the following conclusion:

> I think there are *two terms*, two anthropological personifications, that can
> serve as our guiding thread. Not only do they occupy the whole
> development of Paul's thought in Romans 1-8. They also contest human
> existence as a whole, to the point where Paul can offer this curt summary
> later: "Everything that does not proceed from *Faith* in *Sin*" (14:23).[431]

The predominant term in Paul's "Gospel," the one that makes all the
difference in the world, is "faith."[432] It is by "faith" that a human
being enslaved in Sin is "declared just," and not on the basis of "*works
that are counted up* in order to obtain a legalistic kind of justice."[433]

According to Segundo, this "faith" which characterizes Abraham
and the Christian alike is

> the assertion that *loving is worthwhile* [*vale la pena*], whatever it may
> cost in self-giving and even death. . . . It is a "hope against all hope",
> wagering [*apostar*] on a future that verifiable experience seems to belie.
> Such a future can only come from Someone who values, more than
> anything else in the universe, the hostages created by love's projects and
> works, by true self-giving no matter how imperfect it may be.[434]

Human beings, therefore, are not only "*declared just* by faith," but also through faith get *to live as justified beings*, children of God, cooperators in the kingdom of God.

> The glory of God and the defense of the Absolute do not entail relativizing historical reality in order to make room for the irruption of God alone. The glory of God means seriously making human beings sharers in a joint construction project and giving them all they need to offer this cooperation, without which God alone will do nothing. The personal, creative stamp of each one of these human cooperators (*synergoi* in Greek) with God will be tested and verified in love, in "mutual service". Then it will be inserted in the definitive reality, in the only way that a finite freedom can do that: i.e., by hammering away, like a chisel of a sculptor, at the stubborn solidity of the resistant materials, but with the invisible hope that those materials will be overcome and to some extent turned into God's new heaven and humanity's new earth, the new creation as the joint work of Father and children.[435]

Segundo proposes that Paul *distinguishes* "faith" from "works" in that only by "faith" is one "declared just." However, Segundo also proposes that Paul understood "faith" as that which makes "working in faith" possible, thus rendering "faith" and "faith's works" *inseparable*. This is in keeping with the central thesis of Segundo's theology: *"faith" and "faith's works" need to be distinguished, but they cannot be separated.*

III. An Exegetical Critique of Segundo's Proposal

Our intent in the previous two sections has been to understand and appreciate Segundo's position. The focus here is the *exegetical verifiability* of Segundo's proposal.

Segundo indicates that his assertions are open to critical scrutiny and that he has chosen to follow quite closely the exegetical study in the International Critical Commentary on Romans. This includes both the early edition by William Sanday and Arthur Headlam, and the later edition by C.E.B. Cranfield. Segundo regards his own position as proximate to these exegetes and he refers any and all disagreements of a "scientific", exegetical nature to their commentaries.[436] Segundo's extensive documentation from these sources in his notes seem to bear out that proximity.

While Segundo's right to ally himself with these sources can certainly be honored, he is not excused from exegetical critique, even if he must share that critique with the ICC exegetes. There are several elements in Segundo's analysis that are highly debatable from an exegetical standpoint. Among such elements, we cite the following:

(1)   The concept of Sin (and its "mechanisms") as a problem of "distance" within the human personality per se.

(2)   The "three stage" divine plan of salvation in human history.

(3)   The understanding of Abraham as having "vague faith" and being the paternal figure for all humanity in Romans 4.

(4)   The "necessary universality" of "faith" and reconciliation in Romans 5.

(5)   The reading of Romans 6-8 as the unique understanding and contribution of Christian faith vis-à-vis anthropological faith.

We are not interested here in a detailed exegetical critique of Segundo's analysis. As fascinating as that might be, the immensity of that task would have to be reserved for an exegetical analysis of Segundo's commentary on Romans as a whole. Furthermore, such a detailed analysis would have to be cognizant that Segundo does not follow conventional exegetical norms in his analysis. In that regard, Segundo's commentary may approximate the commentary of Karl Barth who is mildly suspicious of the merits of historical criticism.[437]

For the moment, we will concede that Segundo's analysis is in part debatable, or even erroneous, by exegetical standards. The more pressing question is whether or not Segundo's ultimate *conclusion* about Paul's theology would receive a consensus of exegetical support. In other words, is Segundo accurate in maintaining that Paul *distinguishes* "faith" from "works" in that only by "faith" is one "declared just"; however, "faith" does make "working in faith" possible; therefore, "faith" and "faith's works" are *inseparable*. Does that proposal enjoy a wider consensus of exegetical support as being authentic to Paul?

"Justification by Faith" at the Center of Paul's Theology

Most exegetes of Paul's theology in Romans share the emphasis of Günther Bornkamm: "Paul expounds and develops the *Christian gospel as the gospel of justification by faith alone.*"[438]   Rudolf Bultmann writes, "Paul connects the blessing of salvation strictly, consistently and exclusively to *pistis*. Like Judaism, he describes this blessing as *dikaiosynē.*"[439]   C.K. Barrett comments that "Paul's Gospel" in the saving event of Christ is the basis of "God's righteousness" which "is revealed *on the basis of nothing but faith.*"[440]   Ernst Käsemann similarly echoes that "the justification of the sinner is the centre, not only of the Pauline message but of the whole Christian proclamation."[441]

There is, of course, the minority expression of Krister Stendahl that "the doctrine of justification is not *the* pervasive, organizing doctrinal principle or insight of Paul, but rather that it has a very specific function in his thought."[442]   For Stendahl, Romans 9-11, not the first eight chapters of Romans, is the centerpiece of Paul's theological agenda.[443]   Käsemann challenged Stendahl's position, claiming that Romans 9-11 must be seen in the broader picture of Paul's doctrine of justification. "The doctrine of justification dominates Rom. 9-11 no less that the rest of the epistle. It is the key to salvation history, just as, conversely, salvation history forms the historical depth and cosmic breadth of the event of justification."[444]   In response, Stendahl focused on, and rightly rejected, Käsemann's misrepresentation of Stendahl's position as a polemic against the Jews.[445]   Nevertheless, Stendahl did not give adequate consideration to Käsemann's deeper concern for the *centrality* of justification to Paul's theology, even in Romans 9-11.

It is interesting to note here that Segundo also sides with those who support the "central role of justification" in Paul's theology and that Segundo regards Stendahl's position as an "extreme hypothesis."[446]   Stendahl maintained that "Paul was a man of 'robust' conscience" and "nothing like the *simul justus et peccator* figure seen in him by Augustine, Luther, and the introspective plague of the West."[447]   Segundo counters that "Romans 7, particularly verses 14-25, is obviously introspective and explores the anthropological depths of the human being. Hence, it constitutes the strongest argument against the thesis proposed by Krister Stendahl. . . ."[448]   Nevertheless, Segundo praises Stendahl for bringing about "a Copernican revolution in the exegesis of Paul, explaining why there was no real consideration of any possible justification by faith during the first three centuries of church history."[449]   This tends to confirm Segundo's thesis that "for three centuries after Paul, no one thought of opposing *faith* to *works* and giving faith the decisive role in the face of God's judgment."[450]

"Righteousness of God" as "Righteousness of Faith"

One of the key issues among the German exegetes of Paul's theology is the nature of "God's righteousness."[451] Käsemann, in particular, revolutionized Pauline exegesis with the assertion that "God's power reaches for the world, and the world's salvation consists in the fact that it is led back under God's dominion. *Dikaiosynē theou* is *Heilsetzende Macht*."[452] Käsemann's emphasis on the "righteousness of God" is especially apparent in his commentary on Romans.[453]

Käsemann's renewed emphasis on the "righteousness of God" is regarded by some as an advance over the limited existential-anthropological approach of Bultmann.[454] Bultmann regards "faith" as essential to the "righteousness of God": "The attitude of man in which he receives the gift of 'God's righteousness' and in which the divine deed of salvation accomplishes itself with him is *faith*."[455] Indeed, the two main divisions of Bultmann's text ("Man prior to the Revelation of Faith" and "Man under Faith") make it apparent that Bultmann thinks of "faith" is a predominant Pauline accent. Bornkamm also joins the two themes of "righteousness of God" and "faith." "What Paul teaches is not the general theological proposition that God is righteous. The distinctive feature in his gospel is that *God's righteousness is conveyed to believers*."[456] Similarly, Barrett contends that there is "a close inner relationship between saving righteousness and faith; only those who have faith are restored to a true relationship with God. . . ."[457]

By contrast, the perspectives of Karl Barth and Markus Barth downplay the relationship of "faith" vis-à-vis the "righteousness of God." Karl Barth systematically translates Paul's word "faith" (*pistis*) as "the faithfulness of God," displaying an unmistakable preference for divine faithfulness over human "faith."[458] This is in conformity with Karl Barth's understanding of the Gospel as the proclamation of "a God utterly distinct from men."[459] The role of "faith" is to affirm the "No" of Christ's Resurrection to human and worldly projects.[460] Justification by faith is secondary to christology, as are all anthropological and ecclesiological claims.

> The *articulus stantis et cadentis ecclesiae* is not the doctrine of justification as such, but its basis and culmination: the confession of Jesus Christ, in whom are hid all the treasures of wisdom and knowledge

(Col. 2:3); the knowledge of His being and activity for us and to us and with us.[461]

Anthropological and ecclesiological assertions arise only as they are borrowed from Christology. That is to say, no anthropological or ecclesiological assertion is true in itself and as such. Its truth subsists in the assertions of Christology, or rather in the reality of Jesus Christ alone.[462]

Markus Barth, following Martin Dibelius, asserts that "Paul's theology 'is essentially theodicy.'"[463] The principal meaning of the event of Jesus Christ is not that humanity is saved but that God's faithfulness is vindicated.[464] Faith's role is to be a "doxology" to the "faithfulness of God."[465] "'Jesus Christ was made wisdom for us by God, [that is, was made] righteousness, holiness and redemption.' This proposition is synonymous with the confession: 'Man is justified by faith alone.'"[466]

Käsemann's assertion that "the primacy of christology over anthropology and cosmology" might seem to be a ringing endorsement of the Barthian position.[467] Käsemann, however, does not intend that christology be understood apart from "justification by faith." "The righteousness of God manifests itself as the righteousness of faith. . . . Whatever else God's eschatological righteousness may be, at any rate it is a gift that comes to man *dia pisteōs*."[468] Hence, the assessment that Käsemann says very little about "the coordination of God's righteousness and faith, a special and decisive feature for Paul" is perhaps mistaken.[469] In Käsemann's perspective, the justification by faith is not subsumed under christology, but it is only properly understood and appreciated when it is intimately related with christology.

While it is true that for Paul christology must be interpreted and established in terms of the doctrine of justification, it is equally true that the doctrine of justification makes sense and is necessary only when viewed christologically. . . . It [justification] is and remains applied christology. Only thus is it gospel.[470]

Within the context of this broader christological framework, therefore, Käsemann can appreciate "faith" as "the acceptance of the divine address, . . . a decision of the individual person."[471] However, "faith" remains a gift of God's creation.

The essential thing is still that we do not set ourselves in motion, but that we are called out of ourselves through God's Word and miracle. We cannot therefore interpret our faith as our own work, but only as a grace, which is conferred on us, in the face of the world, without our deserts and in the midst of unavoidable temptation. Faith is brought about by the creator by means of his mighty Word.[472]

Käsemann maintains that "Faith is thus the 'condition' of salvation, not as a human achievement, but as receiving and keeping the word which separates us from all lords and all salvation outside Christ."[473] In this regard, he approximates Bultmann who argues against the understanding of "faith" as an *ergon nomou* (W. Mundle).[474] Käsemann, therefore, seeks to maintain a dialectical balance between "faith" and the "righteousness of God."

Faith is not a substitute for righteousness . . . , and one may not infer from the "reckon" that God treats faith as though it were righteousness. . . . It is a condition as poverty is, or waiting for blessing. It is the place where the Creator alone can and will act as such. . . . *Faith is recognized to be righteous* because, in a way that is past human comprehension, it allows God to act on it instead of wanting to be and do something in itself and thereby seeking a ground of boasting. It lets itself be placed by the word in the possibility of standing outside self before God through Christ.[475]

Compared to Käsemann's masterful presentation, Segundo's resolution of the issue of faith's relationship to the "righteousness of God" is much too simplistic. Segundo understands faith as a universal gift. In this way, he is able to maintain the absolute necessity of faith as the basis for justification while upholding at the same time christological and soteriological universality. Nevertheless, one can also conclude that Segundo is in line with Käsemann and others (with the exception of Karl Barth and Markus Barth) in maintaining that "faith" is the key to justification.

One might further conclude that Segundo enjoys wide exegetical consensus in understanding "faith" as a gift of God's grace and not as a "work of the law." However, there is a distinct difference in Segundo's understanding of the relationship of grace and faith. Segundo understands "faith" as a creational datum existing in all human beings, with Christ's victory having cosmic implications for enhancing that faith. Käsemann is perhaps closer to Paul in accenting that "faith" is created in the *proclamation* of Christ's victory. "Faith only lives from hearing. . . . Hearing has a primacy which cannot be replaced by anything else [cf. Romans 10:14]."[476]   Käsemann also affirms (with implications *contra* Segundo) that the Lord who speaks to the listening believer "cannot be replaced by institutions, theologies and convictions [or 'transcendent data'?!], even when these interpret themselves as being the documentations of that Lord."[477]

Ergon pisteōs: The Work of Faith

There is unanimous agreement among exegetes that Paul repudiates any justification "by works of the law" (*ex ergon nomou*, Romans 3:20).   Justification comes "by faith in Christ" (*ek pisteōs Christou*).[478]   But what about the Pauline concept of the "work of faith" (*ergon tēs pisteōs*)? What is the understanding among exegetes with regard to this Pauline relationship of faith and work?

Karl Barth, who did not revere the role of "faith" as much as others, nevertheless did value the relationship of faith and its work in love.

> Where there is faith, there are also love and works. The man who, justified by faith, has peace with God has also peace with his neighbor and himself: That he lives as one who is righteous by faith to the exclusion of all works is something that he will establish and attest in his works--the particular doctrine of justification that we find in the Epistle of James. If in relation to justification no work is important and every work indifferent, in relation to this confirmation every work is important and none indifferent.[479]

Nevertheless, we must not overlook Barth's qualification from his earlier writing.

> *Works*--our doing and our not doing, our inner disposition and the outward ordering of our lives--are significant only within the inner and outer course of our temporal existence. Notable our *works* may be; but we must not overestimate them, we must not raise them to the order of infinity. God alone is the merchant who can pay in the currency of eternity.[480]

Markus Barth argues for the inseparability of faith and love on christological grounds.

> Thus faith in God (or better, faithfulness to God) and love for men are
> realized in Jesus Christ at the same time in the same deed. Faith and
> love in their fullness and depth are triumphant in him. Also, he shows
> that they are ultimately identical with each other and are therefore
> *inseparable*.[481]

In the lives of Christians, "there is no end to the forms" of the
"doxology" of faith; and love is one of those forms.[482]

Bultmann claims that "'faith' both as to degree and to kind realizes
itself in concrete living: in the individual acts of the man of faith."[483]
"Hence Paul can speak of an *ergon pisteōs* (1 Th. 1:3), and he uses the
phrase *pistis di' agapēs energoumene* (Gal. 5:6) for the whole sphere
of that wherein *pistis* must work itself out in individual life."[484]
Bultmann also stresses that John and Paul share an "inner unity" in
their understanding of faith, and that John also upholds "the unity of
faith and love."[485]

Bornkamm affirms that faith working through love (Gal. 5:6) is
"the all-embracing importance of faith as entirely determinative of
man's whole existence."[486]   However, he adds the caveat that "love
and other 'fruits of the spirit' (Gal. 5:22ff.) are not to be conceived as
preconditions of justification."[487]

E.C. Blackman states boldly: "The moral effects of faith can be
expressed in terms of love (*agapē*). Paul never argues this point; he
assume it."[488]

Ernst Käsemann also affirms that the "faith which accepts God's
promise, and is thereby justifying faith, lays claim to that participation
in the universal kingdom of its Lord. . . . The hearing of the promise
does not end with the listener, but sends him out to be tested in the
world and in history."[489]   Käsemann is unique in bringing faith and
faith's work together by accenting the "gift-character" and "power-
character" as part and parcel of the one righteousness under the
lordship of Christ.[490]

> The distinction between justification and sanctification and the sequence
> derived from it were possible only when the gift was separated from the
> Giver, justification was no longer viewed at its center as transferal to the
> dominion of Christ, and instead anthropology was made its horizon. . .
> Gift and task coincide in the fact that both designate standing under
> Christ's lordship.[491]

Georg Bertram contends that the word "*synergoi*" is predominantly used by Paul in the New Testament, and means "God's 'helpers' and 'handymen'" and "'workers' in the kingdom of God."[492] Bertram also contends that the term *ergon* implies a "unitary character . . . to Christian action evoked by God and proceeding from faith. For this reason this action can and must be for Paul the standard by which man is judged (Rom. 2:6). Nor is this self-evident basis of judgment ever challenged in the New Testament."[493]

This brings into focus the controversial text of Romans 2:6-11. John Reumann, drawing heavily from the insights of Käsemann, is undoubtedly correct in asserting that

> "the doctrine of judgment according to works" that Paul retains from the OT (cf. Ps. 62:12) is to be understood now "in light of" his doctrine of justification, the two linked *inseparably*. "A doctrine of justification which avoids the concept of judgment loses its character as proclamation of the lordship of God. . . . A concept of judgment which does not receive its meaning from the doctrine of justification leaves no more room for assurance of salvation."[494]

Reumann believes that Protestant and Roman Catholic exegesis has come closer on this issue.

> Obviously, Protestant exegesis has gone far in recognizing that (and how) Paul speaks of a judgment based on works. Catholic exegetes now insist that the principle of Rom. 2:6, repayment according to deeds, "does not contradict Paul's ideas of justification by faith" (JBC 53:29). Total consistency in Pauline thought eludes most commentators. But the role of God's judgment in the service of justification *by God* is now more widely recognized.[495]

William Sanday and Arthur Headlam speak of "justification as a past act," belonging "to the beginning, not to the end, of the Christian's career."[496] There is "no real antithesis between Faith and Works in themselves. Works are the evidence of Faith, and Faith has its necessary outcome in Works. The true antithesis is between *earning* salvation and receiving it as a gift of God's bounty."[497] Käsemann, however, rejects the perception of Sanday and Headlam.

> [Paul] certainly does not teach that faith and works are complementary (Sanday and Headlam; Filson, *Recompense*, 127ff.), which would

necessarily bring with it either a sequence of justification and
sanctification, or the assumption of a double justification in baptism and
in the eschatological judgment (J. Jeremias, "Paul and James," 370f.;
Lyonnet, "Gratuité," 106; Black), and hence a possible compromise with
Jas. 2:14ff.[498]

But Käsemann's criticisms grow out of a concern that the final
judgment "by faith alone" is not compromised.

> If retribution according to works is no longer a recognition of human
> achievement, as in the Judaism which Paul combats, but the definitive
> revelation of the lordship of Christ in judgment on all human illusions,
> the believer stands with Gentile and Jew under the same measure of the
> same Lord. . . , and the law of the last day is none other than the "law
> of faith" which is already experienced now, namely, acceptance and
> confirmation of the lordship of Christ. Here "by works alone" in fact
> coincides with "by faith alone" (Althaus). The misunderstanding of
> 'partly by faith and partly by works' is ruled out."[499]

Cranfield is less precise that Käsemann in this regard. According
to Cranfield, in Romans 2:6-11, Christians are not ultimately judged on
the basis of "their faith itself but their conduct as the expression of
faith, and similarly by *erga* in v. 6 each man's conduct as the
expression of faith or of unbelief."[500] Cranfield does not disagree
that justification is only by faith, a point which Protestant scholars have
rightly (in Cranfield's estimation) upheld. However, Cranfield does
observe that

> Roman Catholic scholars have generally maintained that justification
> includes moral renewal . . . . Protestants have generally taken the
> opposite view . . . . [A] good many Protestants have put far too little
> emphasis on sanctification, and some have even seemed inclined to frown
> on the appearance of moral earnestness as though it must necessarily be
> evidence of a weakening loyalty to the doctrine of *sola fide*.[501]

Cranfield concludes that "while sanctification is *distinct* from
justification, the two are *not to be separated*."[502] Compare this to the
analogy of H.P. Liddon which Sanday and Headlam cite and claim as
their own position: "Justification and sanctification may be
distinguished by the student, as are the arterial and nervous systems in
the human body; but in the living soul they are coincident and

inseparable."[503]   This understanding of the relationship between justification and sanctification (between "faith" and "faith's works") need not be contradictory to Käsemann's position. However, Cranfield maintains that

> Paul was probably actually thinking only of Christians [in Romans 2:6-11]; but there is little doubt that, had he been asked whether what he was saying also applied to OT believers, his answer would have been affirmative, and it may well be that he did also recognize the possibility that among the heathen there were those in whose deeds God would see evidence of a secret faith unknown except to Himself.[504]

This vague concept of "a secret faith" would probably be regarded with greater suspicion by Käsemann and other exegetes.

The exegetical consensus on the "work of faith" (*ergon pisteuō*) tends to confirm Segundo's position that "faith" and "faith's works" are *not to be separated*, even though they need to be properly *distinguished*. Segundo's concept of "faith" would also find some support in Cranfield's interpretation of Romans 2:6-11. But there is less exegetical consensus for that position.

Conclusion

The exegetical evidence we have examined in this final section confirms the Segundo's central understanding of Paul's theology of the relationship of "faith" and "works": namely, that Paul *distinguishes* "faith" from "works" in that only by "faith" is one "declared just"; however, "faith" does make "working in faith" possible; therefore, "faith" and "faith's works" are *inseparable*. Given the weight of this exegetical support, we maintain that Segundo has Pauline support for the central thesis evidenced in his [Segundo's] theology as a whole: *"faith" and "faith's works" need to be distinguished, but they cannot be separated.*

These first two chapters have presented this central thesis as a capsulation of the constructive proposal in Segundo's theology. The next two chapters examine how this central thesis is at the heart of Segundo's polemical encounters with contemporary theological and ecclesiological understandings, as well as with Luther.

While Segundo's central thesis is grounded in Paul's theology, there are significant unresolved issues in Segundo's understanding of "faith." These issues include the relationship between "faith" and God's grace, the "object" that faith trusts, and what role "faith" actually plays in the last judgment. The significance of these issues await further development in the final chapter.

Chapter 3
The Faith that Works in Dispute: Part One

Segundo's Theology in the Context of Contemporary Catholic and Protestant Theology

The previous chapters outline the constructive proposal of Juan Luis Segundo's theology. We argued that his entire theological enterprise revolves around a central thesis: *"faith" and "faith's works" need to be distinguished, but they cannot be separated.* Furthermore, this thesis unites Segundo's own theology with the biblical theology of Paul, to which Segundo appeals.

In this chapter, we will seek to demonstrate how this thesis is in contrast to the theologies of Segundo's contemporaries. Specifically, we will focus on Segundo's encounter with the theology of the Chilean episcopacy (1970-1973), with European political theology (particularly, Jürgen Moltmann), and with Joseph Cardinal Ratzinger (the lead representative of the present Vatican Congregation for the Doctrine of the Faith). Each of these theological parties appear to be challenged by Segundo on separate theological issues: namely, ecclesiology, eschatology, and ecclesiastical authority, respectively. However, it will be demonstrated that the central thesis on the relationship of "faith" and "faith's works" is at the heart of these differences. That is, according to Segundo, all of these theologies in some way separate "faith" from "faith's works." The significance of this point for Segundo may be briefly stated: when "faith" and "faith's works" are uncoupled or when concrete historical "works" are somehow depreciated, "faith" itself is diminished in its importance and value.

I. The Chilean Episcopacy (1970-1973): Ecclesiology and the Relationship between "Faith" and "Faith's Works"

In the early 1970's, the Chilean bishops clearly regarded ecclesiology to be a central issue. Two documents were issued on the doctrine of the Church. "The Gospel, Politics, and Brands of Socialism," published on May 27, 1971, presented the major doctrinal position of the Chilean bishops.[505] The second document, "Christian Faith and Activity" (October 16, 1973), was primarily a disciplinary document.[506]

In this latter document, the bishops prohibited anyone from belonging to the "Christians For Socialism" movement. The bishops regarded this movement to be promoting "*a new idea of the Church and its relationship to the world.*"[507] The prohibition of the bishops clearly demonstrates that they believed an ecclesiological issue was at stake:

> The activity of the group known as Christians For Socialism is riddled with ambiguity and calls for clear definition on its part. . . . The ambiguity cannot continue because it is prejudicial to the Church and causes disorientation in many of the faithful--besides being an abuse of the faith and the priesthood in itself. The Church of Christ will not tolerate this sort of damaging harm. *For this reason, and in light of what we have said above, we prohibit priests and religious from belonging to that organization; and also from carrying out the kinds of activity we have denounced in this document in any form whatsoever--institutional or individual, organized or unorganized.*[508]

The bishops do offer a few brief remarks about the involvement of Catholics at the other end of the political spectrum; but here, the bishops are less prohibiting. Such actions on the part of right-winged forces are only described as "grieving," with cautions from the bishops for greater "discretion." The bishops' rationale for this less emphatic stance is as follows:

> The utilization of the faith in the opposite direction is just as regrettable. But it does not call for such extensive examination for obvious reasons. It is not crystallized in organized groups, it does not have the same impact on public opinion, it does not invoke the label "Christian" so explicitly, it does not entail militancy on the part of priests and religious, it is not formulated in written documents, *it does not propound a distinct*

doctrine or vision of the Church, it does not call the fundamentals of faith into question in the same way, and it does not oppose the ecclesiastical hierarchy in the same measure.[509]

Most of the doctrinal rationale for the bishops' prohibition was a restatement of themes from their earlier document. Perhaps that explains why Segundo focuses primarily on the 1971 document for his critical engagement with the Chilean episcopacy. The only comment Segundo makes on the 1973 document has to do with the ironic timing of its release: at the height of the military coup against Salvador Allende and the persecution of his socialist supporters.[510]

Capitalism--Socialism: A *Historical* Crux

Segundo's introductory remarks on "Evangelio, política y socialismos" outline the historical situation in Chile in 1971. One of the dominant political parties in Chile's history was the Christian Democratic Party. Formed by Catholic intellectuals and composed largely of Catholic leaders, the Christian Democratic Party, for the most part, was the normative party of many Catholics in Chile.[511] Enrique Dussel traces its origins to Latin America in the 1930's with "the great effort at reconquest on the part of Catholicism" that "sought to be triumphant and to dominate education, politics, and even economics."[512] The Christian Democratic Party took its cue from the "social doctrine of the Church" that derived its norms from "divine revelation" and natural law theory. As Segundo notes, "the 'social doctrine of the Church' started out by trying to guide Christians to lead a societal life more in conformity with the gospel within the existing capitalist structures."[513] It was the role of the "Catholic hierarchy to determine and spell out the 'specifically Christian contribution' to the process of bettering and improving the existing real-life situation."[514] This social doctrine received its impetus from the encyclical *Rerum novarum*, which precluded the recognition of the legitimacy of socialism.[515]

> The concrete world to which the encyclical was addressed, and within which a more consistently Christian line of conduct was envisioned, was completely dominated by the principle of private ownership of the means of production. Socialism was condemned as an abstract ideal opposed to the natural right of all human beings to own private property.[516]

As political parties go, the Christian Democratic Party was at "the center spot of the political spectrum, operating as *a third possibility* between the socialist parties on the one hand and the conservative parties on the other" and tended to "attract a growing number of members from the middle class, who were afraid of both extremes."[517] As Christian Democrats increased in political power, they recognized that their power base was rooted only on "the failures of the parties on the left and the right" and that they needed "to work out a political platform of their own."[518]

> In other words, it became clearer and clearer that the "social doctrine of the Church" could not pass for a political program--either in the eyes of the electorate or in the eyes of the Christian Democrats who might eventually win power. Realistically speaking, a sermon on socio-economic morality could not take the place of consistent and effective political policy. If the Christian Democracy movement was to differentiate itself politically from the extreme right and the extreme left, it would have to do something more than preach a sermon. It would have to introduce some clear and consistent modification into the law of supply and demand.[519]

It was precisely this Christian Democratic concern to be a "third possibility" that led to the "gradual evolution" of the Church's social doctrine. "It began to call for an ever-increasing 'socialization' of the means of production--deliberately avoiding the use of the word 'socialism.' And it also began to condemn capitalism in clear-cut terms because it was a system based on the pursuit of individual, private profit."[520] Hence, the Christian Democratic Party attempted to win an election on the platform of "communitarian ownership" and "revolution in liberty."

> Both slogans pointed to what was clearly and unmistakably a Christian ideal. . . . The call for "communitarian ownership" clearly represents a middle road between the alleged evils of private ownership on the one hand and of dehumanizing state ownership on the other hand. In a more subtle way, the call for a "revolution in liberty" was also a third-way out, standing between the revolutionless exercise of power by the conservative socialism proclaimed as the necessary way to bring about any radical change in the economic and political system.[521]

The Christian Democratic Party gained power in 1964 under this platform, but it failed to follow through on its initiatives. "It refused to transfer ownership to the community or to revolutionize the capitalistic economic system."[522]   Recognizing growing unrest within the Christian Democratic Party, Christian Democrat leaders began to adopt a platform more to the left.   Nevertheless, the Christian Democrats lost the 1970 election, partly because members had "lost confidence" in their Party's ability to implement its platform and partly because the people of Chile recognized that the necessary guarantees of change were already present in the "socialist" platform of Allende and the Popular Unity Front.[523]   Even though Allende secured only 36.3 percent of the popular vote, in accordance with the constitution he was elected to the presidency and his office was confirmed by the Chilean parliament on October 24, 1970.[524]

While the Popular Unity Front pursued "by legal means" to further the socialist changes in Chile, "the fact is that the structures of Chile continued to remain capitalist" and Allende was going to need the support of the Chilean parliament to enact his new measures.[525]   The Christian Democratic Party could make the difference *if* it "came to feel that it had more affinities with the construction of a socialist society than with the extreme right. *Hence the political judgment made by Christians would prove to be decisive in spelling out Chile's future.*"[526]

Chile was at a historical crossroads in the decision for its political future. The situation was such that a "third position" did not meet the pressing need, however well-intentioned it may have been.[527]   The key issue had become whether Chile was going to continue fostering the existing capitalist system or give itself to the construction of the socialist program under Allende. In actuality, the Christian Democratic Party abandoned its "third position" and embraced the conservative parties that sought to keep capitalism in Chile. Christian Democrats allied themselves with the right-winged fascist movement known as the "Fatherland and Freedom" calling for the violent overthrow of the Allende regime. Christian Democrats also used their slight majority in parliament (under the leadership of Eduardo Frei) to paralyze the reforms of Allende.[528]

The events leading to the demise of Allende's regime are well-documented. National Party members, representing the landowning aristocracy, joined forces with right-winged efforts in Chile to sabotage Allende's reforms. Allende also had to contend with forces outside the country, including the following: the covert operations of the CIA and the National Security Council in secret collaboration with ITT; United States' funding of the Chilean military which functioned independently of the executive branch; controls on wages, prices, credit and investment in Chile by the Nixon Administration and banks and multinational corporations based in the United States, all of which served to undermine Allende's efforts to nationalize the economy.[529] Segundo notes with bitterness that the Christian Democratic Party slogans were "only its way of saying that it was not with the left--not even when the left was trying to put through those very objectives. . . . [The] Christian Democrats handed over the reigns of government to the military junta."[530]

It is important to note that the bishops of Chile had already encouraged the search for a more just economic system, having already denounced ten years prior to Allende's reign "the profound injustice of the capitalist system."[531]

> Using official statistics, they pointed out a host of unpleasant facts: e.g., that ninety percent of the national income was distributed among only ten percent of the population. Whereas the per capita income of the vast majority came to about forty-five dollars a year, the privileged ten percent of the population had an annual per capita income of $3,500.[532]

What would they do when they were confronted with the historical situation they themselves helped to create and in which "the political judgment of Christians would be decisive"?[533]

"The Gospel, Politics, and Brands of Socialism"

In 1971, the Chilean bishops issued their draft document entitled "*Evangelio, política y socialismos.*" Three statements in that document capture the thrust of the bishops' position and they are the basis of Segundo's critiques.[534] The first statement is the consistent reply of the bishops concerning the "Church's option" in every historical context: "The Church opts for the risen Christ."[535] The second statement is the reply of the bishops when pressed about their political option: "Before the different human groups, the Church *does not opt.*"[536] The third statement is the reply of the bishops to the historical situation in Chile with regard to socialism as an option: "Marxist socialism up to now cannot be accepted as a *true alternative* to capitalism, since both remain precisely in the same materialist and economic plane."[537]

These three responses form a coherent ecclesiological perspective that remains to be spelled out clearly. More significant for our consideration here, however, is Segundo's claim that the bishops' document is "a history-making document in *the relationship between faith and ideologies* in the Latin American Church."[538]

"The Church Opts for the Risen Christ"

"The Church opts for the risen Christ" is the succinct response of the Chilean bishops to questions about the role of the Church in the socio-economic situation in Chile in 1971.[539] The answer does not fit the question, or is at least unclear compared to the bishops' earlier denunciations of capitalism. Nevertheless, it is revealing of their particular ecclesiology. The Chilean bishops understand the Church's faithfulness to the Gospel to mean that the Church is a transcendent reality beyond all historical circumstances. Segundo demonstrates this on the basis of the following claim from the bishops' document:

> The Gospel is *another thing*: it is a calling from God to the human being and to the human community to infinitely pass beyond themselves, opening themselves to the divine life which Christ brings to them. . . . Whoever lives the Gospel makes himself in turn more human--more for love and more for Love--even *more than human*, because the freedom which is enjoyed in Jesus Christ is that [freedom] of the children of God."[540]

Segundo expresses three concerns with regard to the bishops' assertion. First, "'being a Christian' is [regarded as] a greater privilege than 'being human.'" Segundo regards that understanding of unique "privilege" to be the "guiding thread of the entire document," taking precedence over any understanding of socio-political involvement.[541] Second, "only Jesus Christ can promise and work" the full liberation that ultimately matters.[542] The document "does not think that Jesus Christ promises and works *by the means of* liberative options (even if they are historically ambiguous)."[543] According to the bishops, since the Church alone possesses the unique "salvation" in Jesus Christ, the Church's proper role is to uphold that "salvation" in order that all Christians may be one in the face of potentially

troublesome socio-political differences.   The Church regards any
"opportunities and guarantees" of socio-political systems as a
responsibility belonging solely to the proper technicians.[544]   The
Church, therefore, becomes a *"Church-in-itself,"* with emphasis on
"unity in our absolute and fundamental option for the risen Christ."[545]
Third, Christians who engage in collaboration with any political system
must recognize the "risk" that such collaboration engenders.   That
"risk" is understood by the bishops' document as jeopardizing one's
right to belong to the *Church*.   That is, being a partisan of an
ambiguous political cause (in particular, a socialist cause) is to risk
one's identity as a Christian.   According to Segundo, "this is the
decisive confirmation of valuation [in the bishops' document] for the
'Church-in-itself.'"[546]   Segundo asks, "Would it not be possible to
consider that an alternative understanding is that the Christian *is
prepared*, or prepares himself efficaciously, for collaborating with the
system which seems most liberative?"[547]

Segundo characterizes the bishops'"conception of the Church as a
separate community, sinful to be sure, but perfect in its possibilities in
offering to the rest of the world what the world seems to be
lacking."[548]   Segundo regards the bishops' ecclesiology as
synonymous with the ecclesiology of some Evangelical Protestants,
particularly that of C. Peter Wagner. Segundo advances six points
from Wagner' understanding of the nature and value of the Church:

1. The function of the Church is the *individual reconciliation* of all
human beings with God. . . .
2. Among the different functions of the Church, priority goes to *the
salvation of souls*. . . .
3. The work of Christ is reduced to his activity through the gospel
message *within the Church*. . . .
4. The *unity of the Church* and membership in it is more important than
any socio-economic-political option. . . .
5. The "theology of the radical left" does not take into account the
dualism of the Bible and, in particular, the *negative supernatural forces*
that rule this world. . . .
6.   Finally, according the Wagner, there is no *universal plan of
salvation*, but only a salvation which passes through evangelism and
individual conversion.[549]

Segundo concludes by saying that the Chilean bishops should have been
as forthright in making similar points "instead of trying to arrive at the

same conclusions while concealing, in a more sophisticated manner, the real theology that is at the base of their document."[550] In Segundo's estimation, the bishops' ecclesiology attributes "an absolute value to those objects, words, gestures and authorities which appear to form a vertical link between the faithful and God, and a purely relative value to the historical functionalism of all this."[551] Segundo labels this as the "heteropraxis of absolutized Churches [which] rests on a radical heterodoxy--the progressive *loss of faith in the gospel of Jesus Christ. . . , the loss of faith in its human functionality.*"[552]

Segundo contrasts this "absolutized" ecclesiology that he perceives in the Chilean bishops with the kind of "functional" ecclesiology that he sees evidenced in Vatican II and affirms as his own.

> The two approaches [the Chilean bishops and Vatican II] are incompatible. The first supposes that the Church is in possession of all which fundamentally interests the human being and his destiny, and it grieves the Church that the rest of humanity does not recognize and accept it for its own good. The second presents the Church as a messenger of truth which has not yet arrived at its end: historic efficacy. Therefore, the purpose of the Church is not accomplished . . . if that truth received by Christians does not carry them to "be united with the rest of humanity in order to seek the truth and to resolve with wisdom the numerous problems . . . which present themselves to individuals and to society" (Gaudium et Spes, para. 16).[553]

Segundo believes that the bishops are "embarrassed by the new guidelines spelled out by Vatican II and their own Medellín Conference."[554] He further recognizes that the bishops use the lack of a "homogenous line of thought" in the documents of Vatican II as an excuse for "defending the older view of faith as an autonomous value."[555] For example, Segundo cites Gaudium et Spes, para. 42, which reads: "Christ, to be sure, gave His Church no proper mission in the political, economic, and social order. The purpose which he set before her is a religious one." He then comments that this would seem to suggest that "we are dealing here not only with different *functions* but different *values*. Thus it has not been easy for the Catholic Church to move through the postconciliar world, for one can find at least two opposing views of faith within the very documents of Vatican II."[556]

In an article that appeared a full year before the Chilean bishops' document, Segundo dealt with the Conciliar understandings on the role

of the Church in the world.[557]   There, Segundo sought to uphold the
distinction-without-separation inherent in the contrasting concepts of
"sacred" and "profane", "religious" and "temporal", "natural vocation"
and "supernatural vocation", "Church" and "world", etc.[558]   In
Segundo's estimation, the Church's pastoral practice too often embraces
a "separation" (and not simply "distinction") between these concepts.
This represents one position in the Conciliar documents.[559]   A second
position calls for a "conceptual distinction" but "not a separation."[560]
Finally, a third position is that there is a "distinction" that is more than
merely conceptual (i.e., that the Church brings something unique in its
"revelation"); but nevertheless, there is "no separation" between the
Church and the world. This third position (which Segundo affirms as
his own) is distinguished from the second position in that the unique
role of the Church is neither "minimized" nor separated from the
world.[561]   Segundo believes that all three of these positions are
evident in the Council, but "for the sake of the laity" only the second
and third positions can have any lasting value for the Church's pastoral
practice.[562]

In summary, it is erroneous to conclude that Segundo criticizes per
se the idea that "the Church opts for the risen Christ." What he is
really criticizing is the "ethereal or inaccessible" use that the Chilean
bishops have made of that "option."[563]

"The Church Does Not Opt"

In light of the Chilean bishops' ecclesiology, the document's
response to any question of political option is not surprising:

> If we take the word "opt" in the strict sense, that is, *choosing* one group
> and *excluding* another, then it is clear that the problem is being posed on
> the basis of a simplistic and dualistic view of realty that attempts to
> divide human beings into two groups: "the good guys" and "the bad
> guys." Furthermore, it forces us to speak out in *favor* of one of these
> groups and *against* the other. . . . Therefore, before the different human
> groups, the Church *does not opt.* In and with Jesus Christ, the Church
> decides for those whom Jesus Christ himself has decided: *for all the
> people of Chile.* . . . To opt for one determined party would imply the
> exclusion of other Chileans, for whom Christ also shed his blood.[564]

The bishops reaffirmed this position in 1973: "The Church can truly say that she is *a-political*."[565]

Segundo certainly perceives the consistency of the bishops' position.

> Why can't the Church choose sides? According to the Chilean bishops, it cannot do that because in practice it would mean excluding from the Church that portion of Christians who have opted for the other side. But in their view the Church belongs to all the people of Chile. In other words, to use our terminology, it means that *the one faith must not be put in the service of ideologies*, which are many and varied by very definition.[566]

Segundo also perceives that the bishops' position maintains two important critical presuppositions: On the one hand, the bishops basically admit that ideologies are primary in the minds of the Chilean people, much to the dismay of the bishops. On the other hand, the bishops assert that faith is something to be prized above any and all ideologies. Thus, even those ideological decisions made in the light of the gospel are regarded by the bishops as a threat to faith rather than a conscious living out of that faith.[567]

Segundo's critical response, however, points out that a price must be paid for the bishops' position. First, there is "the relativization of the condition of those who are exploited and of those who do the exploiting."[568] Segundo is willing to affirm the bishops' claim that greater emphasis should be placed on the "interior attitude" and not on the external condition of people.[569] But Segundo also notes how the bishops misuse that line of argument. For example, the bishops state that Jesus' Sermon on the Mount

> deals with a *spiritual* poverty, consisting in an *interior* attitude. . . . But the same Lord has said that this *interior* poverty is more easily accessible for those who live in conditions of *exterior* poverty. Therefore, the love of the Church for the socio-economic poor is not only based on their condition of "suffering" and being "oppressed" by their misery, but it also is based on this *greater facility* which the people have for being poor *always inwardly*, remaining open to love.[570]

Segundo rebukes this claim by the bishops as being totally antithetical to the message of Jesus in the Sermon on the Mount and a perverse justification of the condition of poverty.[571]

Secondly, the price to be paid for the bishops' position is to relativize all political involvement. Segundo quotes the bishops:

> Therefore, remaining united in our *absolute and fundamental option* for
> the Resurrected Christ [?], we can, in practice, arrive at the different
> political options. We all wish [?] to open our step into history in the
> liberating strength of Christ; but we differ in the appreciation of paths.
> The Gospel only requires the sincere decision for the former. For the
> latter, the conscience of each person ultimately decides. . . . The
> Church, *as a whole, in all the people of God*, does not opt politically for
> any party or specific *system*.[572]

The bishops embrace this "neutral stance" toward all political options
because they have "another kind of liberation" in mind--one that
"restores value to the 'actions' of the Church." That "decisive
alternative" for the Church is to work toward "a diminution of conflict"
by offering "the service of unity and dialogue."[573] However, such a
posture, Segundo argues, looks the other way when people are
experiencing "institutionalized violence."[574] As Segundo says
elsewhere,

> not choosing at certain critical junctures in history is really choosing
> anyway. If a person or group refuses to choose because they have *higher*
> values to defend, then they are downgrading the values that are at stake
> in a given specific situation. They are saying that the latter values are
> dangerous, inferior, or at the very least secondary. Whether they realize
> it or not, whether they want to or not, they are thereby helping to
> perpetuate the existing situation.[575]

The bishops' ecclesiological perspective envisions the role of the
Church as embracing everyone. Segundo counters: "A massive church
is not in the service of the mass. It is intrinsically conservative."[576]
Segundo points out that Jesus was able to tell the difference between an
oppressor and one who is oppressed. Furthermore, Jesus was not
afraid to take the side of the oppressed.[577] However, the bishops, in
their stated desire to offer a gospel to "all the people of Chile," are
unwilling to allow the gospel the freedom to become involved in the
world, protecting the gospel from any chance of "relativization" in the
world. Segundo regards that as a gospel with "no value at all."[578]
In sum, the ecclesiological stance of the Chilean bishops comes at the
cost of a gospel that is concretely meaningless to the people of Chile
in their political circumstances.

The "Great Sin" of Marxism

As Segundo sees it, "the great sin of an ideology is evident from the way in which the Chilean bishops analyze the *socialist* ideology."[579] Hence, Segundo traces the steps that the bishops have taken in their critique of socialism, adding his own counter-criticisms along the way.

Segundo observes that the bishops are confronted with a problem at the outset. The bishops assume that Christians already "know and have experienced" the "dehumanizing effects of capitalism." It is assumed, however, that Christians "do not know" the dehumanizing effects of socialism. Segundo quotes from the bishops' document:

> We have already in large measure experienced the dehumanizing effects of capitalism, and we *know* where they reside. Furthermore, the Pope and we ourselves have previously denounced [those effects] on repeated occasions. . . . Many Christians, but contrast, *do not know* enough exactly about those aspects of Marxism which deserve special objections in the light of the Christian vision of humanism. In reaction to a *known* and endured suffering of evil--the excesses of capitalism--we can tend, at times, to incline ourselves sympathetically and *too candidly* toward a socialism which, even though it is not yet experienced, we imagine as idyllic.[580]

The bishops believe that Marxist socialism is not a "true alternative" to capitalism, and set their agenda to demonstrate the dehumanizing effects of the former. Segundo, however, raises some serious questions about this approach. First, he asks whether or not capitalism is really "known and experienced" as dehumanizing. "Will those who are already rich and "happy" [through the benefits of capitalism] know where its dehumanizing effects reside? Will it be enough to have those effects denounced such that the dehumanizing ingenuity will be regarded as already defeated?"[581] Second, Segundo regards the bishops' "very significant" use of the phrase "excesses of capitalism" as an ideological bias that does not really allow for any kind of socialism to receive a fair hearing. Can something that is "known" (capitalism) be equated with the knowledge of a socialism that has "not yet been experienced"?[582]

Segundo also points out the bishops' prejudicial language in their analysis of socialism. Segundo notes that in the third part of the bishops' document ("Christians and socialism"), the words "danger" and "risk" are used repeatedly, mostly in reference to socialism. Furthermore, the bishops encourage the avoidance of the "seduction" and "preoccupation" with socialism, expressing their own "uneasiness," "caution," and "fear." Segundo argues: "That already forms a climate, and one certainly opposed to all motivation and enthusiasm."[583] By contrast, the negative inferences with regard to capitalism are meager.

> Even more serious is the lack of such references to capitalism, perhaps because that was taken for granted. In any case, these words ["danger" and "risk"] are applied twenty-four times to socialism, once to capitalism and socialism, and only once to capitalism. Terms denoting dehumanization are used fifteen times: e.g., "dehumanizing," "inhuman," "anti-human," "destructive of the human being," "mutilating," "trampling," "staining with blood." Of these, twelve references are to socialism, one to capitalism, and two to both.[584]

When Segundo's text here was quoted by the "Christians for Socialism" in their convention report, the Chilean bishops responded that Segundo had made an "unacceptable and injurious statement" in light of all the Church has done "on behalf of the poorest."[585] Segundo, however, does not deny that the Church may have done work in providing "alms" for the poor; but he is criticizing the bishops for undermining the relationship between faith and its expression in any kind of socialist ideology.

The next step for the bishops is to develop their method for analyzing socialism in Chile. The bishops believe that because Allende was a Marxist, all future socialism in Chile must necessarily be "of *markedly Marxist inspiration.*"[586] Segundo laments at the bishops' lack of imagination:

> Christians ought not as such look to their own goal of socialism, but to a future which Marxism will fabricate. That is their option [according to the bishops], and the document points constantly to that risk--a risk not counterbalanced, at least thematically, by the Christian incapacity for humanizing the reigning capitalism.[587]

The method of analysis which the bishops have chosen helps them to solve their epistemological problem vis-à-vis the nature of socialism in Chile by pointing to other experiences of Marxist socialism. This allows them to gauge Marxism by its "internal dynamic," which they regard as "economic determinism." Furthermore, they note that economic determinism "*tends* to lead to anti-human excesses."[588] Therefore, Chile can only become like all of the other problematic historical realizations of Marxist socialism. Segundo poses serious questions about the underlying presuppositions of the bishops' position. First, Segundo queries how an "internal dynamic," once "known," could "serve as a guidebook to contingent reality in the midst of a complex international panorama with innumerable variables!"[589] Second, have the bishops really made a serious effort to understand the "internal dynamic" of Marxism, let alone Marx's thought?[590] Segundo notes the bishops claim that Marx fostered an "economic determinism": "The material strengths of *production* (that is, of technology) and the situation of human beings in the relation of *production* and *property* (that is, the social classes) not only *condition* but also *determine* the consciousness."[591] Segundo questions the legitimacy of the bishops' interpretation of Marx's use of the word "determine." "Without a doubt some of the Chilean bishops are not very well-read in Marx, but ought to have contacts with the most simplistic, many times official, [representation] of his thought. They interpret it smoothly and easily as economic *determinism*."[592] Segundo establishes his case against the bishops' by quoting the very next sentence from the bishops' document: "Lenin writes, following Marx's logic, 'Our morality is entirely subordinated to the interests of the proletariat and the demands of the class struggle.'"[593] Segundo comments:

> If the sense of the phrase of Marx was economic determinism, then the first two words cited by Lenin would be the most solemn contradiction of Marx, and not a consequence of Marx's logic. There does not exist some possible morality, not even the most perverse, where there exists an economic determinism.[594]

Third, Segundo does not see how the bishops could disregard the papal decrees of John XXIII "that Christian faith should not view ideologies as dogmatic monoliths; that it should evaluate them in terms of their historical embodiments and the changes produced by real-life implementation."[595] Segundo laments:

> Could one not question how it is possible that a Church, which

recognizes the dominant orientation in the national process as Marxism, does not make an effort to even understand it? It is not enough to excuse the Church by claiming that the Marxists ignore, on their part, any revised and more original vision of Christianity. . . . The Church officially maintains, "The faithful live *in very close union* with the rest of humanity in their time, and they must seek to penetrate their manner of thought and experience" (Vatican II, Gaudium et Spes, para. 62).[596]

Nevertheless, what is most problematic, according to Segundo, is the ultimate rationale for the bishop's approach. Segundo notes how the bishops want to convict both capitalism and socialism for committing the "same error" of an "economicist mentality" which deprives human beings of what is "*most important: their spiritual transcendence, their ordination to God.*"[597] The bishops do not think it is bad enough that Marxist totalitarianism has "trampled and stained with blood the history of many peoples."[598] They are more concerned with what they consider to be the "greatest sin" of Marxism: its denial of transcendence or, stated positively, its "atheism." Overlooked by the bishops is "the fact that Marxism is not an ideology that subordinates society to atheism but rather an ideology that subordinates atheism to the construction of a more just society."[599] Segundo then adds, "Marxism poses a real challenge to the Christian faith, which claims to have the same commitment: i.e., to subordinate the Sabbath to man, and *the faith to the solution of historical problems.*"[600] Segundo notes that the bishops, in their anti-ideological position,

have often denounced the same dehumanizing elements in capitalist society without making any reference to its atheism or religiosity. And it is worth noting that the elements overlooked in their analysis are precisely those elements which have to do with the relationship of *faith and ideologies.*[601]

Hence, we arrive at the heart of the bishops' assertion that "socialism is not, in Chile, an alternative to the existing capitalism."[602] Segundo believes that the bishops have in effect made an option in spite of their desire to avoid such an option. "What it in fact means is that one is to accept the *status quo.*"[603] The bishops opt for the existing capitalism that they denounced earlier rather than the possibility of an untried socialism.

So long as no ideologies about this *reality* arise, faith has nothing to fear from the *fact* that extremely wealthy human beings live alongside extremely poor human beings. The problem arises when an *ideology* challenges this *reality*. The great sin of "Christians For Socialism," in other words, is that there is no party of "Christians For Capitalism." Of course such people exist, but they do not have to join together under a banner to exercise their influence and carry out their program. But any attempt to put through a radical change in the existing structures must present itself as an *ideology*. It must knock on the door of the Christian heart and appeal to its relationship with the authentic values of the faith.[604]

Conclusion: The Ecclesiological Separation of "Faith" and "Faith's Works"

Segundo's analysis of the theological position of the Chilean bishops demonstrates that they are operating with an ecclesiology that regards the Church as basically aloof to their contemporary historical challenges. This was dramatically evident in 1973 when the bishops met again to prohibit membership in the "Christians For Socialism" movement because it did not accept that "the existing reality is sufficient for the faith."[605] The bishops were essentially correct in asserting that "Christians For Socialism" were fostering a "new idea of the Church and its relationship with the world."[606] But the newness of this idea was traceable to the ecclesiology of Vatican II and Medellín.[607]

The issue here is greater than ecclesiological differences. The theology behind the ecclesiology of the Chilean bishops calls for "faith" to be *separated* from "faith's works," and not merely distinguished. According to the bishops, the Church is to be separate from the world, and faith is to be separate from ideologies. Whenever the "works of faith" get too close to being seen as actual expressions of the faith, the bishops draw back, fearing that the "absolute" (i.e., the *Church's* faith) will somehow become "relativized." They are unable to perceive "faith" and its transcendent quality as a radicalizing agent that does not take one out of this world but empowers one to live fully and concretely in the world for others. This may entail undertaking the political task of working for "socialist" change. The result of the bishops' theological position, as Segundo has demonstrated, is not only a depreciation of concrete historical "works" but also a depreciation of "faith" itself.

II. Moltmann and European Political Theology: Eschatology and the Relationship between "Faith" and "Faith's Works"

In early 1976, Jürgen Moltmann addressed "An Open Letter to José Míguez Bonino" in a prominent journal of theology and ethics.[608] It was a response to public criticisms several liberation theologians were making about European political theology. Moltmann was a major figure of the latter, and one who had specifically been targeted in the criticisms. Moltmann's intended his response in "An Open Letter" to include not only the criticisms of Míguez Bonino, but also the criticisms of Hugo Assmann, Rubem Alves, Juan Luis Segundo, and Gustavo Gutiérrez.[609]

Moltmann's Criticisms of Liberation Theology

Moltmann has three basic criticisms of Latin American liberation theology. First, Moltmann claims that there is nothing indigenous about the liberation theology coming out of Latin America. Moltmann regards this theology as simply a combination of Marxism and theological concepts about eschatology that are already present in European political theology. In fact, Moltmann contends that both of these components are imported from Europe into Latin America. Hence, there is nothing "new" or "interesting" about Latin American liberation theology. Moltmann believes that liberation theology would be better served if it would "work in concert at a new construction of theology rather than in a rivalry."[610]

A second criticism is that Latin American liberation theologians comment too much about the need for Marxism and Marxist analysis, and not enough about the suffering of the Latin American people. Furthermore, "moral appeals and biblical language about the poor" to indict the whole Western civilization, including those who are supportive (e.g., political theologians), are a distraction from what is truly needed: "a radical turn toward the people."[611]

Third, Moltmann believes that Latin American liberation theologians need to do a better job of "assessing the historical situation."[612] Moltmann notes the divergent opinions of liberation theologians in this regard. Alves speaks of the contextual struggle as "pre-revolutionary;" but Míguez Bonino regards the situation as "revolutionary."[613]   Moltmann asks whether or not the "historical subject of the revolution"--namely, "the oppressed, exploited people themselves"--are ready for the revolution.[614]   The revolution will appear "elitist" if it is only "the intellectuals and the students" who favor it.[615]   "One is justified in speaking of a revolutionary situation only when the common misery is generally experienced, when it is unbearable, when the one necessary thing is recognized, and when the potential to realize what is necessary is at hand and ready."[616] Speaking from his experience of elitist forms of socialism in the European context, Moltmann concludes "it seems more important to maintain a connection with the people than to travel alone into the paradise of the future."[617]   Moltmann believes the most promising route to be followed is that of "democratic socialism." He implies that liberation theologians, in their zeal for socialism, have not been equally concerned about democracy.[618]   In closing, Moltmann appeals for mutual respect and cooperation among Latin American and European theologians so that they might work for the common goal of "a world society in which human beings no longer live against each other but with each other."[619]

The Shift Within Latin American Theology

In 1984, Segundo delivered a lecture on the theme of "the shift within Latin American Theology."[620]   According to Segundo, there is a shift from an "older" form of liberation theology (beginning around 1960 and principally centered around "middle class" persons) to a "newer" form of liberation theology (beginning around the early to mid-1970's and principally centered around "the common people").[621] Segundo helpfully demonstrates how this shift is evident in the early and later works of Gustavo Gutiérrez, Leonardo Boff, and Jon Sobrino.[622]   Thus, this shift was already underway at the time of Moltmann's critique.

In this lecture, Segundo may have addressed some of Moltmann's concerns, particularly those having to do with Marxist praxis, "grassroots" movements, and relationships between Latin American theologians and their counterparts in North America and Europe. Segundo points out that it is a "mistake" to think that liberation theology is derived from European political theology. "Latin American theology, without any precise title, began to have clearly distinctive features at least ten years before Gustavo Gutiérrez's well-known book,

A Theology of Liberation."[623]   Furthermore, Latin American university students were already well-versed in sociological critique of ideologies "before knowing anything about political theology, if it existed at all at this time."[624] While Marxist students did help several Christian students discover the nature of class exploitation in Latin America, Marxism was not necessary to make this "common sense discovery."[625]   Segundo concedes that several of the liberation theologians were educated in Europe; but this does not support the claim that European Marxism and European theology were being imported wholesale into the Latin American context.[626] It certainly does not substantiate the claim that Marxism is uncritically accepted in Latin America.[627]

Segundo also contends that liberation theology, both before and after the shift, has always focused on the plight of the oppressed. The earlier form is an attempt of middle class intellectuals to speak on behalf of the oppressed while the newer form is a "negation" of speaking for those who are quite capable of speaking for themselves. There is, therefore, a greater effort to learn from the oppressed.

> I guess that this conversation of intellectuals and, hence, of theologians (since the latter belong by definition to the former by their task, *intellectus fidei*) had its roots in the painful experience intellectuals often have. In Latin America and everywhere else they try to think and to create ideas for the sake of the common good. They sometimes speak against their own interests in the name of the voiceless people supposedly incapable of recognizing where their actual interest is. And finally they discover not only that they are understood by the people for the sake of whom they have tried to think and to speak, but also that the main stream of history cuts them off from popular victories.[628]

In retrospect, Segundo acknowledges that liberation theology in its earliest form failed to make the kinds of grassroots connections it had hoped to establish. He also expresses regrets on two occasions about the "useless battle" between Latin American theologians and the theologians in Europe and North America. Latin American liberation theology has often been "more a repetitive apology for itself than a constructive theological discourse."[629] This seems to stand in marked contrast with the claim that Segundo is "unwilling to engage in critical dialog with first-world theologians and ethicists who have specifically addressed his work."[630] While the newer form of liberation theology has become generally more appealing for all, it has not yet been able to move the oppressed beyond the "fatalistic conception of God" that often dominates popular religiosity.[631]

It is sometimes difficult to determine where Segundo understands his own thinking vis-à-vis these two lines of liberation theology. However, one gets the distinct impression that he is unwilling to forsake the first form altogether.

> As theologians, we believed at that time, *and some of us still believe*, that this movement among the most active and creative members of the Church could eventually reach, sooner or later, all oppressed people on our continent, through the pastoral activities of a Church following a new line and carrying out a new message. Thus the first theology of liberation was committed to a long-term and far-reaching goal.[632]

Nevertheless, Segundo firmly believes that both forms of liberation theology have contributed to the "mobilization of the poor and the marginalized" such that the "Church of the people" has become a "new phenomenon in Latin American ecclesiology."[633]

The more recent developments in Latin American liberation theology may have helped to ease tensions with the theologies of Europe and North America.[634] Nevertheless, even with these changes, it is erroneous to assume that theological differences are resolved.

The Kingdom of God and Human History

At the heart of European political theology is the eschatological emphasis on the "Kingdom of God." Segundo cites the following text from Moltmann: "Only in and through the dialectic of taking sides does the universalism of the Crucified become a reality in this world. The false universalism of the Church is, on the contrary, a premature and inopportune anticipation of the *Kingdom of God*."[635] The Kingdom of God, not the Church, is "absolute." The role of the Church is to give "full recognition to its *functionality* in relation to the eschatological Kingdom."[636] Only in this way does one avoid "the false universalism of the Church, that is, the Church absolutized."[637]

This emphasis on the eschatological Kingdom and a functional ecclesiology leads Segundo to affirm the "greater affinity" liberation theology has with European political theology vis-à-vis other theologies where these themes are less prominent.[638] Liberation theology and

European political theology diverge, however, in their understanding of the relationship between the Kingdom of God and human history.

Segundo believes that these differences can be traced to different theological presuppositions. Segundo traces his own theological presuppositions to the Catholic concept of "merit" which upholds "the 'eternal' worth of human effort and right intention."[639] Segundo believes that the theology of grace that was elaborated by Karl Rahner and officially affirmed at Vatican II recaptures the basic thrust of this concept and improves upon the concept of grace in Catholic "two planes" theology.

> This point of view . . . served as the background for Vatican II's statement that all human beings are called to one and the same supernatural vocation and, thanks to the grace of God, possess the means needed to fulfill this vocation (*Gaudium et Spes*, n. 22). This holds true both within and outside the Church. The effects of grace within the Christian are the same as those produced by grace in all human beings of good will (*Gaudium et Spes*, n. 22). Thus it was that the Catholic Church officially abandoned the theology of the two planes and opened the way for a theology that was quite different: i.e., liberation theology.[640]

Hence, even though there may be a conceptual distinction between nature and grace, there is no practical or historical distinction.[641]

Segundo traces the theological presuppositions of European political theology to Lutheran Reformation theology, particularly the concept of "justification by faith alone."[642] According to Segundo, this theological presupposition led to "the disappearance of the notion of *merit* from Protestant theology" and the undermining of "the possibility of any theology of history."[643] All that really matters is "the exclusive merits of Christ."[644] Furthermore, Segundo believes that this Lutheran accent has influenced Catholic theology since Vatican II.[645]

Without a doubt Segundo's understanding of his own theological presuppositions are accurate. However, Segundo's assessment that there are Lutheran theological presuppositions in European political theology is questionable, and probably flawed.[646] Segundo cites only Rudolf Weth as evidence of those European political theologians who make direct reference to Luther.[647] Here, Weth quotes Luther's commentary on Matthew 25 from *De servo arbitrio* ("The Bondage of the Will").[648]   But this citation may say more about Rudolf Weth than it does about Luther.   Whether or not Segundo is accurate in his analysis of Luther's theology will become the subject of the next chapter.

For the moment we will concede that Segundo has inaccurately read European political theology as having Lutheran theological presuppositions.   This does not mean, however, that Segundo's essential point about the differences between Latin American liberation theology and European political theology is erroneous.   Segundo regards Latin American liberation theology as upholding the view that *human beings*, "on a political as well as an individual basis, *construct the Kingdom of God from within history now.*"[649]   By contrast, Segundo perceives that European political theology seeks "to counter any attempt to attribute to mankind an historical *causality* in the construction of God's Kingdom."[650]   The significant difference between these two theologies, therefore, is *their understanding of the role human beings actually play in the construction of the eschatological Kingdom.*

According to Segundo, the choice of terms which political theologians use to describe that role tend to diminish human activity. Jürgen Moltmann uses the word "*anticipation*" to describe that role: "The false universalism of the Church is . . . a premature and inopportune *anticipation* [*anticipación*] of the Kingdom of God."[651] This is the only text which Segundo cites from Moltmann with reference to this word.   Nevertheless, the overall direction of Moltmann's theology tends to confirm Segundo's claim.   In Theology of Hope, Moltmann writes:

> Hope's statements of promise *anticipate* the future. . . . They do not seek to illuminate the reality which exists, but the reality which is coming. . . .   Present and future, experience and hope, stand in contradiction to each other in Christian eschatology. . . .   Everywhere in the New Testament the Christian hope is directed towards what is not yet visible; it is consequently a "hoping against hope" and thereby brands the visible realm of present experience as a god-forsaken, transient reality that is to be left behind.[652]

Rudolf Weth claims, "*God himself* brings about the revolutionary action that is decisive for the *coming* of his kingdom.   His action cannot be effected or replaced by *any human action*."[653]   Weth uses the terms "*analogical image*" or "*analogy*" to describe the role of human activity vis-à-vis the kingdom of God:

> Being prepared for the kingdom means something more than "being preserved" for it: it means that the kingdom of God creates already, *here and now, analogies [analogías]* and communicates with human action. . . . For, by the act of divine grace, this world is not created totally (*toto coelo*) different from the kingdom of God, but at the same time it has the capacity and the need to present itself as an *analogical image* [*imagen analógica*].[654]

Johann Baptist Metz uses the words "*sketch*" or "*outline*" to describe the role of human activity vis-à-vis the kingdom.[655] Metz writes: "What distinguishes 'Christian eschatology' from the ideologies of the future in the East and the West, is not that it *knows more*, but that it *knows less* about that future which mankind is trying to discern, and that it persists in its lack of knowledge."[656] Henri de Lavalette, a French Catholic theologian and disciple of Metz, also writes:

> The Christian maintains a certain restraint, a certain reserve, in his "conduct with respect to the future." In this way, no social class, no party, no race, no nation, no generation can identify itself with the Subject who bears the wholeness of human history. But, on the contrary, if the political order is not more than an "*outline* [*esbozo*] of the future age," it is also true that the duty of the Christian is to contribute to the realization of a better anticipation of the kingdom (through a "better organization of the human society").[657]

Segundo concludes: "All these terms systematically and expressly reject every idea of causality."[658] The kingdom of God remains "absolute" while any and all human activity is down-played as "relative" and unable to truly share, in any *real* sense, in the formation of the kingdom.[659]

Moltmann, in his "Open Letter," acknowledges Segundo's criticism about the relativization of human activity. Furthermore, Moltmann affirms that "in his messianic actions Jesus did not 'deabsolutize' but rather--according to our experiences, an activity that is a bit 'unwise'-- 'absolutized.'"[660] Moltmann then adds:

> To be sure, the individual event of liberation or salvation does not gain in this way a "causal character" for the Kingdom of God--even Pelagius

never would have said that--but rather the Kingdom attains a causal character for the experienced event of liberation, for all messianic activity realizes the possibilities that have been made possible through the inbreaking of the messianic time (Lk. 4:18ff.). To this extent the messianic kingdom is the subject of its historical realization and not vice versa. But precisely this "absolutizes" the relative or brings the unconditioned into the conditioned.[661]

Segundo, however, objects because here is no allowance in Moltmann's position for any real sense of "*collaboration*" between the *human being* and God.[662] Moltmann's theology regards "any and all *human cooperation* with God (*synergism*) as a theological deviation."[663] For the moment, and until the final chapter, we will reserve judgment on the weighty theological question implied in Moltmann's charge that Segundo's position might be heretically "Pelagian" (or, as Carl E. Braaten claims, "synergistic").[664] The point here is that *human cooperation and collaboration*, something that the political theologians (and Moltmann in particular) are unwilling to affirm wholeheartedly, *is* affirmed *without reservation* by Segundo. Furthermore, Segundo enjoys Pauline support in that human beings, justified by faith, are *synergoi* ("cooperators") with God in the construction of the kingdom (1 Cor. 3:9).

Moltmann, however, also charges that Segundo's own position is relativized when Segundo says, "This causality is *partial, fragile, often erroneous and having to be remade. . . .* What is at stake, in a *fragmentary* fashion if you like, is the eschatological Kingdom itself. . . ."[665] "In this way," claims Moltmann, Segundo "has only replaced the critical expressions 'anticipation,' 'design' and 'analogy' by the expression 'fragment.'"[666] Segundo never really addresses that criticism directly, perhaps because he regarded the answer as self-evident in his writings. However, we may be able to formulate a response that is consonant with Segundo's thought. Segundo regards "faith" as an "objectively absolute value." "Works" (or "ideologies"), in and of themselves, make "no pretensions to an absolute value"--that is, ideologies are "relative."[667] When "faith" performs its functional task, however, "works" become "faith's works" and lay claim to the same "absolute" character of "faith."[668] That is clearly different than calling such "works" merely an "anticipation," "analogy" or "outline." There is a need, however, to further the analysis. In different historical situations, "faith" may require new and different "works" to

respond appropriately.[669] In such circumstances, the "works" of the
past become "fragmentary." But in the context of the historical
situation in which people actually live, the new "works-in-faith" enjoy
the "absolute" character of "faith." "Faith," therefore, sees beyond the
objective view shared by European political theologians that history is
"fragmentary." "Faith" recognizes that the kingdom of God is
happening *here and now* in the "works" carried out "in faith" in the
midst of human history. This is how Segundo understands the *positive*
import and meaning of the expression used by Jesus, "*signs of the
times*": "concrete transformations effected by him in the *historical
present*, and entrusted by him to his disciples *for then* and for the
future."[670]   By contrast, Segundo perceives that the political
theologians are requiring "*signs from heaven*." Segundo responds:

> When the political theologian of Europe requires Latin Americans to put
> forward a project for a socialist society which will guarantee in advance
> that the evident defects of known socialist systems will be avoided, why
> do we not demand of Christ also that before telling a sick man who has
> been cured "your faith has saved you," he should give a guarantee that
> that cure will not be followed by even graver illnesses.[671]

Segundo's point, therefore, is that the kingdom of God truly
permeates the concrete, historical present in the "faith" and the "works-
in-faith" of the people. By contrast, Segundo asks the European
political theologians, "who consecrates his life to an 'analogy'? Who
dies for an 'outline'? Who moves a human mass, a whole people, in
the name of an 'anticipation'?"[672] Thus, Moltmann is inaccurate to
assert that Segundo and other Latin American liberation theologians
"confirm with their own words exactly the same thing" that European
political theologians are saying.[673]   On the contrary, Segundo's
liberation theology at least is a "radical criticism of European theology,
even the most progressive."[674] European political theology

> ends up being a politically neutral theology. The "revolution" it talks
> about seems to be more like a Kantian revolution than an historical
> revolution. It merely revolutionizes the way we formulate our problems.
> Real-life revolution must have enthusiasm behind it, but the concrete
> circumstances in which this eschatology operates at present seem to
> throw a dash of cold water on any such enthusiasm--not only on the
> phony ideological enthusiasm created by the status quo but also on the
> imaginative enthusiasm for new projects spawned by criticism and hope.[675]

Conclusion: The Eschatological Separation of "Faith" and "Faith's Works"

Segundo affirms with European political theologians that "eschatology" performs a vital function by "deideologizing the human mind, to keep it open and flexible, to liberate it from its ahistorical pretensions."[676] However, "eschatology" is misused whenever it oppresses "our ideological creativity" through premature criticism "even before ideologies have time to be effective and to arouse real enthusiasm."[677] Such a misuse is evident in European political theology when the kingdom of God is valued at the expense of *human causality*. The perspective of European political theology is evident even in some Latin American liberation theologians. For example, Segundo criticizes Rubem Alves whom he considers "a disciple of Moltmann."

> Hope is paradoxically translated into a radically pessimistic view of the whole process of change, even when the latter is not violent, precisely because any and every change prompted by man cannot help but lose out to world-dominating sin. The kingdom of God can only be fashioned by someone who is free from sin, and that comes down to God alone.[678]

It is on this point that Segundo and European political theology finally part company. According to Segundo, the "eschatological vision" of European political theology proposes "*faith and hope in something metaphysical and a disgusted turning-away from real-life history.*"[679] This is an implicit, if not explicit, *separation* between "faith" and "faith's works." "Faith" in the kingdom of God is what ultimately matters, but "faith's works" ultimately do *not* matter.

However, it is not only "faith's works" that are diminished by this perspective. "Faith" is also diminished. Segundo affirms, along with European political theologians, that "faith" is a God-given grace, as we have noted in earlier chapters. Even with regard to the issue of causality, Segundo does not fail to mention the necessity of divine intervention. "The relationship with a liberating event . . . derives, *from the strength of God himself who promotes it*, a genuinely causal character with respect to the definitive Kingdom of God."[680] Nevertheless, what Segundo distinctively brings to the forefront here is that "faith," while it is God's gift, is also the "faith" of *human beings*. Such a concept of "faith" provides the enthusiasm to "work,"

which European political theology cannot provide on the basis of its
theological dampening of all human activity.

III. Cardinal Ratzinger and the Vatican Congregation For the Doctrine of Faith: Ecclesiastical Authority and the Relationship between "Faith" and "Faith's Works"

Historian Enrique Dussel claims that certain events in the early to
middle 1970s placed Latin American liberation theology in a period of
"captivity and exile." This era is marked by the ecclesiastical and
governmental suppression of liberation theology.[681] Military
dictatorships were on the rise in Bolivia (1971), Chile (1973), Uruguay
(1973), Peru (1975), Ecuador (1976), and Argentina (1976).
Furthermore, repressive military regimes continued to foster control in
Brazil, Paraguay, and most of Central America. Only Mexico,
Colombia, Venezuela, and Costa Rica escaped this tyranny by
maintaining a formal democracy. Nevertheless, even in these countries
the "governments were capable of utilizing harsh repression."[682]
These events were coupled with increasing ecclesiastical pressure
directed against liberation theology. In 1971, Belgian Jesuit Roger
Vekemans arrived in Chile and began, with the blessing of his
ecclesiastical superiors, a crusade against liberation theology on the
premises of social analysis and theology. Bishop Alfonso López
Trujillo assisted Vekemans in the publication of the anti-liberationist
journal Tierra Nueva and was elected as the new secretary-general of
the *Conferencia del episcapado latinoamericano* (CELAM) in 1972.
From this position, Bishop Trujillo turned the agencies of CELAM,
once the supportive and enthusiastic base for liberation theology, into
"a platform for the attack on liberation theology."[683]
Segundo keenly felt the effects of the governmental and
ecclesiastical repression of liberation theology. In the 1970s the journal
Perspectivas de Diálogo and the Peter Faber Center, both of which
Segundo helped to establish, were "abruptly shut down by the
Uruguayan government, apparently because of its anger at his critical
reflections on the volatile Uruguayan politics at that time."[684] In spite
of these events, Segundo is sensitive to the charges against the
Uruguayan government for human rights abuses.

We are accused of not being democratic, when we are prevented from
being so. If my country could apply to the rich nations the economic and

political measures that are applied to us today, it would be *we* who would go and investigate, today--hypocritically, of course--the violations of human rights in *those* countries. The tragic thing about the situation is that those who shape and control the defense of human rights--despite undeniable individual good will--are the same persons who make that defense impossible on three-quarters of the planet.[685]

Several years prior to these events, Segundo had lost his personal friend, Camilo Torres, who fell out of graces with the Colombian episcopacy and later died at the hands of the Columbian military.[686] In spite of this loss, Segundo never supported guerilla warfare. He regarded it as disrupting the balance of the "social ecology," i.e., the social complexity of human relationships.[687] Segundo values the non-violent approach of Gandhi and Martin Luther King; but then he offers the following qualification:

> in Latin America, we are not dealing with the attainment of concrete and definite objectives as in such examples, but with the transformation of an entire social structure, and in these circumstances such [non-violent] methods collide again with the problem of Manicheaism inherent in all massive action.[688]

The political attacks on liberation theology would continue well into the 1980s. On March 24, 1980, Archbishop Oscar Romero joined the growing list of priests and laity to be killed by government forces for their association with liberation theology.[689] In May 1980, the "Santa Fe Paper" set the tone for U.S. foreign policy toward Central America. The basis themes of this document under the Reagan administration were to replace President Carter's human rights policies with policies calling for stiffer resistance to the "Marxist-Leninist" forces perceived to be present in liberation theology.[690]

Also noticeable in the early 1980's was a more overt pressure by the Vatican to suppress liberation theology. John Paul II made five visits to Central and Latin America between 1979-1985, each time warning liberation theologians about their unorthodox trends.[691] The most vehement attach was led by Joseph Cardinal Ratzinger.[692] In March 1983, Cardinal Ratzinger addressed a "Peruvian bishops' conference with a document containing ten critical questions directed to Gustavo Gutiérrez's theology."[693] In September 1984, the Sacred Congregation for the Doctrine of the Faith, under Ratzinger's leadership, published the Instruction on Certain Aspects of the

"Theology of Liberation".[694] On May 9, 1985, liberation theologian
Leonardo Boff was silenced and called to the Vatican for questioning
by Ratzinger and the Congregation. "The measure referred, of course,
only to Boff himself, but since he is one of the most widely read
proponents of the 'theology of liberation' nearly everyone interpreted
the silencing as a clear warning to the whole movement."[695] Signs
of lessened repression and a return to civilian rule in Latin American
countries were not manifested until 1985. Better ecclesiastical relations
with liberation theologians followed early the next year with the lifting
of the silencing of Leonardo Boff (March 29, 1986), a cordial letter
from the pope to the Brazilian bishops praising the theological renewal
there, and a second (and more balanced) statement on liberation
theology by the Vatican, entitled, "Instruction on Christian Freedom
and Liberation."[696]

Ratzinger, the Renewal of "Ecclesiastical Authority," and Liberation Theology

"It is beyond doubt that when John Paul II appointed Joseph
Ratzinger as head of the [Congregation for the Doctrine of the Faith].
. . , he made a 'prestige' decision."[697] The fact is that Joseph
Ratzinger was one of "the most famous Catholic scholars," and one of
the most "progressive" in Catholic theology, at least prior to Vatican
II.[698] It was after Vatican II, however, that Ratzinger began to call
into question the "progressive wing" of Catholic theology. Ratzinger
never accused Vatican II itself as the cause of this problem. In fact, he
goes out of his way to defend Vatican II:

> Vatican II in its official promulgations, in its authentic documents, cannot
> be held responsible for this development which, on the contrary, radically
> contradicts both the letter and the spirit of the Council Fathers. . . . I
> am convinced that the damage that we have incurred in these twenty
> years is due, not to the "true" Council, but to the unleashing *within* the
> Church of latent polemical and centrifugal forces; and *outside* the Church
> it is due to the confrontation with a cultural revolution in the West: the
> success of the upper middle class, the new "tertiary bourgeoisie", with
> its liberal-radical ideology of individualistic, rationalistic and hedonistic
> stamp. . . . [We need] to *return to the authentic texts of the original
> Vatican II.*[699]

The problem Ratzinger perceives in the "progressive wing" is that, in the face of modernity, "the authentically Catholic meaning of the reality 'Church' is tacitly disappearing, without being expressly rejected."[700] What Ratzinger means by this is that the *hierarchy* of the Church is being undermined, if not explicitly rejected, as the only true dominical source of *authority* in the Church.

> If the Church, in fact, is our Church, if we alone are the Church, if *her structures* are not *willed by Christ*, then it is no longer possible to conceive of the existence of a *hierarchy* as a service to the baptized *established by the Lord himself*. It is a rejection of the concept of *an authority willed by God, an authority therefore that has its legitimation in God. . . .*[701]

According to Ratzinger, in the "decisive split" between Protestantism and the Catholic Church "the authority of the exegete is put over the authority of the Church and her tradition."[702] Ratzinger believes it is necessary to maintain the emphasis on *ecclesiastical authority* if the Church is to be and remain the Church.

This same evaluation is specifically applied to liberation theology.[703] "An analysis of the phenomenon of liberation theology reveals that it constitutes a *fundamental threat to the faith of the Church*."[704] In fact, Ratzinger implies that liberation theology is heretical. "The very radicality of liberation theology means that its seriousness is often underestimated, since it does not fit into any of the accepted categories of *heresy*; its fundamental concern cannot be detected by the existing range of standard questions."[705] Ratzinger makes some concessions to liberation theology: "The Gospel of Jesus Christ is a message of freedom and a force for liberation. In recent years this essential truth has become the object of reflection for theologians, with a new kind of attention which is itself full of promise."[706] However, he had reservations about limiting the soteriological message of the Church to this "one aspect."[707]

Before we examine Ratzinger's more substantive charges, it is important that we understand what Ratzinger believes to be the underlying cause of the "fundamental threat to the faith of the Church" in liberation theology. Ratzinger believes that liberation theology upholds two principal "elements" which were engendered by the "new theological situation" of Vatican II. These two elements are the

Bultmannian use of "historical criticism" (experiential hermeneutics) and the use of "marxist analysis."[708] Ratzinger contends that these approaches, when regarded as "authorities" in their own right, undermine the "authority" of "the Church's teaching office."[709] This constitutes a "crisis" of almost apocalyptic proportion. Many of the faithful, Ratzinger contends, have become enslaved by the humanist sciences.[710] In the "Instruction on Certain Aspects of The 'Theology of Liberation,'" therefore, Ratzinger is issuing a call to priests and laity to leave the ranks of liberation theology.

Specific Charges and Segundo's Response

Segundo wrote an entire tome (Theology and the Church) to address the concerns of the "Instruction." We can recognize with Phillip Berryman that "it is unusual--practically unheard of--for a Latin American theologian to engage in such a head-on polemics with a major Vatican figure."[711] Nevertheless, Segundo believes that the document presents a "caricature" of liberation theology.[712] Furthermore, the document charges that the "deviations and risks of deviation" in liberation theology are a "practical negation of Christian faith."[713] Segundo ups the ante: "First, I want to make clear that I am profoundly affected by it [the document]. Let me be clear: I understand that my theology (that is, my interpretation of the Christian faith) is false if the theology of the document is true--or if it is the only true one."[714]

Segundo believes that the "Instruction," from beginning to end, is a condemnation of liberation theology. The "Instruction" is presented in two equal parts. The first part is a "lengthy introduction" (chapters I-VI). The second part (chapters VII-XI) deals with specific charges against liberation theology for "uncritically borrowing from Marxist ideology and [having] recourse to theses of a biblical hermeneutics marked by rationalism" (VI, 10). Segundo contends, however, that already in the first half "liberation theology has already been condemned and, what is more, the *theological reasons* have already been expounded for such a condemnation."[715] "[When] the document announces that it 'will be discussing' (see VI, 9), the cause of liberation theology has already been judged. In other words, the decisive criteria for measuring its conformity with Christian faith have been applied and it has been found lacking."[716]

Segundo makes four introductory comments about the "Instruction." First, Segundo does not believe that the "Instruction" was written with malicious intent, but with serious regard for what were considered harmful "deviations" from the faith.[717]   Second, Segundo notes that in the first part the "Instruction" alternates between chapters that express things "positive" (odd-numbered chapters) and things "negative" (even-numbered chapters) about liberation theology. There are two reasons that can account for this alteration. The first reason is that the Congregation does not want to "disavow" that there are truly faithful persons working with "an authentic evangelical spirit" for the poor. The second reason is that the Congregation does not want to subject these truly faithful to a totally harsh treatment that would suggest that they were totally duped. Liberation theology does, after all, have some basis in Christian faith.[718]   Segundo's third introductory remark is that one misrepresents the document's authors if one reads only the affirming positive chapters and disregards the rest.[719] Finally, the document seeks to be pastoral in recognizing that people are torn between "two directions: one toward the voice of Puebla which asks one to opt preferentially for the poor, and the other toward the temptation to make the option simpler and more effective by reducing it to an option for the world and for history."[720]

Segundo perceives four specific "charges" against liberation theology in the "Instruction." One of the charges is substantively *theological*: that liberation theology is inadequately "transcendent" and a "reductionism" of the gospel to historical "immanentism." This charge surfaces early and frequently throughout the "Instruction."

The remaining three charges are regarded by Segundo as being more *practical* in nature: "concepts uncritically borrowed from Marxist analysis,"[721] "recourse to theses of a biblical hermeneutic marked by rationalism,"[722] and the resort to "violence" in "class struggle".[723] Segundo maintains that these last three charges do not apply to him.[724] Nevertheless, Segundo does make an attempt to address the charges in a manner congruent with what we have noted earlier in our analysis of his works.

Segundo affirms the validity of the Congregation's "*warning*" about "concepts uncritically borrowed from Marxist ideology."[725] Nevertheless, Segundo questions much of the Congregation's understandings of the influence of Marxism on liberation theology, especially with regard to the charges of "atheism," "denial of the human person," and "epistemological entrapment."[726]

Segundo notes that the charge against "recourse to theses of a biblical hermeneutic marked by rationalism" never gets elaborated very much in the "Instruction."[727] The thrust of the charge, however, might be traced to Ratzinger's concern about an uncritical reliance on Bultmann.[728] Segundo responds that liberation theologians are certainly familiar with Bultmann's thought by virtue of their education in European schools.

> However, insofar as those liberation theologians are integrated into the Latin American context, there is nothing further from that context than the Bultmannian methodology and agenda. One needs only to think of "demythologization," born of the "death of God" and proper to the "developed" mentality of the modern world; the rejection of the search for the historical Jesus and of the historical causes of his death; the purely eschatological, ahistorical idea of the coming of the kingdom of God supposedly preached by Jesus; the method of personalistic, existential biblical interpretation, without any depth of social analysis; and so on.[729]

Segundo offers a four-fold response to the charge that liberation theology promotes "violence" in "class struggle." First, the idea of addressing "class struggle," while a modern concept, has roots that go back into the foundations of the early Church.[730] Second, "conflict" in "class struggle" is not necessarily the same as "violence." Furthermore, it is certainly not unequivocally "marxist," since "capitalism" also relies on "conflict."[731] Third, the reality of violence is inescapable. The larger issue becomes how to limit it as much as possible.[732] Finally, the suggestion that liberation theology supports violent guerrilla warfare is a "caricature," intentionally oversimplified by hidden agenda of the "Instruction."[733]

Segundo claims that all of the charges and their conclusions "would have been arrived at with or without the use of social sciences, with or without class struggle, and with or without the use of violent means."[734] The "Instruction" has an inherent theological position that is opposed to liberation theology.[735] Hence, what becomes solely important for Segundo is the theological charge of the "Instruction":

> The different theologies of liberation are situated between the preferential option for the poor forcefully reaffirmed without ambiguity after Medellín at the conference of Puebla on the one hand, and the temptation

> *to reduce the Gospel to an earthly gospel* on the other. . . . It will be affirmed that God himself makes history. It will be added that there is only one history, one in which the *distinction* between the history of salvation and profane history is no longer necessary. . . . Affirmations such as these reflect *historicist immanentism.* Thus there is a tendency to identify the kingdom of God and its growth with the human liberation movement. . . .[736]

Segundo believes that this charge is reflected in different ways in the "Instruction," but essentially charge is the same: "liberation theology begins by *separating* the secular from the religious dimension and ends by *reducing* everything to the secular. . . ."[737]

Segundo's choice of terminology ("separating" for "distinction") in his rephrasing of the charge is significant here and hints to his theological criticism of the "Instruction." We have noted all along in Segundo's theology that "faith" and "faith's works" need to be distinguished, but they cannot be separated. Here, Segundo *distinguishes* between religious and secular history, but he does not *separate* these histories. Segundo maintains that in the context of history, there is human activity that has "faith" in the "changes in history that are humanizing" and for the sake of "*temporal* results." But, in the same history, there are also activities that arise from "faith" in God and that transform human history into something that shares "the absolute and the eternal."[738]

In order to further substantiate this claim before the Congregation, Segundo appeals directly to the *ecclesiastical authority* of Vatican II:

> Because it does not *separate* religious history from the profane--without ignoring the singular fact that we are called to live that history with the revelation of the mystery of the individual, hidden by God, within it (Gaudium et Spes, 39 and 22)---it is contradictory to accuse liberation theology of "reducing" the Gospel to an earthly gospel. On the contrary, this theology maintains that the *eyes of faith* illumine this mutual understanding of the earthly city and its history, on the one hand, and the building of the kingdom of God on the other (Gaudium et Spes, 40).[739]

Segundo continues, "from that *union of both histories that Jesus lived* until his death there arises the fact that *Jesus' resurrection carries with it* . . . not only those persons who have died but *also that same "profane" history that seemed subject to corruption.*"[740] Segundo then appeals to the *ecclesiastical authority* of Paul VI. When the Pope was asked, regarding <u>Gaudium et Spes</u>, "Will it not be said that the thought of the Church in Council has deviated toward the *anthropocentric* positions of modern culture?" he answered, "Deviated, no; *turned, yes.*"[741]

> Paul VI, foreseeing that objection, takes the step of denying precisely the "separation" that this accusation of reductionism implies: "it will have to be recognized that this same [human] concern *can never be separated* from the more authentic religious concerns, that is, charity, which is the one that gives rise to these concerns (and where there is charity, there is God), due to the *intimate union, constantly affirmed and upheld* by the Council, that exists between *human and temporal values* and properly spiritual, religious, and eternal values. The Church is inclined toward man and *the earth*, but in so doing, raises it toward *the kingdom of God.*"[742]

Counter-charges against the Congregation

In addition to clearing himself of all the charges of the "Instruction," Segundo makes counter-charges against the Congregation. Segundo claims that the "Instruction" does not simply distinguish between secular and religious history, but *separates* them by calling the human being *out* of secular history into a relationship with the absolute and thereby rendering human history to the dustbin of temporality.[743] This is readily apparent in some of Segundo's exegetical analyses of the document. For example, in the Introduction to the "Instruction," Segundo notes the following claim:

> Liberation is first and foremost liberation from the radical slavery of sin. . . . Faced with the urgency of certain problems, some are tempted to emphasize, unilaterally, the liberation from servitude of an earthly and temporal kind. They do so in such a way that they seem to put liberation from sin in second place and so fail to give it the primary importance it is due.[744]

Segundo makes a number of observations about this statement. First, he observes a distinction between an "emphasis" on the "radical" (*radix*, "root"), or "primary," and an "emphasis" on the "secondary."[745] Second, the "radical" emphasis here is not something that is "visible." Only the "secondary" is visible. "In short, the 'really real' is the invisible world, while the world about us is mere shadow and simulacrum. Thus, this 'theology' is build [sic] on a kind of textbook Platonism."[746] Third, and most important, "the realm of the invisible, because it belongs to the root of reality, to the realm of causes, is opposed to the realm of the visible where consequences flourish."[747] Hence, "there exists one language for speaking of *religious* realities (sin, grace, etc.) and another for secular, earthly, or temporal realities."[748] Furthermore, people are encouraged to avoid the secular realities and to affirm the "religious" realities. In liberation theology, by contrast, "the word 'sin' [is]. . . , *without abandoning its religious context*, . . . translated in such a way that it points to *realities*--individual as well as social--*that are concretely expressed* outside of the religious sphere."[749] The religious experience of "sin," therefore, is understood and presented as present in the concrete, historical experiences where people live.

A second example is the Congregation's understanding of the "signs of the times." The "Instruction" claims: "The powerful and almost irresistible aspiration that people have for liberation constitutes one of the principal signs of the times which the church has to examine in the light of the Gospel."[750] The implication of the document's use of "signs of the times" here is *negative*. The "signs of the times" must be "examined" by something more religious, less earthly.[751] This negative appraisal of the "signs of the times" is confirmed by a statement made earlier by Ratzinger: liberation theology has opted for "an entirely new theological and spiritual orientation. . . to be sought directly from *Scripture* and the *signs of the times*."[752] However, Segundo notes that in the Gospels Jesus places a *positive* emphasis on the "signs of the times" in contrast to the emphasis of the scribes and the Pharisees on "signs from heaven." Jesus was emphasizing that the gospel is something that is present in *history* and is grasped through *"faith."* "The function of the signs of the times is precisely that of helping one break the circle of the dead letter--even in the case of the Gospel."[753]

A third case that Segundo presents is the selective reading of biblical history in the "Instruction." According to Segundo, "the document insists upon a particular theology where the religious and the secular are opposed."[754] Passages that refer to concrete involvement in history are rejected or abused in favor of other passages that are more emphatic on (non-historical) "religious experience." For example, Segundo notes the following sentence in the document: "The

Psalms call us back to an essential religious experience: It is from God alone that one can expect salvation and healing. God, and not man, has the power to change the situations of suffering."[755] This use of the Psalms intentionally argues for "the non-activity of people in history because all concrete change concerning human suffering is taken from the human field of action and attributed to God."[756]

By contrast, Segundo notes that the Psalms were used as instruments of prayer in the context of real-life, concrete, historical activities of people. Hence, liberation theology does not deny the value of "prayer," but it *unites* prayer with "working" (*ora et labora*). "Faced with evils that can and should be corrected in history, it does not question the importance of prayer nor substitute enthusiasm for social change for the experience of divine transcendence."[757] Thus, religious and secular history are joined together, not bifurcated.

Conclusion: "Ecclesiastical Authority" and the Relationship Between "Faith" and "Faith's Works"

The position of Cardinal Ratzinger and the Congregation for the Doctrine of the Faith is in many respects a re-absolutization of the Church. Thus, many of the problematic aspects of the position of the Chilean bishops resurface in this position. In particular, we would note the radical bifurcation between the "religious" and the "secular" realms. Contrary to the charge of the "Instruction" that liberation theology is guilty of "reducing" the gospel to an "earthly gospel," however, Segundo has emphasized that the gospel is down-to-earth, expressed in concrete, historical human activity.

We have also noted that Segundo has superseded the "ecclesiastical authority" of Ratzinger and the Congregation by appealing to the higher "ecclesiastical authority" of the Vatican Council.[758] Unfortunately, neither Segundo nor Ratzinger adequately appeal to *Jesus Christ* as ultimate ecclesiastical authority, though Segundo has the better of the argument by seeking to base his position in the authority of the Scriptures.[759]

The central thesis of Segundo's theology is apparent when we consider that Segundo understands human history as the context for "faith's" role. Thus, human history is re-valued as "religious" and not simply secular. The position of Ratzinger, however, calls for an ethereal "faith" that has no point of connection with human history.

Therefore, as in the previous two theological positions we have studied in this chapter, Ratzinger's theology *separates* "faith" from "faith's works" by separating religious history from secular history.   "His position--one frequently found in official church documents--is that *faith enables one to rise above ideologies.*"[760]   Thus, Segundo expresses his own solemn "warning to the Church at large."[761]   The theological accent of Vatican II on "the Church at the service of humanity" ought not be surrendered in the post-conciliar period.   Quoting the prayer of Cardinal Henri de Lubac, Segundo concludes: "If I lack love and justice, I separate myself completely from you, God, and my adoration is nothing more than idolatry.   To believe in you, I must believe in love and in justice, and to believe in these things is worth a thousand times more than saying your Name."[762]

Chapter 4
The Faith that Works in Dispute: Part Two

Segundo and Luther on "Faith" and "Faith's Works"

We have demonstrated in the previous chapter that the central thesis in Segundo's theology ("faith" and "faith's works" need to be distinguished, but they cannot be separated) is appropriately juxtaposed against some contemporary Catholic and Protestant theologies. The ecclesiology of the Chilean bishops separates the Church from politics. The eschatology of Jürgen Moltmann and other European political theologians separates the Kingdom of God from human history. Cardinal Ratzinger and the Vatican Congregation for the Doctrine of the Faith, in their call for submission to ecclesiastical authority, separate religious history from secular history. In all three cases, Segundo emphasizes that he is most concerned with the implicit, if not explicit, *separation* of "faith" from "faith's works," regardless of the general theological focus of the discussion (ecclesiology, eschatology, ecclesiastical authority).

In this chapter, we turn our attention to Segundo's critical analysis of the theology of Martin Luther. While Segundo recognizes Luther's strength in rediscovering the Pauline concepts of "sin" and "faith," Segundo perceives that Luther's theology of "justification" promotes a "passive" notion of "faith" that undermines any "theology of history" and any and all "human cooperation" in the Kingdom of God. Therefore, Segundo concludes that Luther also fosters an anti-Pauline separation of "faith" from "faith's works." Segundo's case against Luther, however, is seriously weakened by a lack of primary evidence.

In the second part of this chapter, we will explore the primary sources of Luther and the Reformation. The primary sources of Luther will include relevant treatises and commentaries on the issues presented by Segundo. Since Segundo connects Luther's theology with the position of the Augsburg Confession and the Reformation,[763] we will also include relevant material from the Lutheran Confessional writings, especially the Augsburg Confession (1530) and its attendant Apology (1531). Through this examination of primary sources, we will be able to better evaluate Segundo's critique of Luther (and the Reformation) on the issue of the relationship between "faith" and "faith's works."

I. Segundo's Case Against Luther

In the introduction to the five volume series, "Open Theology for the Adult Laity," Segundo claims that liberation theology has two noticeable characteristics. First, it is "reductive." "It does not deal with all the avatars of a doctrine with the accumulations of twenty centuries. We reduce, then, the multitude of dogmatic enunciations to certain fundamental mysteries of the Revelation which gives an account of our faith."[764] Segundo is not interested in simply conforming to the standards of a European and North American "erudite" scholasticism which tends to view liberation theology with "academic disdain."[765] Second, liberation theology "takes into account essentially the world in which our contemporaries live and work."[766] For Segundo, that contemporary audience is the predominantly "Catholic" populace of Latin America.[767]

In light of these characteristics, it comes as a welcome surprise that Segundo not only chooses to deal with Luther's theology, but affirms Luther for having raised "*one of the most profound points of Christian reflection. To the detriment of unity perhaps. Or perhaps so that unity would be based on a deeper truth.*"[768]

Luther's Rediscovery of Paul

What is the "deeper truth" that Luther perceives, and that Segundo commends? In order to answer this question, Segundo returns to Paul's description of "the divided human being" in Romans 7:14-25. Segundo concludes that the entrapment of the "*divided being*" is traceable to the "*pagan stage*" or the stage prior to grace; but *victory* is traceable to the "after" or "now" of *Christian existence* (Romans 8:1-2).[769]

> What, then, is the work, the gift, or the grace of Christ? It is that "we are able *to do the things which the law commands*, because we are no longer living according to the flesh [or human condition], but according to the Spirit [that is, according to grace] (Romans 8:4). Without a doubt, this is so, because [Christ] has "strengthened the inner human being" (Ephesians 3:16) which before wished [*quería*] [the good], but was not capable of accomplishing [it].[770]

However, Segundo notes that in the history of the Church there arose "an oversimplified notion of the human being's potentialities for loving."[771] The assumption was that "the divided human being pertained to a past already superseded."[772] According to this line of thinking, the human being "could choose the good or the bad as he wished [*quería*]." As a result, Pelagius emphasized a "morality of the law," a concept that was challenged by Augustine.[773]

Segundo credits Luther for bringing to the foreground the understanding of "the experience of *sin* which is inherent *in Christian existence*."[774]

> [Luther] possessed a keener and deeper awareness of what lies buried in the depths of every so-called "good" action. He knew, as any reflective person might have, how terribly tenacious our egotism is, how it creeps into our most "virtuous" actions in disguised form. For Luther, in other words, Paul's description of a human being divided between what he wills to do [*quiere*] and what he does continues to be the description of the Christian.[775]

Hence, Segundo extols Luther "for having perceived the radical opposition of Paul's thinking to any simplistic reduction of the problem of Sin."[776] Moreover, Segundo credits Luther for rediscovering Paul's understanding that "faith alone" sets the human being "free" from this "radical problem of insecurity" and allows human beings to stand in a relationship that is "right with God."[777] Segundo adds, "this is not an occasional teaching" in Paul, and he cites several examples: Romans 3:20-28; Philippians 3:9; Ephesians 2:9-10; and Galatians 3:11-12, 22.[778] Segundo affirms that "the Lutheran principle of salvation by faith rather than by works seems, *and certainly is*, central to the New Testament thought of people like Paul."[779]

The Reformation and the Council of Trent

While Luther is praised for the rediscovery of key Pauline concepts, Segundo believes that the controversy between the Reformers and the Council of Trent made the weaknesses in Luther's position more apparent. In one of his earliest works, Segundo makes a modest effort (by his own admission) to recount the controversy. Segundo cites five chief formulas advanced by the Reformation, together with the responses of Trent. Briefly summarized, the Reformation asserted that (1) justification is by Christ alone, because Christ is the "one and only just person" (*un solo justo*); (2) the will of human beings is an *enslaved will* (*siervo arbitrio*); (3) the justification of the human being is a "*forensic justification* in which, akin to that which occurs in a courtroom, the accused is declared innocent but is not converted into an innocent person;" (4) the human being is *simul justus et peccator*; and (5) "faith alone, not works, unites the human being with the saving, justifying grace of Christ."[780]

Trent countered all five formulations, stressing that (1) human beings are *not "formally just"* by Christ's righteousness; (2) the *free will* of human beings is *not "lost and extinguished;"* (3) human beings are *not justified "solely by the imputation of Christ's justice,"* because this would exclude "the grace and the charity which is diffused" into the hearts of people "by the Holy Spirit and which inheres within them;" (4) the *just person does not sin in doing good works*; and (5) "faith" understood as "*confidence* in the divine mercy" is *not "the one and only thing by which we are justified."*[781]

The formulations of the Reformation and the responses of Trent reflect serious differences that are not to be minimized. Hence, Segundo does not agree with others who attribute the differences to some "colossal misunderstanding."[782] Segundo thinks that there is a certain "truth which each side perceived and defended."[783] Nevertheless, in Segundo's estimation, both sides are much too "rigid" and "afraid of freedom" to adequately grasp Paul's concept of the depth of grace.[784]

Segundo valued Luther's contribution to the understanding of the depth of "sin" in the human condition, and the valuable role of "faith" as remedy for that condition. Segundo expresses the valuable contribution of Trent as follows:

Thanks to Christ, then, and despite all the dividedness of the human condition with all its weighty determinisms and snares which weight down our projects to a great extent, *a little love passes into our lives*. This is what the Catholic Church defended against Luther, or against those who would oversimplify the picture.[785]

The principal criticism that Segundo makes of Luther and the Reformation is that they regard the value and significance of all human activity as *worthless*. That assessment is based on the detailed notations that Segundo offers on the Reformation formulations:

Everything depends here on God, on the unique action God exercises, through Jesus Christ, in favor of the human being. *Everything* depends on what reaches the human being *from above*, *nothing* on what the human being brings *from below*.[786]

The fact that Jesus Christ died for the reconciliation of the human being corrupted by sin, "establishes, in a decisive manner, that that *corruption was radical and total*." . . . Within this situation the human being, by virtue of the unity of his being and his action, goes from sin to sin. Such is the corruption in which God encounters him.[787]

At every moment of his existence, the human being who is absolved by God never ceases to be the sinner which he was as well.[788]

This must be kept clearly in mind, *continues Barth*, when one wants to understand the great *negation* of Paul and the Reformationists--particularly, the *sola fide* ("by faith alone") of Luther. His doctrine of justification by faith *opposes faith to all good works*.[789]

It is significant to point out that all of these commentaries are quoted by Segundo from Henri Bouillard's expository tome *on the theology of Karl Barth*. Segundo regards that the position of the Reformation and the position of Barth as *synonymous* or at least as part of a continuing trajectory (in Segundo's words, "lest one might think these formulas belong only to some past stage").[790]

Merit, Grace, and "Two Kingdoms" Theology

Segundo's later writings elaborate on this "weakness" that he believes he has exposed in Luther's theology. Segundo affirms that the concept of "merit" is of "utmost importance for liberation theology."[791] We would be mistaken, however, to assume that Segundo intends to adopt the concept of "merit" uncritically. The fact is that he is very critical of this concept, even in much of its contemporary usage.[792] Nevertheless, the concept of "merit" has some enduring value.

In his discussion of "merit," Segundo cites an example of a medical doctor. In the *old* concept of "merit," what mattered for the doctor most was the "effort expended" and that it was done "for God." It mattered very little whether or not the patient was helped. "The patient is only the occasion of the merit."[793] The intention of one's actions, therefore, were other-worldly.

Segundo maintains that "this [older] conception of merit assumes that there are two very different, if not opposed, planes of value and efficacy."[794] There is "the human and historical plane" in which the doctor's value is measured in terms of his ability to help patients. There is also the more valued "plane of eternal values." Efforts expended in the human and historical plane "not only do not count, but are actually quite dangerous" because they may rival the "eternal" values. "In Catholic theology and spirituality these two planes have been given characteristic names. The *supernatural* plane is the plane of eternal values; the *natural* plane is the plane of temporal values."[795]

Liberation theology is critical of "two planes" theology because it leads to a bifurcation or *separation* of the planes.[796] Nevertheless, Segundo is aware that "two planes" theology possesses a strong hold on the lives of many Catholics because "only *grace*, that is, a free gift of God, enabled the human being to do anything worthwhile in terms of such a divine destiny as eternal life."[797] There are two presuppositions about "grace" in "two planes" theology. First, grace is not universal. Some possess it, and others do not. Second, "the absolutely gratuitous nature of the gift, its supernatural nature, presupposes the existence of purely natural states, persons, and values in real-life history."[798]

A few years prior to Vatican II, the theological concept of "grace" began to change in Catholic theology. Grace is understood in this new theology as a *universal* gift to humanity by which "all human beings [get] to live in essentially *gratuitous* conditions."[799] This concept, elaborated by Karl Rahner, became the official position of the Catholic church in Vatican II:

> all human beings are called to one and the same supernatural vocation
> and, thanks to the grace of God, possess the means needed to fulfill this
> vocation (Gaudium et spes, 22). This holds true both within and outside
> the Church. The effects of grace within the Christian are the same as
> those produced by grace in all human beings of good will (Gaudium et
> spes , 22).[800]

In this new understanding of "grace" there is a "*distinction, not a
separation*" of the planes.[801] As one might gather, this change was
more amenable to liberation theology and allowed liberation theology
to claim official ecclesiastical support.[802]

Segundo then seeks to apply this discussion to the theology of
Luther and the Reformation. Segundo contends that both Catholics and
Protestants share a concern for "the eternal, the last, the
meta-historical."[803] But the Catholic concept of "merit," for all of its
legalistic foibles, at least provides a *link* between the kingdom of God
and human history.[804] The Reformation, according to Segundo,
severed that connection. "Salvation by faith alone" means that one is
saved "by the *exclusive merits* of Christ," and any possibility of a
"theology of history" is undermined.[805]

In Segundo's estimation, "Luther's doctrine of the *two kingdoms*"
is the Reformation equivalent for the Catholic concept of "two
planes."[806] This Lutheran legacy, according to Segundo, is especially
evident in European political theology. Segundo, however, does hold
out some hope for a "possible contribution" that Reformation theology
can make to the Latin American context. That contribution is the
Tillichian concept of "protestant principle," the protest against
ideological absolutizations.[807]

Following the insights of James S. Preus and Reinhold Niebuhr,
Segundo argues that "two kingdoms" theology leads to the radical
separation of "political authority" from "theological authority." It may
even imply that "political authority" is granted autonomous sanction by
"religious authority."[808] Segundo cites Luther's silencing of the
peasants' revolt as evidence of a practical implementation of this
principle.[809]

However, Segundo regards the doctrine of "two kingdoms" as only
the symptom of a deeper theological malady. "The doctrine of the *two
kingdoms* is intimately bound up with other central themes in Lutheran

theology: e.g., the doctrine of justification by faith alone and the key notion that glory belongs to God alone (*soli Deo gloria*)."[810] This leads us to a consideration of the central issue in Segundo's theological quarrel with Luther.

The Problem of Justification

In one of Segundo's early writings, he chides that Luther placed too much emphasis on "faith," especially in regard to "justification."[811] In this regard, his position approximates that of Karl Barth, who believed that the Reformation accent on "justification by faith alone" was "wildly overestimated."[812] From his initial reading of Romans 5, Segundo concluded that "faith" ought not become a "restrictive condition" for a "justification" (*justificación*) that is "universal."[813] After a more detailed analysis of Romans, Segundo continues to maintain his position on "universal salvation." (*salvación universal*)."[814] Furthermore, according to Segundo, Luther "did not insist on" the "*antithetical parallel* between Adam and Christ."[815] Segundo contends that Christ's love is the basis for a "*qualitative disproportion*" over the sins of Adam and, therefore, over the effects of Adam's sin.[816] This critical posture is echoed in some of Segundo's most recent criticisms of Luther:

> *Not everyone is a believer.* Many believe weakly and pass by periods or crises of doubt. For these persons, the freedom [of faith] is a frightful secret. If God graciously provides justification for sin, why does that free gift not reach everyone who depends upon the poverty of their human freedom? This has always remained the terrible danger [in Luther's position].[817]

Nevertheless, Segundo concedes that *Luther's understanding of the liberating quality of "faith" vis-à-vis the enslavement of "sin" is essentially correct and consistent with Paul's theology.* In order to remain consistent with his understanding of universal salvation, Segundo proposes that "faith" be understood as a attitudinal "wager" and as a special grace given by God to *everyone*, even if in varying degrees: "In how many human beings will God find or place the wager [*apuesta*] that love is *worthwhile* [*vale la pena*], the hoping in love against all hope? . . . [Answer:] *in all the children of Adam.*"[818]

In spite of this modest concession to Luther, Segundo never

rescinds his primary criticism of Luther. Segundo still believes that Luther *separates* "faith" from "faith's works." Segundo seeks to illustrate this point by examining what he calls "the *cultic-legal* key" in Romans 3:23-25.[819] Segundo contends that there is a "strict" and a "loose" interpretation of the "cultic-legal" in this passage. The "strict" interpretation is described in this way:

> we might imagine a courtroom where a defendant has been convicted of Sin. The judge asks: Has Christ died yet? If the answer is no, the defendant continues to be declared convicted because he or she has not paid for Sin. If the answer is yes, the defendant is declared innocent or just (pardoned). The death of Christ, in the words, was the precondition and the decisive, immediate, sufficient factor for our reconciliation with God.[820]

On the other hand, Segundo contends that Paul may have been employing a "loose" interpretation, which could be depicted as follows:

> When Christ consented to die for love of us while we were still God's enemies, he freed us radically from our moral fears and thus opened up a whole new possibility for us. Despite all our human limitations, we can now forget our own destiny compromised by Sin and move out creatively and freely to build the kingdom of God insofar as the latter depends on us. Or, to use a Pauline synonym for the kingdom of God, we might say that our task now is to effect the real humanization of the human world. Note that the symbolism is still framed in the juridical scheme. The fear that would be ours if Christ's death had not freed us is metaphorically that of a sinful defendant standing before the most just of judges.[821]

Both interpretations convey the concept of a "forensic justification." However, Segundo believes that the former, strict interpretation is too static. It resembles an understanding of "vicarious satisfaction" and does not address the importance of human freedom and causality in shaping the kingdom of God. The loose interpretation, by contrast, depicts Christ as sharing in the human destiny *and also* conveys the dynamic of human causality of the Kingdom. Therefore, Segundo affirms the Pauline and Lutheran emphasis on "forensic justification." In fact, he commends Luther for appropriately understanding "the recognized meaning in the New Testament and in Paul of the Greek term, to 'declare just,' as in a court of law."[822]

However, Segundo is opposed to any kind of understanding that denies the value of human causality. He thinks that Reformation expressions about "human causality" are rare. "At the time of the Reformation [Martin] Bucer may have been the only person who attempted to clarify the relationship between justification by faith alone and historical effort to build up the kingdom of God."[823] In Segundo's estimation, Bucer remains one of the bright examples from the Reformation.

> Bucer tried to balance himself between two opposing tendencies. His first treatise, That Nobody Should Live for Self Alone, but for His Neighbor (1523) distinguished him, by its very title, from Luther. Whereas Luther's point of departure was on the problem of personal salvation, Bucer began with the neighbor: "The human being," he wrote, "can stop being preoccupied with himself, because he is sure that God, the eternal Father, is concerned about him as his own beloved child."[824]

Luther, according to Segundo, was never able to get beyond "a *paralysing concern* with justification of self."[825] However, in discussing the Lutheran understanding of justification, Segundo cites *Karl Barth's* "rejection of the Catholic attempt to connect God 'and' man, *faith 'and' good works*."[826] Segundo concludes: "the *Lutheran* rejection of this 'and' in the problem of justification turns *faith* into the confident but *essentially passive acceptance of God's fixed plan for human destiny and the construction of his eschatological kingdom*."[827] As if to clinch the argument, Segundo quotes from Luther's own De servo arbitrio:

> How could [the Sons of the Kingdom] merit what already belongs to them and has been prepared for them since before they were created? It would be more exact to say that it is the Kingdom of God which merits us as possessors. . . . The Kingdom of God is already prepared. But the children of God must be prepared in view of the Kingdom, so that it is the Kingdom which merits the children, and not the children who merit the Kingdom.[828]

For Segundo, this means that Luther's understanding of the Kingdom is something which "*only* awaits the entry of it of every man by faith."[829] Hence, while Luther may have been accurate in affirming "faith" as a dynamic freedom *from* "Catholic legalism," his understanding of "faith" did not adequately grasp the concept of freedom *for* the "building of the Kingdom of God."[830]

There can be no denying that Martin Luther rediscovered central features of Paul's theology. But his juridical, magical view of justification by faith led him to a position that is thoroughly *anti-Pauline*, in my opinion. His view of "*soli Deo gloria*" implies that God's glory is protected all the more, the less human causality collaborates with God's plans.[831]

Segundo perceives that this erroneous understanding of justification and "*soli Deo gloria*" is pervasive in the Reformation tradition. For example, Segundo criticizes Rudolf Bultmann: "Before any exegetical effort has been made, [Bultmann] defines the kingdom of God as 'a miraculous event which will be brought about *by God alone without the help of human beings.*'"[832] Segundo also has Jürgen Moltmann in mind when he states that "'synergism' (cooperation), which Paul explicitly made his own, is considered as a theological deviation by some Lutherans."[833]

Conclusion: Summary of Segundo's Critique and Inherent Difficulties

Segundo credits Luther for rediscovering the importance and depth of the Pauline concepts of "sin" and "faith." Nevertheless, any positive contribution by Luther is far outweighed by Segundo's criticisms against Luther's theology. First, Segundo has argued that Luther bifurcates the "religious" and "secular" planes or realms. Second, Segundo does not believe that Luther has an antithetical parallel between Christ and Adam, or that Luther does not understand or appreciate the concept of qualitative disproportion. Third, Luther has a paralyzing concern with justification of the self. Fourth, Luther operates with a passive notion of "faith." Finally, Segundo believes that Luther denies all human causality and cooperation in the Kingdom of God. Because of these critical factors, Segundo contends that Luther is ultimately anti-Pauline and, like much of contemporary Catholic and Protestant theology, *separates* "faith" from "faith's works."

However, on the basis of the *evidence* provided in establishing the case against Luther, there are at least three factors that seriously weaken Segundo's argument. *First, Segundo relies exclusively on "secondary" sources.* This is an extremely peculiar phenomenon, given that Segundo cites evidence from "primary" sources when criticizing the theologies of his contemporaries. It is possible, of course, that Segundo may have been familiar with Luther's writings; but it is curious that he never demonstrates that fact, even in his most recent and more sympathetic treatment of Luther and the Reformation.[834]

The objection could be made that Segundo did quote Luther at least once directly, in the quote above from De servo arbitrio. However, this text is also from secondary material. In all three cases where Segundo quotes this text, the context is identical and almost verbatim.[835] Segundo is seeking to delineate the position of Rudolf Weth and quotes Weth's use of Luther, including Weth's parenthetical insertion ("the Sons of the Kingdom").[836] It is unlikely that Segundo consulted Luther directly, since Weth provides the exact reference from Luther's De servo arbitrio.[837] Furthermore, Segundo credits Weth for the Luther reference, though this credit is more concealed in Segundo's "Capitalism--Socialism" article.[838]

Second, Segundo's polemic against Luther's theology is principally a polemic against the theology of Karl Barth and European political theology. Segundo's early description of Luther's theology is based on formulations derived from Henri Bouillard's commentary on the thought of Karl Barth. Furthermore, on one other critical occasion, *Barth's* position on the relationship of faith and works is explicitly cited as an example of *Luther's* position. The differences, and perhaps similarities between Segundo and Barth are no doubt worthy of further investigation. It is *Luther*, however, and not Barth who is explicitly criticized by Segundo. Segundo is aware of critical differences between Barth and Luther on the role of faith and christological universalism. This should have suggested to Segundo that Barth probably should not be taken at face value as an authoritative representative for Luther's theology.[839]

Segundo's weightier criticisms against Luther concerning human causality and the Kingdom of God are mired in Segundo's critique against European political theology. We have already investigated Rudolf Weth's quotation from Luther. Segundo's citation of Jürgen Moltmann as representative of a "Lutheran" understanding is curious as well as erroneous. Segundo would have found stronger support by claiming a relationship between the theology of Moltmann and *Karl Barth*. One authority on Moltmann's theology claims that Barth was "the pervasive theological influence" in Moltmann's life.[840] Also of interest is the following quote from Rubem Alves, whom Segundo himself recognizes as "a disciple of Moltmann":

Indeed, "the revelation of the risen Lord does not become 'historic' as a result of the fact that history continues willy-nilly, but it stands as a sort of *primum movens* at the head of the process of history." It is not historical, but "pulls" history. It is qualitatively "wholly other," *as in Barth*. In terms of relation it is tangential, *as in Barth*. The impact of its announcement is the advent of "crisis," *as in Barth*. Its promise is a new world that comes when all human possibilities are ended, *as in Barth*. *Moltmann's position suggests itself compellingly to me as 90-degree rotation of the idea of transcendence of the early Barth.*[841]

If the position of Alves is correct, then the theological presuppositions for Moltmann may be found in Barth, not Luther.

Third, Segundo's criticism are based on insubstantial or superficially presented evidence. For example, none of the Pauline exegetes we have examined refer to a differentiation between a "strict" and "loose" cultic-legal key in Paul's theology in Romans 3:23-25. This would tend to indicate that Segundo is a maverick on this point.[842] Furthermore, Segundo provides no evidence to fault Luther for fostering a "strict" interpretation vis-à-vis a "loose" interpretation of the "cultic-legal" key.

Segundo's critique of Luther's "doctrine of the two kingdoms" is also lacking in critical support. In actual fact, there are a number of critics, including Karl Barth, who have noted the tragic use (or misuse) of "two kingdoms" theology in the last two centuries.[843] However, of the three critics (Harvey Cox, James Preus, and Reinhold Niebuhr) cited by Segundo, only Preus traces his argument back to Luther. Preus raises the concept of "two kingdoms" in connection with Luther's response to the peasant's revolt. Preus depicts Luther as an agent for law and order and strict obedience to secular authorities at the expense of any political liberation.[844] Luther may well deserve the criticism of political naivete for his role in the peasant's revolt. However, the deeper theological and historical factors are neglected by Preus.[845] This leaves Segundo with very weak evidence to warrant the claim that Luther separated "political authority" from "theological authority," or sanctioned the "political realm" as an autonomous reality.

It is regrettable that much of Segundo's argument is based on vague references to Luther from "secondary" sources. These citations may provide us with sharper insights into Segundo's own theological agenda, but they do not present Luther's theology in the best possible light. Hence, we need to examine Luther's sources directly to provide a clear or credible picture of Luther's position vis-à-vis Segundo's central thesis on the relationship between "faith" and "faith's works."

II. Luther and the Confessions on the Relationship between "Faith" and "Faith's Works"

In this part, we will examine the theology of Luther and the Reformation on the basis of the original texts. Our specific agenda will be to examine whether or not Luther and the Reformation did in fact separate "faith" from "faith's works" as Segundo contends. Furthermore, we will also look closely at the critical points that Segundo has raised against Luther. These criticisms claim that Luther (1) bifurcates the "religious" and "secular" planes or realms; (2) lacks an antithetical parallel between Christ and Adam or an understanding of qualitative disproportion; (3) demonstrates a paralyzing concern with personal justification; (4) operates with a passive concept of "faith"; (5) denies all human causality and cooperation in the Kingdom of God.

Iustificatio sola fide, For the Sake of the Gospel

Segundo rightly focuses on Luther's "doctrine of justification by faith alone" as a "central theme," not only for Luther, but for the Reformation as a whole. "Justification by faith" is "the single great proposed dogma of the Reformation" and "the doctrine by which the church 'stands or falls.'"[846]

For our purposes, it is more important to understand *why* "justification by faith" was centrally valued by the Reformers. The Reformers came to recognize that "justification by faith" speaks more clearly than all the other "articles" of faith of the *one* doctrine that matters for the life of the Church and the world: the *doctrina evangelii*, the "good news" of Jesus Christ.[847] Historically speaking, the Reformers were not aware, even at Augsburg in April, 1530, that this "article" was a problem for their critics. The "article" on "justification" (*De Iustificacione*) was listed fourth in the Augsburg Confession, and was not considered by the Reformers among the "Articles About Matters in Dispute."[848] At Augsburg, the article was presented as follows:

> It is also taught among us [i.e., our Churches] that we cannot obtain forgiveness of sin and righteousness before God by our own merits,

works, or satisfactions, but that we receive forgiveness of sin and become righteous before God by grace, for Christ's sake, through faith, when we believe that Christ suffered for us and that for his sake our sin is forgiven and righteousness and eternal life are given to us. For God will regard and reckon this faith as righteousness, as Paul says in Romans 3:21-26 and 4:5.[849]

The Confutatio Pontificia (August 3, 1530) affirmed with the Reformers that certain heresies were to be condemned (notably, "Pelagianism"). It varied with the position of the Reformers by affirming the divinely-graced value of "merit" as something "worthy of eternal life." Furthermore, the Confutatio stated that justification was not to be limited to "faith alone," but to include "grace and love."[850] It was this response of the Confutation that made it clear that "justification by faith" was the central issue in dispute.[851] Hence, Melanchthon refers to "justification by faith alone" in the Apology of the Augsburg Confession (1531) as "the main doctrine of Christianity." "When it is properly understood, *it illumines and magnifies the honor of Christ and brings to pious consciences the abundant consolation that they need.*"[852] Similarly in the Smalcald Articles (1537), Luther wrote:

> *The first and chief article is this, that Jesus Christ, our God and Lord, "was put to death for our trespasses and raised for our justification" (Rom. 4:25). . . . Inasmuch as this must be believed and cannot be obtained or apprehended by any work, law, or merit, it is clear and certain that such faith alone justifies us*, as St. Paul says in Romans 3, "For we hold that a man is justified by faith apart from works of law" (Rom. 3:28), and again, "that he [God] himself is righteous and that he justifies him who has faith in Jesus" (Rom. 3:26).[853]

We misunderstand Luther and the Reformation if we do not recognize, first and foremost, that the "deeper truth" with which they were concerned is the *gospel*. For this, they would make their appeal to Paul and to the entire biblical witness.

The False Gospel of "Free Choice" and "Merit": "Apart from me you can do nothing" (John 15:5)

Luther's De servo arbitrio, the only source by Luther to which Segundo refers, is in response to the Diatribe or Discourse of Erasmus,

De libero arbitrio. Erasmus maintains that human beings have "free choice" and that even though "damaged by sin," this "free choice" is "not extinguished."[854] Erasmus argues, therefore, that "free choice" can "cooperate" in a limited way through the "successive degrees" of natural, stimulating, cooperating, and conclusive grace toward the eventual goal of salvation.[855] "Hence it was commonly taught that if a man would only do 'what in him lay,' however little that might be, God would reward him with a gift of grace, enabling him to do more and yet more until he had enough to qualify for glory."[856]

Congruent with the concept of "free choice" is the concept of "merit." Scholasticism distinguished between a preparatory "merit of congruity" (*meritum congrui*), and "merit of condignity" (*meritum condigni*).

> The former was ascribed to man's well-intentioned efforts, which, although they were not strictly meritorious, it was "fitting" that God should reward with his grace. The latter, as resulting from good works done with the aid of grace thus received, was regarded as meritorious in the strict sense of the term.[857]

Luther remarks on the issue of free will that "it is not irreverent, inquisitive, or superfluous, but essentially salutary and necessary for a Christian, to find out whether the will does anything or nothing in matters pertaining to eternal salvation."[858] Luther asserts that the human will can do "nothing" *coram Deo* to affect (positively or negatively) the relationship between human beings and God (John 15:5), not even "a very little."[859] Luther provides a whole series of biblical examples (the hardening of Pharaoh's heart, Ex. 4:21; Paul's rebuke of the questioner, Rom. 9:20; etc.) that depict the necessity of and human dependence upon God's sovereign freedom.[860]

Luther claims that Erasmus is unable to grasp the promise of the gospel. Luther maintains that the relationship between human beings and God is totally in the control of God. Erasmus clings to something in the human being (viz., free choice) that can control the outcome of that relationship.[861] Luther refers to Erasmus as a "wriggling eel"[862] and an "uncatchable Proteus"[863] because of Erasmus' evasiveness from outright Pelagianism. In Luther's estimation, Erasmus was steering a course between the "Charybdis and Scylla" of Pelagianism and the merit of condignity.[864] Similarly, the Apology charges that the Confutatio and the critics of the Reformation were guilty of a thinly-veiled "Pelagianism" by promoting "two modes of justification ["merit" and "initial grace"], one based upon reason, the other based upon the law, neither one based upon the Gospel or the promise of Christ."[865]   Living in faith is first and foremost a "theology of the cross":

> through the cross *works are destroyed* and *the old Adam, who is especially edified by works, is crucified.* It is impossible for a person not to be puffed up by his good works unless he has first been deflated and destroyed by suffering and evil until he knows that he is worthless and that *his works are not his but God's.*[866]

Luther regarded the concept of "free choice" as particularly deceptive because it assumes that the human will is on "neutral ground," as if "God and the devil. . . were only observers of that mutable free will."[867] "As long as he [Satan] reigns, the human will is not free nor under its own control, but is the slave of sin and Satan, and can only will what its master wills."[868]   Satan's reign is challenged through the "ministry of the Word,"[869] "the preaching and offering of divine mercy throughout the world";[870] indeed, the work of Christ's kingdom in the world.

> For Christians know that there are *two kingdoms* in the world, which are bitterly opposed to each other. In one of them Satan reigns, who is therefore called by Christ "the ruler of this world" (John 12:31) and by Paul "the god of this world" (2 Cor. 4:4). . . . In the other Kingdom, Christ reigns, and his Kingdom ceaselessly resists and makes war on the kingdom of Satan. Into this Kingdom we are transferred, not by our own power but by the grace of God, by which we are set free from the present evil age and delivered from the dominion of darkness.[871]

God's activity is not restricted to the preached Word. The fact that God's rule in the world, even where the Word is not being preached, is the basis for Luther's more developed concept of the "*two* kingdoms"--the "kingdom of Christ," to be sure; but also "the kingdom of the world."[872] This is also the basis for Luther's understanding of the "hidden God" (*Deus absconditus*): "To the extent that God hides himself and wills to be unknown to us, it is no business of ours."[873] Drawing on Paul's reference in 2 Thess. 2:4, Luther argues that even if the God who is revealed in preaching and worship is not heeded,

God's majesty remains intact, and "all things are under his mighty hand."[874] God's will is "immutable and infallible, and it governs our mutable will."[875]

Luther concedes that this truth is offensive to human reason (often personified by Luther as "Reason").[876] Nevertheless, while the "immutability" (or "necessity," as opposed to "contingency") of God's will is offensive to Reason, it is the greatest consolation to faith.

> Christian faith is entirely extinguished, the promises of God and the whole gospel are completely destroyed, if we teach and believe that it is not for us to know the necessary foreknowledge of God and the necessity of the things that are to come to pass. For this is the one supreme consolation of Christians in all adversities, to know that God does not lie, but does all things immutably, and that his will can neither be resisted nor changed nor hindered.[877]

Luther returns to this theme in a more pastoral way at the end of his treatise, in the discussion of the "three lights" of nature, grace, and glory. The "*light of nature*" cannot get beyond the "insoluble problem how it can be just that a good man should suffer and a bad man prosper."[878]

> God so orders this corporal world in its external affairs that if you respect and follow the judgment of human reason, you are bound to say either that there is no God or that God is unjust. "The tents of the ungodly are at peace," says Job [Job 12:6], and Psalm 72 [73:12] complains that the sinners of the world increase in riches. . . . Tell me, is it not in everyone's judgment most unjust that the wicked should prosper and the good suffer?[879]

The "*light of grace*" or the "light of the gospel" brings into being "Word and faith" and moves one beyond the "light of nature." This "light of grace" teaches that "there is a life after this life, and whatever has not been punished and rewarded here will be punished and rewarded there, since this life is nothing but an *anticipation, or rather, the beginning* of the life to come."[880]

Nevertheless, even this "light" cannot get beyond the "insoluble problem how God can damn one who is unable by any power of his own to do anything but sin and be guilty."[881] Hence, to all appearances, God is "unjust." Neither the "light of nature" nor the "light of grace" can "judge otherwise of a God who crowns one ungodly man freely and apart from merits, yet damns another who may well be less, or at least not more, ungodly."[882] The "*light of glory*," however,

> tells us differently, and it will show us hereafter that the God whose judgment here is one of incomprehensible righteousness is a God of most perfect and manifest righteousness. In the meantime, we can only *believe* this, being admonished and confirmed by the example of the light of grace, which performs a similar miracle in relation to the light of nature.[883]

We recognize here just how important this theme is, then, for the gospel. Faith believes in God's righteousness, despite everything to the contrary. However, Luther concludes from his own experiences that relying on "free choice" is a path of "anxious doubt."[884] That is why Paul writes in Romans "against free choice and for the grace of God."[885]

The "Passive" Righteousness:
"Christ redeemed us from the curse of the law" (Gal. 3:13)

Luther attributes the adjective "passive" only to "righteousness." "Passive" righteousness is "the righteousness of grace, mercy, and the forgiveness of sins," "the righteousness of Christ and of the Holy Spirit" granted to us through God the Father.[886] This "passive" rightcousness is set in juxtaposition to "active" righteousness, "the righteousness of works, or moral and civil righteousness,"[887] which is the "righteousness of my own or of the divine Law."[888]

Luther sometimes speaks of these two kinds of "righteousness" needing to be "*distinct and separated.*"[889] More commonly, however, the emphasis is on "*distinction.*" "Therefore let us learn diligently this art of *distinguishing* between these two kinds of righteousness, in order that we may know how far we should obey the Law."[890] Similarly, Luther notes how Paul in Romans 4 makes a "distinction" (*partitionem*) between the "twofold righteousness of Abraham."[891] In regard to the article of justification by faith, the Apology also upholds "the *distinction* [*discrimine*] between the law and the promises or Gospel."[892]

There is more than simply a semantic issue involved here. Luther perceives that the two kinds of righteousness (*duplex iustitia*) are *already conjoined in the Christian life*, accounting for the two forums of Christian existence (*coram Deo, coram mundo*).[893]   In fact, it is because they are inseparably intermingled that Luther perceives the need for the *distinction*:   "in the hour of death or in other conflicts of conscience these two kinds of righteousness come together more closely than you would wish or ask."[894]   Luther maintains, therefore, that there can be "no middle ground" between the "passive" righteousness and the "active" righteousness.[895]   Because "passive" righteousness alone can place human beings in a right relationship with God, it is the primary righteousness.[896]   The insistence on the primacy of "passive" righteousness is essential in order to keep the promise of the Gospel central.   Otherwise, one may "fall into a trust in his own works."[897]

While *human beings* are "passive" in receiving the gift of righteousness, *God*, who is the giver of the gift through Christ, is *not* passive.   Luther expounds upon this in his commentary on Galatians 3:13.   There is first of all the very active identification that Christ makes with human beings and their history in their theological state of Fallenness.   In so doing, Christ actively becomes one "among thieves," "an associate of sinners."[898]   So much does Christ identify with us that he becomes "wrapped up in our sins, our curse, our death, and everything evil."[899]   This is how far "the indescribable and inestimable mercy and love of God" is willing to go for the redemption of humanity.[900]

> When the merciful Father saw that we were being *oppressed* through the Law, that we were being held *under a curse*, and that we *could not be liberated* from it by anything, He sent His Son into the world, heaped all the sins of men upon Him, and said to Him: "Be Peter the denier, Paul the persecutor, blasphemer, and assaulter; David the adulterer; the sinner who ate the apple in Paradise; the thief on the cross.   In short, *be the person of all men, the one who has committed the sins of all men.*[901]

It is here that Luther advances what he believes to be *Paul's* "invincible and irrefutable *antithesis*" between Christ and the sin of Adam:

> If the sins of the entire world are on that one man Jesus Christ, then they are not on the world.   But if they are not on Him, then they are still on the world.   Again, if Christ Himself is made guilty of all the sins that we have all committed, then we are absolved from all sins, not through ourselves or through our own works or merits but through Him.   But if He is innocent and does not carry our sins, then we carry them and shall

die and be damned in them.[902]

Far from ignoring this antithetical parallel, Luther asserts that the "one man" Christ actively enters into mortal combat for our sakes and takes on the "sin" that is "dominating and ruling," "capturing and enslaving" all people.[903] The Law calls for Christ's death as a "sinner," and indeed "attacks Him and kills Him."[904] Furthermore, the sins of the world, "past, present, and future, attack Him, try to damn Him, and do in fact damn Him."[905] However, "in Christ all sin is conquered, killed, and buried; and righteousness remains the victor and the ruler eternally."[906] Furthermore, Luther does not understand this activity of Christ as a static, "vicarious satisfaction." Christ enters into this saving activity freely and by his own choice. "He took upon Himself our sins, *not by compulsion but of His own free will*" and "of His own free will and by the will of the Father He wanted to be an associate of sinners."[907] Christ did this "because of His great love."[908]

Luther consistently depicts the role of Christ as one of active and complete involvement in everything that conditions the human experience, including the experience of suffering under the weight of sin. Hence, Christ suffers for us physically, emotionally, and spiritually: "For all the curses of the Law were gathered together in Him, and therefore He bore and sustained them *in His body* for us. Consequently, He was not only accursed; but He *became a curse for us.*"[909] "It is something awful to bear sin, the wrath of God, the curse, and death. Therefore a man who *feels* these things in earnest really becomes sin, death, and the curse itself."[910]

Christ "took upon Himself our sinful person and granted us His innocent and victorious Person."[911] Luther describes this "fortunate exchange" with a list of superlatives: "the most joyous of all doctrines," "delightful comfort," etc.[912]

The Righteousness of Faith: "Abraham believed God, and it was reckoned to him as righteousness" (Gen. 15:6; Gal. 3:6)

Faith is never depicted by Luther as something "passive," but as "*fides apprehensiva*--a faith which seizes Christ, and holds him fast, in order that his righteousness may be ours, and our sin his."[913]

We must look at this image and *take hold* of it with a firm faith. He who does this has the innocence and the victory of Christ, no matter how great a sinner he is. . . . Therefore we are justified by faith alone, because faith alone *grasps* this victory of Christ. *To the extent that you believe this, to that extent you have it.* If you believe that sin, death, and the curse have been abolished, they have been abolished, because Christ conquered and overcame them in Himself; and He wants us to believe that just as in His Person there is no longer the mask of the sinner or any vestige of death, so this is no longer in our person, since He has done everything for us.[914]

It is of course true that Luther and the Reformation regarded *propter fidem* as nothing unless it is also *propter Christum*.[915] But this ought not drive a wedge between these Christ and faith. The Augsburg Confession connects the two, claiming that justification is *propter Christum per fidem*.[916] The discussion of this distinction (*propter fidem/propter Christum*) may only make better sense in the light of a much later controversy within Lutheranism between "fideists" and "objectivists."[917]

Luther cites the example of Abraham in Gen. 15:6 in order to establish this connection between faith and the righteousness of Christ. Abraham's faith is "reckoned as righteousness" for Abraham "because it [faith] renders to God what is due to Him; whoever does this is righteous."[918] Luther also examines in this regard the antithesis between "faith" and "reason."

[Reason] fought against faith in him [Abraham] and regarded it as something ridiculous, absurd, and impossible that Sarah, who was not only ninety years old now but was also barren by nature, should give birth to a son. Faith certainly had to struggle with reason in Abraham. But faith won the victory in him; it killed and sacrificed God's bitterest and most harmful enemy. Thus all devout people enter with Abraham into the darkness of faith, kill reason, and say: "Reason, you are foolish. You do not understand the things that belong to God (Matt. 16:23)."[919]

"Faith alone attributes glory to God" precisely because it recognizes God as "merciful, truthful, and faithful to His promises" and "not as an angry judge, who must be placated by their works."[920] It is in this light that Luther will speak of "faith" as "our chief work" and "first, highest, and most precious of all good works."[921]

Luther understands the totality of "Christian righteousness" to consist of both "*faith in the heart and the imputation of God.*"[922] "The sacrifice of faith began in Abraham, but it was finally consummated only in death. Therefore the second part of righteousness had to be added, which perfects it in us, namely, divine imputation."[923]   Luther hardly thinks that Abraham's faith was abounding. In fact, Luther claims that Abraham had "barely a little spark" of faith."[924]   The same understanding of the quantity of faith is carried into Christian existence. "We have received the first fruits of the Spirit, but not the tithes."[925]   Luther maintains that "reason, . . . lust, wrath, impatience, and other fruits of the flesh and of unbelief still remain in us."[926]   "Not even the more perfect saints have a full and constant joy in God."[927]   Even for the prophets and apostles "feelings change; sometimes they are sad, sometimes joyful."[928] Nevertheless, one can argue that Luther's *"qualitative disproportion"* is advanced in this manner:

> On account of this faith in Christ God does not see the sin that still remains in me. For so long as I go on living in the flesh, there is certainly sin in me. But meanwhile Christ protects me under the shadow of His wings and spreads over me the wide heaven of the forgiveness of sins, under which I live in safety. This prevents God from seeing the sins that still cling to my flesh. My flesh distrusts God, is angry with Him, does not rejoice in Him, etc. But God overlooks these sins, and in His sight they are as though they were not sins. This is accomplished by imputation on account of faith by which I begin to take hold of Christ; and on His account God reckons imperfect righteousness as perfect righteousness and sin as not sin, even though it really is sin.[929]

This is the appropriate meaning of Luther's *simul justus et peccator*. "The Christian man is righteous and a sinner at the same time, holy and profane, an enemy of God and a child of God."[930]   Faith, therefore, is not something to be measured *quantitatively*, but *qualitatively through Christ*. Despite all appearances to the contrary, the Christian is made whole, holy and complete through faith in Christ (the object of one's faith).

The Faith that Works:
"Faith working through love" (Gal. 5:6)

The *distinction* of the righteousness of faith and the righteousness of works does not mean *separation*. Luther affirms that passive righteousness received through Christ "is the basis, the cause, the source of all our own actual righteousness" as "its fruit and consequence."[931]   "We say that justification is effective without works, *not that faith is without works*. For that faith which lacks fruit is not an efficacious but a feigned faith."[932]   "When I have this righteousness [of Christ] within me, I descend from heaven like the rain that makes the earth fertile.   That is, I come forth into another kingdom, and I perform good works whenever the opportunity arises."[933]

"Faith" provides the connection between passive righteousness and active righteousness.

> *Faith is a living, daring confidence in God's grace, so sure and certain that the believer would stake his life on it a thousand times.*   This knowledge of and confidence in God's grace makes men glad and bold and happy in dealing with God and with all creatures.   And this is the work which the Holy Spirit performs in faith.   *Because of it, without compulsion, a person is ready and glad to do good to everyone, to serve everyone, to suffer everything, out of love and praise to God who has shown him his grace.   Thus it is impossible to separate works from faith,* quite as impossible to separate heat and light from fire.[934]

We are justified by "faith alone."   "But after a man is justified by faith, now possesses Christ by faith, and knows that He is his righteousness and life, he will certainly not be idle but, like a sound tree, will bear good fruit (Matt. 7:17)."[935]   Faith is "abstract" and "absolute" when it comes to justification; but "when Scripture speaks about rewards and works, then it is speaking about faith as something compound, concrete, or incarnate."[936]   "Everything that is attributed to works belongs to faith."[937]   Faith is "effective" (*efficax*) and "active" (*operosa*) through love.[938]   In a manner that is compellingly similar to the example we have noted from Martin Bucer, Luther writes:

> We conclude, therefore, that a Christian lives not in himself, but in Christ and in his neighbor.   Otherwise he is not a Christian.   He lives in Christ through faith, in his neighbor through love.   By faith he is caught up beyond himself into God.   By love he descends beneath himself into his neighbor.[939]

Faith is not, in the Thomistic interpretation of Galatians 5:6, "formed" or "fashioned by love" (*fides charitate formata*).[940]   That leaves too much room for the *opinio legis* to exploit the role of faith in justification.[941]   The Reformers emphasize that "whatever does not proceed from faith is sin" (Rom. 14:23), "apart from me you can do nothing" (John 15:5), and "without faith it is impossible to please God" (Heb. 11:6).[942]   Nevertheless, one who is justified can truly affirm that "God is pleased" by the works done in faith.[943]

On at least one occasion, Luther will go so far as to say that "faith without works is worthless and useless."[944]   Such an unproductive faith is "a false faith and does not justify."[945]   In this way, Luther's position approximates (but only approximates) the position of James.[946]   Melanchthon, however, is more emphatic about the truth in James. "James is not against us when he distinguishes between dead and living faith."[947]   Faith is not an "idle knowledge."   It "resists the terrors of conscience and encourages and consoles terrified hearts."[948]   "Since this faith is a new life, it necessarily produces new impulses and new works.   Accordingly, James is *correct* in denying that we are justified by a faith without works."[949]

It is important to observe here that the relationship of "faith" and "works" is the outgrowth of the Reformation doctrine of "justification." Luther may well have wanted to address this relationship more fully in a work which he never completed, De Iustificatione.[950]   Melanchthon, however, explicitly states that the article on "Justification" as it is addressed in the Apology (Article 4) combines the "articles" of the Augsburg Confession which address not only "Justification" (AC 4), but also "The Office of the Ministry"(AC 5), "The New Obedience"(AC 6), and *"Faith and Good Works"* (AC 20).[951]   The Apology maintains an emphasis on the *connection* between "faith" and "works," even as it seeks to *distinguish* their roles, as some of the following examples demonstrate. "Love and good works must also follow faith. So they are not excluded as though they did not follow, but trust in the merit of love or works is excluded from justification."[952]   "Our opponents slanderously claim that we do not require good works, whereas we not only require them but show how they can be done."[953]   "In commending works, therefore, we must add that faith is necessary, and that they are commended because of faith as its fruit or testimony."[954]

This distinction-without-separation might even account for the concept of "double justification" advanced by Gropper (together with Bucer, and Pighius) at Regensberg in 1541.   In this concept, justification is in reality a combination of *iustitia infusa* and *iustitia*

acquisita (or *iustitia inhaerens*).[955]   But this posture does not allow
for the concept of a "double *formal cause* of justification" (in which
one needs not only faith, but also love, to be justified) advanced by the
Catholic participants at Regensberg.[956]   In Luther's estimation, the
Catholic position cannot be embraced because it fails to make a proper
"distinction" between faith and works.   Therefore, Luther later assessed
the results of Regensburg as a specious *zusammenleimen* (gluing
together) of antithetical positions.[957]

Human Cooperation in the Kingdom:
"For we are fellow workers with God" (1 Cor. 3:9)

Luther also addresses the issue of human cooperation with God in
advancing the work of the kingdom. His treatment of this issue is most
explicit in <u>De servo arbitrio</u>, in the context of his discussion of
"Precepts and Rewards in the New Testament: The Question of
Merit."[958] Luther notes that all "precepts in the New Testament" are
exhortations which follow the preaching of the gospel.

> [First] the gospel is preached. . . in which the Spirit and grace are
> offered with a view to the remission of sins, which has been obtained for
> us by Christ crucified; and all this freely, and by the sole mercy of God
> the Father, whereby favor is shown to us, unworthy as we are and
> deserving of damnation rather than anything else.   Then follow
> exhortations, in order to stir up those who are already justified and have
> obtained mercy, so that they may be active in the fruits of the freely
> given righteousness and of the Spirit, and may exercise love by good
> works and bravely bear the cross and all other tribulations of the
> world.[959]

For example, when Christ says, "Rejoice and be glad, for your reward
is great in heaven" (Matthew 5:12), he is "exhorting. . . the apostles,
who. . . were appointed to the ministry of the word. . . [and] bearing
the tribulations of the world."[960]

This emphasis on exhortations stemming from the gospel is also
evident in Luther's discussion of "merits" and "reward."   Human
beings are unable by their merit to make themselves "worthy" of the
kingdom of God.[961]   But there are rewards as a "consequence" of
their action. The ungodly are rewarded with "hell and the judgment of
God."   The godly are rewarded with the Kingdom (Matthew

25:34).[962] This does not mean that the godly seek to "merit" or "obtain" the Kingdom like "the ungodly who with an evil and mercenary eye 'seek their own' even in God."[963] Nevertheless, "the children of God do good with a will that is disinterested [*gratuita voluntate*], not seeking any reward, but only the glory and will of God, and being ready to do good even if--an impossible supposition--there were neither a kingdom nor a hell."[964]

It is in the context of this discussion that we encounter the text quoted previously by Segundo: "How could they merit that which is already theirs and is prepared for them before they are born? . . . For the Kingdom is not being prepared, but has been prepared, while the sons of the Kingdom are being prepared, not preparing the Kingdom."[965] This text is intended to be an evangelical promise that the Kingdom has been "merited" for us through Christ. Whenever there are references to "reward" in the Scriptures (for example, II Chron. 15:7; Gen. 15:1; Rom. 2:6-7), these point to the hope of "eternal life" and are "for the purpose of *exhortation* and commination, whereby the godly are awakened, comforted, and raised up to go forward, persevere, and conquer in doing good and enduring evil, lest they should grow weary or lose heart."[966] Thus, Paul exhorts the Corinthians in the gospel by saying, "'Be courageous, knowing that in the Lord your labor is not in vain' [1 Cor. 15:58; 16:13]; and similarly, God upholds Abraham by saying, "'I am your exceeding great reward' [Gen. 15:1]."[967]

Luther notes that "Reason may turn up her nose" at the suggestion that these words of exhortation make a difference: "Why should God will these things to be done by means of words, when nothing is accomplished by such words, and the will is unable to turn itself in either direction?"[968] Luther responds:

It has thus pleased God to impart the Spirit, not without the Word, but through the Word, so as to have us as *cooperators* [*ut nos habeat suos cooperatores*] with him [1 Cor. 3:9] when we sound forth outwardly what he himself alone breathes inwardly wherever he wills, thus doing things that he could of course do without the Word, though he does not will so to do. And who are we that we should inquire into the cause of the divine will [cf. Rom. 9:20]? . . . Similarly, he could nourish us without bread, and in fact has provided a means of nourishing us without bread, as Matthew 4[:4] says: Man is not nourished by bread alone, but by the Word of God, though it has pleased God by means of bread and together with bread brought to us from without, to nourish us with the Word inwardly.[969]

Luther, therefore, affirms that human beings are "cooperators" and agents in the Kingdom of God through their faith and their concrete words and messages of hope and promise. Hence, Luther posture toward the concept of human "cooperation" is quite positive. However, Luther does not accept Erasmus' premises that such "cooperation" is a matter of "free choice." For Luther, such premises constitute an alien gospel and confuse the concepts of "free choice" and "cooperation" rather than help to elucidate them in the best possible light.

> Where, then, is our orator [Erasmus] running off to, who was going to speak about a palm [cooperation], but talks of nothing but a gourd [free choice]? "It started out as a wine jar, why does it end as a water jug?" We too know that Paul cooperates with God in teaching the Corinthians [1 Cor. 3:9], inasmuch as he preaches outwardly while God teaches inwardly, each doing a different work. He also cooperates with God when he speaks by the Spirit of God [1 Cor. 12:3].[970]

In fact, Luther is more bold in claiming that "all things, even including the ungodly, cooperate with God."[971] One gathers, however, that they do not cooperate in the same promising sense as "those whom he has justified, that is, in his Kingdom."[972]

In the Formula of Concord, the issue of "cooperation" is again addressed with regard to a dispute that resurfaced within the Reformation over the nature of "free will." The position of the "synergists" (John Pfeffinger, Victorine Strigel, and Erasmus) maintained that human beings cooperate by the "natural power" of their free will in their salvation.[973] This position was clearly rejected. But the Formula affirmed that "*we can and must cooperate by the power of the Holy Spirit*, even though we do so in great weakness."[974]

Conclusion: Luther and Segundo on the Relationship between "Faith" and "Faith's Works"

On the basis of the "primary" sources of Luther, we conclude that Luther also affirms that *"faith" and "faith's works" need to be distinguished, but they cannot be separated*. Furthermore, the criticisms that Segundo has made against Luther are inadmissible on the basis of Luther's own writings. *First, there is no bifurcation or separation of the "two kingdoms".* In the theology of the Reformation, the concept of the "two kingdoms" refers either to the ongoing conflict between Christ and Satan or, more commonly, to the *two different ways that God rules* (law and gospel). *Second, there is a very definite understanding of the antithetical parallel between Christ and Adam.* However, Luther locates the qualitative disproportion in faith, whereas Segundo tends to locate that disproportion in love. As we have indicated, Luther has an essentially evangelical reason for locating that qualitative disproportion in faith rather than love. *Third, there is no "paralyzing concern with the justification of the self."* In fact, that is the very problem Luther overcomes through his evangelical focus. *Fourth, there is no understanding of "faith" as passive.* The primary righteousness that God brings to human beings is a "passive" righteousness. That is, human beings cannot earn their salvation. Faith, however, is *fides apprehensiva, efficax, operosa*, and actively participating in works of love. *Fifth, there is an explicit affirmation of human causality and cooperation in the Kingdom of God.* Luther's understanding of evangelical exhortation invites human cooperation.

However, we also conclude that Segundo and Luther are not in total theological agreement. There are definite differences with regard to their theological *presuppositions*.[975] Luther's presuppositions are grounded in the evangelical doctrine of "justification". Segundo's presuppositions are based in a "theology of grace" that received clear expression in the theology of Karl Rahner and Vatican II. Considerations with regard to Segundo's presuppositions are the subject matter of the final chapter.

Chapter 5
Foundations for the Faith that Works

The Inherent Problems in Segundo's Theological Presuppositions

Thus far we have established that Segundo is promoting a central thesis in his theology: *"faith" and "faith's works" need to be distinguished, but they cannot be separated* (Chapter One). Furthermore, we have demonstrated this thesis in Segundo's theology is in continuity with biblical and Pauline sources (Chapter Two). Segundo is especially critical of what he perceives as the situation in much of contemporary theology--a *separation* of "faith" from "faith's works." We have explored and affirmed this criticism in regard to Segundo's polemical encounters with Catholic and Protestant theologies (Chapter Three). Furthermore, we have explored Segundo's charge that Luther is also culpable for such a separation. However, we have demonstrated that Segundo's criticism of Luther is flawed. We have demonstrated that Luther affirms not only the central Pauline thesis, but also Paul's evangelical presuppositions for that thesis--"justification by faith" as the heart of the Christian gospel (Chapter Four).

We have made an effort to present Segundo's central thesis, and to suspend judgment on any theological presuppositions that serve as a foundation for that thesis. However, it is clearly the case with Luther and perhaps also the case with contemporary theology (especially Moltmann) that the basis for their objection to Segundo's theology has more to do with Segundo's *presuppositions* than with Segundo's central thesis.

In all of the previous chapters, but especially in the chapters in which we considered Segundo's polemic against other theologies, the emphasis on "universal grace" has been presented as *the* major theological presupposition for Segundo's theology. In this concluding chapter, we turn our attention to the fuller implications of that presupposition. First, we will examine Segundo's theology of "universal grace" in light of its origin and development in recent trends in Catholic theology, including Segundo's own proposal for an "evolutionary" gospel. Second, we will note that this theological presupposition is not the same as Paul's evangelical presupposition ("justification by faith"). This poses a inherent problem for Segundo's claim of being continuous with Paul's theology. Finally, we will note some of the inherent problems that Segundo's theological presupposition poses for the relationship between "faith" and "faith's works" in his central thesis.

I.   Segundo's Theological Presuppositions: Recent Trends in Catholic Theology of "Grace"

In this part, we will begin by tracing the recent trends in Catholic theology on the understanding of "grace." Specifically, we will examine the theological understandings of Leopold Malevez and Karl Rahner, and how their understandings of "grace" culminated in the official theology of Vatican II. We will note how these understandings have influenced Segundo's unique proposal for a "political theology of grace" and how that understanding of grace is evident in Segundo's "evolutionary" gospel for the contemporary situation.

Malevez, Rahner, and Vatican II

In a candid "*personal* testimony of the origins of liberation theology," Segundo recounts that the most influential event in his education happened in 1953, in "the course on the theology of grace given by an excellent theologian, Leopold Malevez."[976] "On the intellectual and theological level, *what I have always understood as my own 'theology of liberation' began with him*--a theology I amplified once I had returned to Latin America."[977]

The particular contribution of Malevez was the rediscovery of deep historical roots for a new concept of "grace." Malevez traced the concept of grace back to the Second Council of Orange (529) which "intervened in the dispute between the disciples of Augustine and those of Pelagius (the pseudo-Pelagians) to declare that the 'beginning of faith,' or rather, the preparation for it, was *already supernatural.*"[978] This understanding of grace as "*initium fidei*" (the beginning of faith) commonly circulated in theology well through the Middle Ages.[979] Malevez's uniquely discovered, however, that the *initium fidei* historically applied to "the *human virtues* that the pagan world of antiquity seemed to exhibit."[980]   Hence, the Church Fathers (notably, Eusebius of Caesarea) considered these "human virtues" as a "preparation for the Gospel." "For virtuous persons and, in some way more generally, for the entire march of human good will in history, there must be the understanding that no one is prepared or begins something that totally exceeds his or her possibilities."[981]   Thus the Second Council of Orange resolved the debate between the Augustinians and pseudo-Pelagians by claiming that

> the entire road traveled by the pagans (guided by good will and love)-- toward the God who is love and toward the Christian message of that Mystery hidden in love--was already (even though it did not lead to the faith) from God, from freely-given grace, and related to the plane of supernatural efficacy.[982]

According to Segundo, Malevez "anticipated" Karl Rahner's more popularized concept of "*the supernatural existential.*"[983]   Segundo comments:

> I said "anticipated" because, although the term "supernatural existential" was already well known (I do not know exactly when Malevez began to work theologically with this idea), Karl Rahner did not at that time accept the wider interpretation of the *initium fidei* or the preparation for faith, proposed by Malevez. He would accept it later, perceiving its truth at the same time as that doctrine converged with his concept of the concretely supernatural existence of every person.[984]

Rahner eventually emended his concept of the "supernatural existential" in such a way that it became synonymous with Malevez's concept of "*initium fidei.*"   However, Rahner's concept was more explicit about the "*universal dimensions*" of grace.[985]

The theological concept of grace developed by Rahner and others (including Blic, L. Malevez, C. Boyer, Garrigou-Lagrange, A. Michel, de Broglie or Philippe de la Trinité) eventually replaced the concept of grace advanced by the older school of "nouvelle théologie" (Lubac, Bouillard, Delaye, von Balthasar, Rondet).[986]   According to the teachings of "La nouvelle Théologie,"

> the grace of God lifted the individual to a *supernatural plane*, beginning
> with the acceptance of faith (and consequent baptism). Before that, the
> person moved on a level where, it was supposed, the destiny and efficacy
> of human actions led only to *natural* and temporal ends. One's intimate
> relationship with God and heavenly destiny *began with faith*, a gift from
> God which inaugurated that habitual gift of the supernatural.[987]

Rahner referred to this older concept of grace as "extrinsecism" or a
grace that "comes purely *from outside*" the human being.[988]   The
newer concept of "grace," however, recognizes that the *human being*
"is the event of God's absolute self-communication."[989]   The
"supernatural existential," therefore, made a *conceptual or theoretical
distinction* between nature and the supernatural (what human beings
might have been apart from God's grace), but not a *historical or
chronological* distinction (what human beings *are in fact* before and
after God's grace).

> It signifies that the human beings we know are born within an existence
> whose structure is supernatural; in it everything is related to their one
> and only destiny, and they can do nothing that does not have a positive
> or negative value vis-à-vis eternal life. This does not mean that grace or
> nature are confused with each other. The two concepts are different.
> And this forces us to remember at all times that human beings could have
> existed without the gift which God, *in reality*, made to them from the
> very beginning, in calling them to a supernatural existence.[990]

Thus Segundo concludes, "From the beginning of humanity, God's
grace placed *all persons* on the path toward the intimate relationship
with him and with celestial life."[991]

The understanding of "grace" advanced by Malevez and Rahner
was adopted at Vatican II (1962-1968).   Segundo appeals to the
Dogmatic Constitution on the Church (Lumen Gentium) and especially
to the Pastoral Constitution on the Church in the Modern World
(Gaudium et Spes) more than all the other texts produced by that
Council.[992]   One of the texts of special interest to Segundo is
paragraph 16 of Lumen Gentium.   The paragraph begins by claiming
that "those who have not yet received the Gospel are related to the
People of God in various ways."[993]   Specific examples are then cited:
Paul's appeal to the Jewish "people to which the covenants and

promises were made" in Romans 9-11, the Moslems who "profess to hold the faith of Abraham," and "those who in shadows and images seek the unknown God" (cf. Acts 17:25-28).[994] The paragraph then concludes:

> Those who, through no fault of their own, do not know the Gospel of Christ or his Church, but who nevertheless seek God with a *sincere heart*, and moved by grace, *try in their actions to do his will* as they know it through the dictates of their conscience--those too many [sic] achieve eternal salvation. Nor shall divine providence deny the assistance necessary for salvation to those who, without any fault of theirs, have not yet arrived at an explicit knowledge of God, and who, not without grace, *strive to lead a good life*. Whatever good or truth is found amongst them is considered by the Church to be a *preparation for the Gospel* and given by him who enlightens all men that they may at length have life.[995]

The text is obviously influenced by Rahner's concept of "anonymous Christianity."[996] Although Segundo values "this great theological principle" in <u>Lumen Gentium</u>, he thinks that it "is minimized by the fact that the interest of the Constitution is the Church, still conceived in the traditional way as 'perfect society.'"[997] Therefore, <u>Gaudium et Spes</u> is valued by Segundo because it made significant advances in the understanding of ecclesiology. First, there are some important paragraphs on the "kinds and causes of atheism" and "the attitude of the Church towards atheism" (para. 19-21), stressing better relationships and understanding between the Church and those who are atheistic).[998] Then follows the section on "Christ the New Man" (para. 22). Christ is the "image of the invisible God" (Col. 1:15) and "the perfect man who has *restored in the children of Adam that likeness to God which has been disfigured ever since the first sin.*"[999] The Christian, in accordance with Romans 8, is "conformed to the image of the Son who is firstborn of many brothers" and therefore is also duty bound "to struggle with evil through many afflictions and to suffer death; but, as one who has been *made a partner in the paschal mystery*, and as one who has been configured to the death of Christ, he will go forward, strengthened by hope, to the resurrection."[1000] We then come now to the text that Segundo quotes more than any other from Vatican II:

All this holds true *not for Christians only but also for all men [and women] of good will in whose hearts grace is active invisibly.* For since Christ died for all, and since all men [and women] are in fact called to one and the same destiny, which is divine, we must hold that *the Holy Spirit offers to all the possibility of being made partners, in a way known to God, in the paschal mystery.* Such is the nature and the greatness of the mystery of man as enlightened for the faithful by the Christian revelation.[1001]

Segundo's Theology of "Grace"

Segundo claims that "there does not exist any human being who is totally alien to God's grace."[1002] Therefore, he perceives his own position in line with the positions of Malevez and Rahner. Furthermore, Segundo borrows from Rahner's understanding that "grace" makes possible the exercise of human freedom vis-à-vis concupiscence or Sin.[1003] Sin is perceived as that which alienates the human being, not from God per se, but *from oneself.*[1004]

All of us human beings possess an incipient liberty that seeks fulfillment. But in the power of nature that invades us and dwells within us, *our incipient liberty encounters something which belongs to us and conditions all our executions even though it is indeed alien to the innermost core of our own ego.*[1005]

If there is any alienation from God, it is due to our not being the graced creatures God wishes us to be. The human being needs to be reconciled *with oneself.* "Grace" is that which "heals" human beings so that they can *recognize* their accomplishments as in conformity with their own inner freedom.[1006] That is, "grace" means that the human being can "determine for oneself one's own existence" and not be conditioned by the ever present forces (flesh, world, and devil, to use the biblical categories) at work outside one's "inner core" of freedom that control and enslave one's actions.[1007] Segundo distinguishes this from Pelagianism because he regards the latter as having "oversimplified the picture of the human condition."[1008] Pelagianism suggests that the "natural" will is "totally free" to choose between good and evil as the law prescribed, had it not been for the "allure of concupiscence."[1009]

Segundo believes that he has developed a uniquely "*political* version of a theology of grace."[1010] Segundo frequently quotes the passage from <u>Gaudium et Spes</u> (para. 38-39) concerning the fulfillment of human activity in the fullness of the paschal mystery.

> The Word of God, through whom all things were made, became man and dwelt among men: a perfect man, he entered world history, taking that history into himself and *recapitulating* it. . . . Far from diminishing our concern to develop this earth, the expectancy of a new earth should spur us on, for it is here that the body of a new human family grows, foreshadowing in some way the age which is to come. That is why, although we must be careful to distinguish earthly progress clearly from the increase of the kingdom of Christ, such progress is of vital concern to the kingdom of God, insofar as it can contribute to the better ordering of human society.[1011]

Segundo then connects this Vatican II emphasis with the thought of Teilhard de Chardin. The keen influence of Teilhard is evident in the abundant references to Teilhard in Segundo's early writing.[1012] In Segundo's later "evolutionary" christology, the references to Teilhard are also quite apparent, but Segundo's disquiet toward Teilhard's "optimism" is also more pronounced.[1013] Despite these reservations, Segundo himself puts forward an "evolutionary" understanding of sin and grace. We have touched upon this briefly in our discussion of Segundo's "mass-minority" distinction. It deserves fuller elaboration here because it is the basis for Segundo's own elaboration of the meaning of the "gospel."

By way of analogy, Segundo develops the principle of physics which is most conducive to his theological goals: "the principle of the conservation of energy. Or, if you will, *entropy*."[1014] "It states simply that every natural transformation is effected with the same sum total of energy. *None of it is lost, and no new energy is introduced.*"[1015] There are four consequences, characteristics, or features of entropy. First, for any evolution to take place, energy must be *expended*. Segundo cites the example coal that must be transformed into heat, heat to water, and water to steam in order for a steam locomotive to run.[1016] The second feature is that, while energy is conserved, it is also *degraded*, making it "more difficult to concentrate and put at the service of the human being again."[1017] Using the example above, it is difficult to reuse heat or steam. "It is like a wave in the ocean. . . . When the wave is dispersed, . . . this energy is dispersed into the infinite. It is not lost, but it becomes imperceptible."[1018]   The third feature is that evolution "moves toward ever more complex and potent concentrations of energy."[1019]   This presupposes something that "runs counter to the thrust of entropy; it is *negentropy*."[1020]   The fourth features recognizes that "*simpler syntheses of degraded energy*" are "*statistically greater.*" Nevertheless, the process of *negentropy* continues to function like "a minority current running against a majority tendency."[1021]   "Maintaining this delicate balance between majorities and minorities, evolution keeps passing *new thresholds* and moving toward higher forms of life and superior structures."[1022]

Segundo then applies these categories to the two major events of "Adam's sin and Christ's redemption."[1023]   Concupiscence is equated to the first two features of entropy because it runs counter to the evolution of human beings (first feature) and becomes mired in mechanisms making evolution more and more inaccessible (second feature).   Nevertheless, redemption (like the third feature of negentropy) delivers one from this spiralling trend.   Even though concupiscence remains "quantitatively" dominant and the basis of guilt, redemption is "qualitatively" greater (fourth feature).[1024]   Thus, the cosmic forces of "love, grace, life, and God's gift constitute the positive vector of evolution," while "egotism, sin, enslavement to the world and the flesh constitute the negative vector of evolution."[1025] "Faith" is that which recognizes the direction of the cosmic process.[1026]   But Segundo understands that "faith" is something within every human being.   "In how many human beings will God find or place that wager that love is worth the trouble [*el amor vale la pena*], the hoping in love against all hope? . . . [Answer:] *in all the children of Adam.*"[1027]   This "wager that love is worth the trouble" is the "*beginning of faith*" (*initium fidei*).[1028]

Segundo's "Evolutionary" Gospel

Segundo perceives that there are at least two principle challenges that church needs to address today.   "Our task is *ecological* and *political*."[1029]   There is a need to address not only the "exploitation of natural resources," but also the "mad desire to possess more and more" in political consumerism.[1030]   From the vantage point of the poor nations, these tasks are not separate, but conjoined through the interconnectedness that weaves together all of humanity.[1031]   While

Segundo recognizes the need for "flexibility" in the process of developing adequate ideologies for the contemporary experience,[1032] the church cannot afford to be passive. What vision will the church bring to meet these challenges?

Segundo believes that "evolutionary categories" can best convey the gospel of Jesus of Nazareth for today.[1033] We have already noted in Segundo's thought that the church is not unique in possessing "grace" or "faith." The church is unique because it possesses *"full-fledged faith."*[1034] "The Christian is *he who already knows*. This, undoubtedly, is what distinguishes and defines him."[1035] Therefore, in *the ministry of the Word* (2 Cor. 5:19; Rom. 5:6) the church engages in the task of "*conscientization*: i.e., making people consciously aware of a process that is going on *without their knowing it*."[1036] In evolutionary terms, this means that the role of church is to *reveal* the true nature of the evolutionary process which is already happening in the world.

> From *Christian revelation* we know that a divine force carries individual human beings, the human race, and the whole universe toward their recapitulation in Christ. "Recapitulation" here does not mean a mere summing up. It means that each and every element of human history and the universe is united with its head: i.e., with its deepest inner meaning. . . . We know that this cosmic force is love (GS 38). It is the life of God himself given as a present to man. Thus it is the gift par excellence: *grace*.[1037]

Segundo regards it as the task of every human being to live their "faith" today by traversing the "new thresholds" that lie before humanity. He also thinks that only a minority are willing to lead the way. Segundo finds helpful Teilhard's analogy of passengers who move from the hold of a ship and take command of the vessel from the bridge.

> Up to now human beings have been living at once dispersed and closed in on themselves, like passengers who have met by accident in the hold of a ship whose movement they did not even suspect. Living on earth that brought them together in groups, they could find nothing better to do than to argue with each other or amuse themselves. Now, by chance, or better, by the normal effect of organization, our eyes have just opened. The *most daring of us* have mounted the bridge and seen the ship that has been carrying us all. They have glimpsed the foam produced by the

prow as it cuts through the water. They have caught on to the fact that there is a boiler to be fed and a helm to be directed. Above all, they have seen the clouds floating by and smelled the fragrance of the islands beyond the circle of the horizon. The agitation of the hold is no longer possible. Mere drifting is no longer possible. The time has come to pilot the ship. It is inevitable that a different humanity must emerge from this vision.[1038]

Teilhard's analogy breaks down, however, when it gives the impression that humanity has crossed a single threshold (from mere passengers to commanders of destiny). Humanity crosses several thresholds in the ongoing process of evolution.[1039]   As humanity crosses these thresholds, faith plays a dramatic role. "Only *faith* makes the human being an 'heir of the world.' . . . My hypothesis, then, is that 'the most daring' of us must be those who most felt themselves to be the 'heirs of the world,' in line with the basic anthropological *faith* that is part of the Christian message in its pristine sense."[1040]

The same understanding of faith's role in the evolutionary process applies to the life of Jesus. "Jesus is part of that process. He is integrated into it and conditioned by it, just as he conditions the process to the extent that he is meaningful."[1041]   Jesus enters into the evolutionary struggle by bringing his *negentropy* of love and the kingdom of God to bear on the *entropy* of a socio-political order in Israel which marginalized the poor and oppressed.[1042] Jesus' living proclamation "*that God is love*" makes him a minority individual who reveals the divine plan in spite of obstacles to the contrary.[1043]   In this light, the "faith *of* Jesus" is more important than "faith *in* Jesus."[1044]

The divinity of Jesus is also affirmed, however, when anthropological faith elevates "the concrete values perceived in the history of Jesus to the category of absolute and to wager that to them the entire universe bows and submits in a personal way."[1045] Through "faith" Jesus is the regarded as the "primordial" being who makes the traversing of thresholds possible. *"In this world, nothing could ever burst forth as final across the different thresholds successively traversed by evolution (however critical they be) which has not already existed in an obscure and primordial way."*[1046]

Segundo, of course, acknowledges "the seeming victory of *entropy*" in the world. "The overwhelming weight of experience, of what goes on inside us and outside us, shows us the universal work of

. . . the principle of entropy. We constantly experience the bitter taste of the degeneration of energy into evermore undifferentiated and unusable forms."[1047]   Nevertheless, Jesus also shares in the those qualities of entropy (Sin and Death) and overcomes them, even though his victory is now "invisible," that is, "an object of faith rather than of verifiable experience. Only when the ultimate reality is presented to faith with the resurrection, will the whole transcendent datum of Jesus' victory over Sin fit into it."[1048]

As the church seeks to traverse *new* thresholds, it must avoid two temptations. On the one hand, the church must "reject ideological purism." This means that the church must not look for the "faithful copy of Jesus' own faith" because Jesus' faith was fleshed out in particular ideologies which were strictly relevant for his time.[1049] On the other hand, the community of faith must not seek to "avoid Death by quantitative increases." The result of following this path is that "the very mechanism of the real world threatens its [the church's] life and Sin enters it."[1050]   The church, as the community of "faith," must live the "daring" existence in the world of "evolutionary" struggle together with the rest of "the most daring," lest, Segundo warns, we "deny the gospel."[1051]

> Like Jesus, you see, his community must die and rise day after day. The death is visible, the resurrection is not. There is a wager involved, which only faith can make. Only thus will Jesus continue to be a factor of flexibility for *a humanity that holds in its hands the future evolution of the world.* Only thus will the latter get as close as possible to that Omega point that is its horizon.[1052]

Living in "faith," therefore, is not done in hopelessness. It trusts that through Jesus there will indeed be a "recapitulation" (*anakephalaiosis*; Eph. 1:3-14) that gives "meaning" to the "negentropy that has been slowly and painfully elaborated by God and the human beings who are God's collaborators (*synergoi*)."[1053]   In this way, Segundo is consistent with his own summary of the gospel: "No love is lost on this world."[1054]   Segundo regards this as the "good news" for people who are suffering from the "anxiety" of proffering "their love, but in the end it seems to be in vain."[1055]   In Segundo's estimation, people most need to hear the exhortation that their "labors are not in vain." The exhortation has Pauline support.[1056]   But *is there adequate gospel in Segundo's theology to support the exhortation?*

II. The Problem of Segundo's Presuppositions:
Inherent Difficulties in Segundo's Reading of Paul

Segundo appeals to Paul as an early Christian proponent of the "evolutionary" gospel. In this section, we will examine Segundo's claim together with a critical appraisal based on Paul's theology.

Segundo's Portrayal of Paul's Gospel

In Segundo's estimation, Paul's "antithetical parallel" of Christ and Adam establishes the basis for "a complex eschatology crying out for evolutionary categories, which of course were not available at that time."[1057]   Segundo claims that there are three "evolutionary" insights already in rudimentary form in Paul's theology.   First, Segundo claims that Paul understood the "*creation*" to be "*incomplete*" and crying out to human beings to exercise their freedom and provide completeness. "Indeed Paul goes so far as to talk about a universe subjected to uselessness and corruption unless *human beings are capable of redeeming it with their creativity.*"[1058]   According to Segundo, Paul presupposed that the human self was already justified. "Paul felt it essential to displace the attention and the infantile fear of the human being focused on its own salvation, the latter being conceived as a successful passing of a test whose stipulations had been fixed in the Law by God."[1059]   "Faith" is a characteristic of "the mature, adult, human being" who does not rely on any "calculations based on the fulfillment of the Law (i.e., works)."[1060]   According to Segundo, Paul perceives that people have difficulty moving away from the infantile fear of the Law. "The problem was that one had to move beyond the conception of freedom as a *danger*. And so Paul . . . ignored the option of our 'inner humanity,' simply assuming that it was good."[1061]   In other words, Segundo believes that Paul is principally interested in encouraging human beings to exercise their God-given creativity rather than succumb to the mechanisms that would reduce them to something less than human, "between the good of being free and a person and the evil of not being that but a mere thing."[1062]

Second, Segundo contends that Paul sought to resolve the conflict between a sense of "optimism" and a sense of "pessimism." "Optimism seemed to be implied in the conception of our 'inner humanity' being always oriented by the Spirit toward love and goodness."[1063]   But there is also the "pessimism about inscribing in reality the projects of that seemingly well-intentioned inner humanity."[1064]

> On the one hand, *everything* is new. If Jesus has any meaning and significance, it is that there is nothing to fear (obviously from the enemies: the Law, Sin, and Death). . . . But all that runs counter to our concrete experience. There we would be inclined to say that *nothing* has changed.[1065]

Segundo argues that Paul's solution in Romans 6 is to move from "a *fact* to the urging [*exhortación*] of that fact on us as a *duty*."[1066] The *fact* is implied in the "antithetical parallel" between Christ and Adam and the victory of Christ over Sin (Romans 5). This allows for the *duty* of human creativity. However, the evidence of "concrete experience" (Romans 7) tends to point to an alternative fact: that Death "has the last word."[1067] This leads to Paul's eschatological solution in Romans 8.

> Twice the words alluding to that [eschatological] perspective (*apocalypse* and *glory*) are linked up with one alluding to history (creative *adoption* and *freedom*), as if to tell us we should not expect to see what is still an object of hope. It is an object of the hope that is incorporated into our activity as a fundamental, transcendent datum of that activity.[1068]

Third, Paul understands "faith" to be an "wager" that "Death is defeated."[1069] The definitive validation of that wager must wait for the eschatological results: "*in the end* we shall see who was right in giving this or that axiological direction to his or her life and activity."[1070] Paul's wager is placed in "the universal resurrection" with the anticipation for "the outcome of a victory of Grace over Sin" and "the manifestation of the freedom proper to the children of God the creator."[1071]

> Only a resurrection that liberates us from Sin's condemnation to meaninglessness can justify the risk entailed in freedom. And justify it to the point where, whatever the real-life discharge of that freedom may have been, the human being can say "at the end": it was worthwhile [*valía la pena*].[1072]

For Paul, this wager is not made in a vacuum. It is "drawn from the experiences of the risen Jesus and set against the backdrop of the experience of the divided human being."[1073] As sure and certain as Paul was about the validity of this wager, the results must still wait for an eschatological confirmation.

> It is thus that human freedom meets up with the *definitive* on the road of meaning. That meeting is "outside" history, in the sense that, so long as history lasts, the "Flesh" will always subject that freedom to Sin, hence failure on the plane of meaningfulness. But the meeting is "inside" history because what is called to be definitive, once tested and examined closely, is what was done by the human being in the face of history and its complexities, and to give meaning and value to the latter.[1074]

In the language of Segundo's evolutionary categories, the gospel of Paul is summarized as follows:

> The significance of Jesus of Nazareth for every human being will appear only when Death is defeated, only when negentropy (i.e., growing consciousness) can peek over the barrier now placed in its way by time (subjected to entropy) and be conscious not only of the fragile, present moment but of the total and definitive meaning constructed in history.[1075]

A Critical Appraisal of Segundo's Reading of Paul

Segundo's "evolutionary" reading of Paul's theology is creative and manages to portray many of the edifying themes in Paul's gospel. However, there are at least three critical points in Segundo's reading of Paul that from an exegetical standpoint ultimately distort the message of Paul's theology.

First, Segundo has a unique and exegetically unsubstantiated reading of the Pauline understanding of Sin. Romans 1:18-30 is ultimately read through the lens of Romans 7:14-25. This is apparent when Segundo locates the problem of Sin strictly within the human personality. Sin is *the distance between "spontaneous intention" and "concrete performance."* "In effect, there would be no enslavement if the human being were master of his actions, no matter how bad they were."[1076]

Paul, however, locates that the root problem of sin in an alienated relationship between the human being and God. Paul opens his argument on the problem of sin by pointing to *the distance between*

God and his creatures: "For the wrath of God (*orge theou*) is revealed from heaven against all ungodliness (*asebeia*) and wickedness (*adikia*) of people who by their wickedness suppress the truth" (Romans 1:18). The exegetical consensus tends to support this latter reading of Paul. Käsemann states: "The whole world even in its secularity belongs to the Creator. This is its *aletheia* (truth). . . . The reality of the world and the basic sin of mankind consist in *not recognizing God* in his reality that opens itself to us."[1077] C. K. Barrett also confirms this viewpoint: "As God's creature, man was bound to render glory and thanksgiving to his Creator. . . . This men failed to do; instead they *rebelled against God*, and their fault lay not in lack of knowledge but in their rebellion."[1078] Similarly, Bornkamm emphasizes that Paul begins the epistle to the Romans with "the subject of *mankind's and the world's lost state in the sight of God*," and that "all whom God summons to life. . . are 'without excuse' and objects of his wrath."[1079] Furthermore, Käsemann claims that the radical sins of "ungodliness" (*asebeia*) and "wickedness" (*adikia*) "are comprised, as a kind of hendiadys, in *adikia*, which . . . obviously stands opposed to the righteousness of God and for this reason can be associated with *asebeia*."[1080] The root of Sin, therefore, is not the cravings for "injustice" *between human beings* (though that is clearly a manifestation). The primary "injustice" in Romans 1:18 is the rebellion against God the Creator, meriting God's wrath.

Segundo acknowledges that Paul's thrice-repeated phrase, "handed them over" (*paredoken autous*; Romans 1:24, 26, 28), suggests "a fairly clear process: disavowal of God in favor of idolatry, divine punishment leaving the human being abandoned to itself, and, finally, the aberrant and dehumanized conduct of the human being in its interpersonal relations."[1081] However, he regards this scheme of "idolatry/punishment/dehumanization" as only an "infantile" first reading of Romans 1:18-32 and one to be ultimately rejected.[1082] Segundo chooses to bypass this interpretation in favor of a "second reading" of the text based on the four-fold scheme of "the desire for injustice/deceitful justificatory reasons/creation of an infrahuman idol which justifies injustice/the fall into infrahuman mutual relations."[1083] This allows him to present the image of Sin as an internal struggle within the human personality. Segundo acknowledges that this interpretation is influenced by his reading of Romans 7:14-25 and other texts (Romans 6:18; 1 Cor. 3:1-2; 2 Cor. 11:16-21).[1084] However,

Romans 7:14-25 comes later in the development of Paul's epistle, in what Segundo himself claims is a depiction of the "Christian *now*."[1085] The critical issue here is whether there is a *reason* for the order in which Paul presents his argument in Romans. Is there a difference in Paul's theology between *human beings* standing under the "wrath of God" and in need of justification (Romans 1:18-3:20) and *Christians* standing in the light of "justification" and favorable standing with God looking back over their sinful past (Romans 7:14-25)?[1086] Segundo believes that there is no difference because he does not believe any individual is without justification and "faith." But for that argument, Segundo does not appeal to Paul but to his theological presuppositions on the meaning of "grace."

Segundo's understanding of "grace" also weakens the Pauline concept of the "wrath of God." According to Segundo, God's wrath is not a mortifying event, but an event that "enlightens the human being."[1087] There is, therefore, no connotation of hostility per se. The covenant with God "cannot be vitiated by man's infidelity."[1088] The judgment of God, therefore, cannot place human beings at an irreconcilable disadvantage vis-à-vis their salvation.

> To say that there is no relation between the work of the human being and the judgment of God is to profoundly dehumanize human existence. . . . That view would also seem to be very cold-blooded and devastating for the two million years of humanity that preceded the manifestation of the "Divine Person." They would appear to be *out of favor* with a God who, according to Paul, does not show favoritism to anyone.[1089]

What Segundo does not entertain, however, is the possibility that the human being may still have his or her work taken into consideration before the judgment of God and still be judged "out of favor." Segundo might have been closer to Paul had he recognized the dynamic of the "wrath of God" at work in the massive negativity of the "evolutionary" process.

Our conclusion here is that Segundo is reading his own theological presupposition on the nature of "grace" back into Paul when he takes the uniquely Christian struggle between Spirit and Flesh (Romans 7:14-25), and attributes that to all humanity (Romans 1:18-3:20). Paul does not concede a "universal grace" in his notion of the sinful human being in Romans. Paul only concedes a "universal wrath."

Second, Segundo has a unique and exegetically unsubstantiated reading of the Pauline understanding of "faith," particularly the "faith" of Abraham. Segundo has two premises in his reading of the "faith" of Abraham. First, according to Segundo, Abraham is part of the initial stage of "universality" in the overall working of God's plan. It is apparent, however, that this is part of a larger Hegelian reading of Romans. The stage of "universality" (thesis) is followed by second stage of the Jewish "religious particularity of the Law" (antithesis). These culminate in the final "Christian" stage (synthesis).[1090] Second, Segundo is quite emphatic that Abraham believed "*in God*" and more specifically, in the vague "*minimum content*" of the victory of life over death that God makes possible and promises.[1091]

Clearly, the emphasis on the promise of God to Abraham is central.[1092] Paul's usage of this theme in Romans 4 (after 3:21-31), however, suggests that Abraham is "the prototype of *Christian* faith," not "faith" as a universal category.[1093] Galatians 3:16 is even more specific in this regard, where the "seed" of Abraham is understood to be messianic.[1094]

Furthermore, the "faith" of Abraham was "brought about by the creator by means of his mighty Word."[1095] "Faith only lives from hearing. . . Hearing has a primacy which cannot be replaced by anything else."[1096] This conforms to what Paul says later in Romans 10:14-17: "Faith then comes from what is heard, and what is heard comes by the preaching of Christ." Käsemann claims that "faith is clearly described as acceptance of the kerygma, and to that extent--only to that extent!--it is characterized as obedience."[1097] Barrett affirms that people "call on the Lord because they believe; they believe because they hear; they hear because others preach; these preach because they are sent--by the Lord, with whom the whole process begins, as it ends with him."[1098] This does not suggest, especially in its context (preaching to the unbelieving of Paul's "kinsmen by race," Rom. 9:3), a mere "conscientization" of an already existing process in the lives of people, but the creation of something new that did not exist prior to the event of the Word.

Segundo's conclusion, therefore, that the "faith" of Abraham is "universal" is without substantiation in the theology of Paul. Segundo's reading seeks to render "justifying faith" as something accessible to everyone:

> We could say, without too much risk [!], that all those whose actions imply in their work that there exists in the universe *a power* which is

able to give life to the dead and call into being what does not exist, share the faith of Abraham. [This means that] a child of Abraham, a "believer," is *every atheist, pagan, Jew or Christian*, who renounces having a contractual relationship with *the Absolute*, and *who believes in the promise inscribed in the same human values offered by existence*, fighting for them as if death could not render his fight in vain.[1099]

It is readily apparent that the *reason* Segundo understands Abrahamic "faith" this way is because he has read his own "theology of grace" (especially the concept of "anonymous Christians") back into the Pauline text. This may explain the liberties that Segundo takes in developing his concept of "faith;" but it does not represent Paul's theology.

Third, Segundo has a unique and exegetically unsubstantiated reading of the Pauline understanding of Christ's "universal victory." For all the emphasis that Segundo places on the "universal victory" of Christ in antithetical parallel to the Sin of Adam, it is curious that the victory is so remarkably paltry compared to Paul's description of that victory. Christ's victory is a "qualitative disproportion" over the Sin of Adam.[1100] But the victory is understood to mean that all human beings are gifted with a "transcendent datum": that "loving is worthwhile."[1101] Paul and the biblical witnesses are quite clear that human beings do not need a victorious Christ for that datum. It is readily available in the Law.[1102]

The victory of Christ over Adam in Romans 5 is much more dynamic and universal in Paul's presentation. Transgression (*paraptoma*) is overcome by grace (*charisma*); death (*thanatos*) is overcome by life (*zoe*); condemnation (*krima/katakrima*) is overcome by acquittal (*dikaioma*); disobedience (*parakoe*) is overcome by being under the word of obedience (*ypakoe*); and the rule of death (*o thanatos ebasileusen*) is overcome by those who reign in Christ (*outos e charis basileuse*). In effect, there is nothing in the adamic subjection of human beings to the universal "wrath of God" that cannot be overcome through Christ's victory to those who believe in Him. The Adam-Christ parallel is regarded by Barrett as the progenitors of two different races.[1103] Nygren regards the parallel as "two aeons."[1104] Käsemann refers to the parallel as "the apocalyptic antithesis of primal time and end-time" and he rejects the Barthian formulation that Christ has a "material priority" to Adam.[1105]

The antithetical parallel between Christ and Adam in Romans

5:12-21 follows the Pauline understanding of *the faith of the Christian* who is now "standing in the peace of God" and no longer under God's wrath (Romans 5:1-11).[1106] Segundo, of course, does not bifurcate the reading of Romans 5. He still maintains the connection of "faith" to the universal dynamics of Christ's victory. But Segundo reads Romans 5:12-21 in the light of his own concept of a universal *"anthropological" faith*. Segundo does not entertain the concept of a specific "Christian" faith until Romans 6. Segundo rejects any "divine foreknowledge" of those who "will and will not accept the redemption and salvation *offered to all*."[1107] He posits instead that *Paul predicts a universal salvation by claiming that all people will sometime in their lives make use of the transcendent datum, "loving is worthwhile."* "If the freedom of the human being is capable of carrying out what it chooses and, thanks be to God, chooses the good, one single performance of the good means more than all the 'alien' stuff that has accumulated in that human life."[1108] We must acknowledge that Segundo has *some* exegetical support for this position: "something has been accomplished by Christ which does not just concern believers but is as universal in its effects as was the sin of Adam. The existence of Jesus Christ does not only determine the existence of believers: it is also the innermost secret of the life of every man."[1109] Even here we would note that Segundo's exegetical support is much more explicitly christological than Segundo himself. However, we must conclude that Segundo's support here is forced. It does not critically engage the understanding of Paul in Romans 5, but posits instead a "speculation" which Paul did not do.

> If . . . Paul's doctrine of justification is seen predominantly from the standpoint of individualistic anthropology, and the cosmic dimensions of 1:18-3:20 is viewed only as a dark foil and not as an antithetical correlate, the logical connection with the context [of Romans 5:12-21] will have to be disputed. . . . The latter designation is correct only to the degree that the apostle does not know any existence outside the reality of the history of salvation or judgment between the first Adam and the last. . . . All the same Paul does not lose himself in historical speculation.[1110]

Segundo's real substantiation for "universalism" is based in his own presuppositions and commitment to a universal "theology of grace" apart from "faith-in-Christ," apart from means (the event of the Word), and quite apart from the theological presentation of Paul in Romans.

Conclusion

We would conclude that Segundo reads into Paul his own understanding of a universal "theology of grace." Maintaining a sense of continuity with Paul is only possible if Paul is amended to say what Segundo wants him to say. Segundo is cognizant of the difficulties that this presents. He suggests that Paul poses *problems* in terms that are generally anthropological; but the *solutions* are given "in terms of the Christian *now*."[1111] Segundo is also aware that he is out of the mainstream of exegesis which accents the more specifically christological theme in Paul (i.e., faith "in Christ").[1112] If these exegetes are correct, then Segundo admits that his "whole exegesis of these chapters [of Romans] is mistaken."[1113] Segundo suggests that Paul is *also* quite christological in his answer about the basis for salvation. Nevertheless, Segundo speculates, "the internal logic of Paul's thought" would have to lead Paul to conform to a "more complex answer,"[1114] apparently in keeping with Segundo's own reading of Paul.

Segundo has an overall desire for the Latin American church to "'adapt' the directives of Vatican II to the reality of the continent."[1115] Specifically, this means taking an active role vis-à-vis the people who have been "trampled upon, humiliated, and deformed by centuries of oppression and suffering."[1116] The reason that Segundo appeals to Paul grows out of this basic pastoral concern. According to Segundo, Paul had a timeless sensitivity to the fact that "many . . . reject faith or the Christian community for good reasons, for mistaken but guiltless reasons, or simply for lack of information."[1117] But in the process of addressing that pastoral concern, Segundo has reduced the Pauline concept of "faith" to an "easier" requirement. Ultimately, Segundo's universal concept of "faith" is not all that radically different from the "false universalism" and ecclesiastical abuses he perceives in the formula, *extra ecclesiam non salus*.[1118] However, our key point here is that Segundo is not consistent with Paul's theology. Paul's gospel does not weaken the concept of the "wrath of God" in which all human beings find themselves; nor does Paul's gospel take for granted the promising remedy of "justification by faith in Christ."

III.   The   Problem   of   Segundo's   Presuppositions: Inherent Problems for Segundo's Thesis

As we have indicated, Segundo's theological presuppositions about "grace" render his position without exegetical support in his reading of Paul's epistle to the Romans.   Those same presuppositions also undermine the central thesis with regard to the relationship between "faith" and "faith's works."

We have noted in our analysis of Segundo's theology that the following thesis is supported: *"faith" and "faith's works" need to be distinguished, but they cannot be separated*.   On the basis of the opening chapters, we have noted three foci were this thesis is consistently argued: (1) ecclesiology (the distinction, but inseparability of "faith" and "love"); (2)   methodology (the distinction, but inseparability of "faith" and "ideologies"); and (3)   the biblical perspective (the distinction, but inseparability of "faith" and the "work of faith").

In the remainder of this chapter, we will reexamine these three foci in the light of Segundo's theological presuppositions.   We will particularly note that Segundo's theology of "grace" hampers rather than supports this thesis we have found to be central to his theology.

Ecclesiology: The Distinction, but Inseparability of "Faith" and "Love"

In Segundo's early theology, the relationship between "faith" and "love" was a central issue in the development of an ecclesiology for the Latin American context.   The issue grew out of a real-life struggle between two opposed groups on the nature of the church's mission. One group accented "faith-and-sacraments" to be the mission of the church.   The other group maintained that "love" was central to the church's mission.[1119]   Segundo resolved the issue by appealing to the following argument: the church's "essence" corresponds to "faith-and-sacraments," while the church's "necessity" or "function" corresponds to "love."[1120]   Furthermore, the "essence" supports the "function." "Love would die" without those "essential" expressions present in proclamation and sacraments.[1121]   Hence, Segundo maintains a *formal distinction*, and yet an inseparability of "faith" and "love."

However, the distinction-without-separability is weakened if we press the matter further. Segundo understands "redemption" as a universal constant: "the redemptive work of Christ, carried out within history, goes beyond the limits of time and dominates the whole unfolding development of the universe--both its past and its future."[1122] This is consistent with Segundo's theology of "grace." Since everyone is divinely graced by this redemption, *all that remains* is the necessity to love.

This leads us into a closer examination of Segundo's understanding of the "essential" and "necessary" dimensions of the church's mission. In Segundo's theology, the "essential" contribution of the "faith-and-sacraments" is not "salvation," but "knowledge" (revelation). "The Christian is he *who already knows*. This, undoubtedly, is what distinguishes and defines him."[1123] "Salvation" is achieved *through "love."* "Through Christ, God gave everyone the possibility of loving others, and he joined all people and every individual in solidarity; he thus put *love* in everyone's hands as *the divine instrument of salvation.*"[1124]

Segundo then examines two biblical texts on the meaning of salvation. One text tends to support the understanding that salvation comes through "faith-and-sacraments" (Mark 16:15-16). The other text supports the understanding that salvation is the result of "love" (Matthew 25:31-46). Segundo's solution is *to choose the latter text as more "universal."* The choice is understandable if "faith" is understood as a universal constant given by "grace." It is true to say, therefore, that there is no separation between "faith" and "love" in Segundo's theology. But it is also questionable *whether there is a real distinction.* "Faith-and-sacraments" are *collapsed* into the larger divine plan of "salvation" through acts of "love."[1125]

Furthermore, Segundo's interpretation of Matthew 25:31-46 is highly questionable. First, Segundo understands the Matthean text to be claiming that "the Christian . . . will not ask the Lord: When did I see you?"[1126] The text itself, however, is quite specific that the "sheep," as well as the "goats," *did ask* that very question. As far as the "sheep" are concerned, their focus is on the *neighbor* for the neighbor's own sake because they are supported by their *faith* in Christ the King who has taken care of them and set them free for their mission. Therefore, they ask, "When did we see *you*, Lord?" The Matthean text claims, therefore, that "faith and love" work conjointly in the life of the Christian.[1127] But faith or trust is not to be presumed. The "goats" also ask, "When did we see you?" They, however, are *without* such faith and trust even as they were remiss in their duty of love toward their neighbors.

This leads to a consideration of a second criticism of Segundo's interpretation of Matthew 25. In an effort to determine the meaning of salvation, Segundo sets the Matthean text in an "either-or" juxtaposition with a text that support "faith-and-sacraments." Segundo states that "nothing can take the place of *love* before the judgment seat of God."[1128] Berryman rightly interprets the theological implication of this argument: "people are saved by what the *do* for others, independently of how explicitly 'religious' their intentions."[1129] In other words, despite his efforts to tread lightly around Pelagianism, Segundo's interpretation of the final judgment is unable to avoid falling over the precipice.

Segundo's criticisms of contemporary Catholic and Protestant theology may have neglected the helpful signals within those theologies to this flaw within Segundo's own theology. Moltmann alludes to the danger of Pelagianism in Segundo's theology when he states: "To be sure, the individual event of liberation or salvation does not gain in this way a 'causal character' for the Kingdom of God [that is, that human beings save themselves]--even Pelagius never would have said that."[1130] Moltmann's warning is arrogant and cryptic, as is his concession that European political theology lacks an adequate emphasis on "human causality." But that does not negate Moltmann's vital concern.

Ratzinger may also be echoing that warning when he claims that "liberation theology . . . constitutes a fundamental threat to the faith of the Church."[1131] This might also explain the careful wording in the Congregation's "Instruction" that emphasizes "the *distinction* between the history of salvation and profane history."[1132] There is good reason for Segundo to ignore the document's wording and accuse the Congregation for *separating* these realms.[1133] Furthermore, there is never a specific charge of heresy. Finally, the case against Segundo is considerably weakened by Segundo's adequate demonstration of support for his theology in the conciliar documents of Vatican II. Nevertheless, Segundo may have missed the potentially deeper significance in the concern being raised by Ratzinger and the Congregation.

Finally, it is possible to reconsider the Chilean bishops' statement: "we opt for the risen Christ."[1134] Such an affirmation might be appreciated as a truly gospel-centered "value" and a corrective to any kind of works-righteousness. Segundo is correct in pointing out that the denial of brothers and sisters in their pain and suffering is faithless and a message contradictory to the gospel. But the harshness of Segundo's polemic may have overstated his case.

Ultimately in Segundo's theology, "faith" is relegated to the role of explicating or revealing a process that is already in motion for all people. The ministry of the Word can only give "full consciousness to what before was only spontaneous."[1135] This understanding of the ministry of the Word is strictly exhortative. However, exhortation results in legalism if the "faith" being encouraged is not "faith" *in the gospel*. Luther indicates that the New Testament never took "faith" for granted: exhortation follows gospel.[1136] There is a very essential "human causality" in bringing the benefits of Christ (*beneficia Christi*) to bear on the "faith-in-crisis."[1137] Without the saving proclamation that sets people in right-relationship with God, faith continues to be in crisis. The exhortation to love, however, cannot adequately resolve that crisis.

(2) Methodology: The Distinction, but Inseparability of "Faith" and "Ideologies"

Segundo's methodological framework makes a distinction between "faith" as a "wager" (*apuesta*) or "attitude" (*actitud*) or even absolute "value" (*valor*), and "ideologies" as means of "efficacy" (*eficacia*).[1138] While "faith" is distinguished from "ideologies," there is no separation. "Faith" will necessarily find expression in some "ideology."

Inherent difficulties begin to arise, however, when Segundo seeks to distinguish between "anthropological" faith and "religious" faith.[1139] Of these two categories, Segundo considers "anthropological" faith to be *primary*. "Anthropological" faith is primary because it already contains a "transcendent datum" that makes it worthwhile. "Religious" faith only adds to the "transcendent data" and fosters a "tradition" of referential witnesses. But both of these elements are already technically already present in "anthropological" faith.[1140] Thus, "faith" develops or evolves along a number of "stages," but it is still the same "faith." Any real distinction between "anthropological" faith and "religious" faith *dissolves* into the continuity of their relationship.   "Faith" has existed all along, only in a "primordial way."[1141]

We may underscore the inherent difficulties this presents by observing that Segundo has two ways of talking about the essential "value" in faith. On some occasions, Segundo understands the claim of "faith" to be that "*life* is worthwhile" (*la vida vale la pena*).[1142] On other occasions, Segundo understands the claim of "faith" to be that "*love* is worthwhile" (*el amor vale la pena*).[1143] Segundo apparently regards these claims as synonymous and shared by all human beings.

If that is the case, however, it is not demonstrated adequately in the anthropological example he consistently chooses to talk about the relationship between "faith" and "ideologies," namely, Camus' tragic figure of Caligula.[1144] We might concede that Caligula values "*life*" as worthwhile (at least initially) in his vain pursuit of "happiness." He did not, however, value "*love*" as worthwhile. It is possible, of course, that Segundo is citing this example to make the case that "lovelessness" leads to an empty life.   That point may well have merit, even theological merit. One might, therefore, consider that Albert Camus regards "morality" as the best response to a life that is otherwise "absurd."[1145]   But even Camus acknowledges that some people do not consider life worthwhile, let alone love worthwhile.[1146] The only basis for Segundo to maintain otherwise is inherent to his theology of "grace." That theological presupposition leads to the claim that Camus (and others like Karl Marx and Milan Machoveč) are people with "faith," even though they themselves would not cherish that description.[1147]   Nevertheless, Camus, Marx, and Machovec are necessarily viewed as anthropological "believers" because the (prejudicial?) "faith" and insight of Christians claims that for them on the basis of their participation in the divine plan of "love." The result, however, is to make the concept of "faith" meaningless and, ironically, to dehumanize persons by not respecting them for their stance.

(3) The Biblical Perspective: The Distinction, but Inseparability of "Faith" and "Ideologies"

Segundo claims that there is also a distinction-without-separation between "faith" and "ideologies" in the biblical perspective.   The framework for this biblical perspective is provided in the concept of the "hermeneutic circle."[1148]   "Faith" allows one to leave behind a dead or dying "ideology" and to replace it with a new ideology and a "new hermeneutic." In Segundo's concept of biblical revelation, therefore, "faith" is the "permanent and unique" element in the Scriptures, and "ideologies" are the "changing" elements.[1149] Different "ideologies" could be used in different times and circumstances (e.g., slaying of enemies in the Old Testament or turning the other cheek in the New Testament), but the "faith" has remained constant.[1150] The tradition of "faith" is therefore an ongoing "liberative process" of learning from past ideologies, but fashioning new ones more relevant for the time.[1151] Jesus also becomes part of that learning process and his gift of the Spirit assures that the process will continue in the lives of people.[1152]

Segundo's biblical perspective is flawed on two points, both of which find their basis in Segundo's theological presuppositions. First, Segundo says that "faith" itself does not have any distinctive "truth content." It is simply "freedom for ideologies." "If someone were to ask me what I have derived from my faith encounter as an absolute truth that can validly give orientation to my concrete life, then my honest response should be: *nothing*."[1153] "Faith," therefore, is not simply expressed in ideologies. It ultimately is *insignificant*. The only truly significant "value" of human existence is ideologies; and this is contrary to Segundo's distinction between "faith" and "ideologies."

Second, precisely *because* "faith" expresses itself in ideologies, Jesus is strictly a figure of the past. Christianity can "abandon its teacher to launch out into the provisional and relative depths of history."[1154] "Faith," therefore, trusts in a *process* that involves *all* humanity. The onus of *Christian* faith, therefore, is to join the "heroic minorities" in shaping new ideologies in the process. The means of grace are already presupposed for living in that process. The result, however, is that the Judeo-Christian tradition (with its "faith" and "ideologies") becomes diluted in the larger panorama of world history (with its "faith" and "ideologies").[1155] The biblical perspective sheds light on a preestablished process that exists for all human beings. Technically, however, one does not need that perspective and can simply observe the process in world history. Therefore, there is nothing all that "*new*" about the "good news" of Jesus Christ, and nothing all that ultimately "*good*," given that the onus of salvation lies squarely on the shoulders of the "heroic minorities." One must question, therefore, whether their "anxiety" is going to be really lessened or increased to unbearable proportions.[1156]

Conclusion

We have argued throughout these chapters that the central thesis on the proper relationship between "faith" and "faith's works" is present in Segundo's theology. However, Segundo's own theological presuppositions in his understanding of "grace" proves to be an insufficient foundation for that central thesis. With his foundational presuppositions, his distinction between "faith" and "faith's work" cannot be maintained, and the inseparability is maintained only at the expense of collapsing one "faith" into "faith's works".

We have also demonstrated that Segundo's theological presuppositions lead him into other significant problems. His ecclesiological understanding of salvation results in Pelagianism. His methodological understanding of "faith" ends up dehumanizing those who do not understand themselves as having any kind of "faith." His biblical understandings deny any real significance to the Judeo-Christian gospel.

A more adequate foundation for the central thesis may be found in the Paul-Luther trajectory. This latter perspective maintains that human beings are universally subjected to the wrath of God as a consequence of their sin. Nevertheless, God's grace in Jesus Christ creates faith in the hearts of human beings *through the ministry of the Word*. This liberates believers, first of all, to *grasp* the promise of liberation and redemption and, secondly, to *act freely* for the liberation and redemption of the world as God's causal agents, in the name of their promising Lord, Jesus Christ.

Conclusion

Toward Dialogue on the Relationship Between "Faith" and "Faith's Works"

Segundo presents an essentially evangelical point of view on the relationship between "faith" and "faith's works." Segundo seeks to distinguish between "faith" and "ideologies" (or "faith" and "love") without separating the categories. We have noted that this central thesis is characteristic of the two major themes in Segundo's theology-- ecclesiology and methodology. Furthermore, this central thesis is present in Segundo's understanding of the biblical tradition, and especially in Paul.

Segundo presents a crucial challenge to contemporary Catholic and Protestant theology on the relationship between "faith" and "faith's works." He argues that some contemporary theologians (specifically, the Chilean bishops, European political theologians, and Cardinal Ratzinger) make a distinction between "faith" and "faith's works" that results in a separation. Segundo affirms the need for distinction, but criticizes the separation that is often made between "faith" and "faith's works."

Segundo's attempt to bring this same challenge to Luther fails. Segundo's criticisms against contemporary theologies is credibly supported by his careful and painstaking analyses of primary sources. In his analysis of Luther, however, Segundo only consults secondary sources. Luther is viewed primarily through the lens of European political theology or through the theology of Karl Barth. It is not unreasonable to suspect, therefore, that Luther will appear to reflect whatever weaknesses are present in those contemporary theologies. We have demonstrated on the basis of Luther's primary sources that Segundo's presentation is a caricature.

We also find that the presuppositions in Luther's theology are markedly different than Segundo's, even though both Luther and Segundo share an evangelical concern: to bring the "good news" to bear on human beings who are experiencing a "faith-in-crisis." Segundo's theological presuppositions are traceable to recent trends in Catholic theology about the meaning of "grace." These presuppositions lead to unique but exegetically unsubstantiated interpretations of Paul's theology, particularly the Pauline concepts of "sin," "faith," and the Christ-Adam parallel in Romans 5.

Furthermore, Segundo's theological presuppositions present inherent difficulties for Segundo's theology as a whole. In Segundo's ecclesiology, there is a formal distinction between "faith" and "love" on the church's role vis-à-vis salvation. Practically speaking, however, there is no real distinction. "Faith" is collapsed into the larger divine plan of "salvation" through "love." Theologically, this results in "works-righteousness." In Segundo's methodology, there is no real distinction between "anthropological" faith and "religious" faith as the latter is collapsed into the former. Furthermore, "faith" as a universal category becomes meaningless or, worse, dehumanizing. In Segundo's biblical hermeneutic, "faith" carries no discernible value outside of being a freedom to continue in the preexisting process of creating "ideologies." As a whole, therefore, any distinction between "faith" and "faith's works" is confused, and separation is avoided only at the expense of minimizing one of the elements ("faith") in favor of the other ("faith's works").

Segundo shows no sign of open dialogue with any understandings of "grace" outside of his own Catholic tradition. While he criticizes ecclesiastical institutions, he never carries that criticism to the theological perspectives on "grace" presented in Vatican II (Malevez, Rahner, Teilhard). No one, including Segundo, diminishes the value of recent trends in Catholic theology to ecumenical dialogue with Protestantism in general, and Lutheranism in particular.[1157] There is greater mutual understanding between these traditions on issues that have long divided them and a recognition that the divergences are not as massive as they once were. However, the fundamental issue of "justification by faith" remains unresolved, despite Rahner's magnanimous overtures and the fine work of Lutheran-Catholic dialogue.[1158]   There are definite differences between Segundo and Luther on the understanding of "justification by faith." Segundo understands "justification by faith" to be a "transcendent datum" that "loving is worthwhile." Furthermore, that datum is a universal gift to human beings that carries an implicit, but not explicit, christology and a pressing urge to find fulfillment in "ideologies." Luther understands "justification by faith" to be a trusting grasp of Jesus Christ as one's Lord. "Faith" comes by the grace present in the ministry of the Word, and such faith is alone saving. However, works necessarily follow faith.

The differences between these two perspectives follows along the lines of each tradition. Catholic theology understands personhood in terms of "love." Lutheran theology understands personhood in terms of "faith."[1159]   Segundo's theology makes some conscious overtures in the direction of the validity of the Lutheran position, but his concept of "faith" lacks adequate "ideological suspicion" of the Catholic tradition.

While Segundo's critique of Luther is weak, he may have a more powerful case against some contemporary Lutheran theologies on the relationship between "faith" and "faith's works." Lutheranism has developed an unmistakable reputation of quietism.[1160]   Lutherans need to clarify their understanding of "justification by faith" in light of the massive problem of injustice in the world today. There have been some recent discussions among Lutherans on this subject. One might consider the statements, presentations, and responses that several Lutheran theologians shared at the conference on "Justification and Justice" held in Mexico City in December, 1985. However, the conference was not without considerable disagreement on the issue of "faith" and "faith's works." One observer of that conference remarks:

> Dr. [Gerhard] Forde, often designated *the* Lutheran theologian of justification by faith, is insistent that justification by faith cannot be related to justice in "any sort of positive or artificial synthesis." . . . From his critics' point of view, he emphasizes that point to the extent that his theological position *endangers an integrated understanding of the relationship between faith and works.*[1161]

There have also been some recent attempts to reinforce the connection between Luther and liberation theology. The Departmento Ecumenico de Investiogaciones (DEI) in San Jose has brought together

Protestant Latin American pastors and lay persons "to study their particular confessional heritages in light of the liberation struggle and liberation theology."[1162]   The Instituto Superior Evangelico de Estudios Teologicos (ISEDET) in Buenos Aires has also made efforts to examine "Luther's positions on some key social-ethical questions."[1163]   Elsa Tamez has recently published a text in which she asserts that "justification by faith must be oriented toward the affirmation of life--real life for real persons."[1164]   While all of these efforts are to be applauded, they ultimately fail to grasp the full depth of liberation inherent in Luther's understanding of forensic justification.[1165]

In spite of unresolved difficulties, all theologians should be able to perceive that one of the forms of "love" in today's world is socio-political justice, for which Christians and non-Christians may work side by side.[1166]   That calling needs to be made more explicit. We need to consider that it is not only our fellow human companions (which is cause enough) but also our brothers and sisters *in the faith* who are suffering from the socio-economic oppressiveness of our own nation. Perhaps then we being to recognize that there is a very serious "faith-in-crisis" present in our own backyard.   Indeed, the North American "faith-in-crisis" may be greater than the "faith-in-crisis" in Latin America.   Human causal agents of the kingdom of God have a great responsibility to address these challenges.   Segundo appropriately asserts that when we engage in the task of collaborating in the process of liberating human beings, we have an ecumenism that is far greater than Catholic-Protestant dialogue.   It is an ecumenism that "extends beyond the boundaries of Christianity."[1167]

Appendix

The Life and Works of Juan Luis Segundo, S.J. *(from 1925 to 1994)*

YEAR	EVENTS IN LIFE OF SEGUNDO	MAJOR HISTORICAL EVENTS
1925	Born in Montevideo on March 31	
1929		"Great Depression" Failure of the British oligarchy in Latin America
1930		Beginning of "Catholic Action" and Christian Democratic Party in Latin America Rise of the military class
1936		Chile forms Christian Democratic Party Maritain's Humanisme Integral (ET: 1968)
1937		Yves Congar's Divided Christendom (ET: 1939), and the attack against nouvelle théologie
1939		World War II begins

YEAR	EVENTS IN LIFE OF SEGUNDO	MAJOR HISTORICAL EVENTS
1941	Enters Society of Jesus; begins study of philosophy at seminary in San Miguel, Argentina	
1945		World War II ends
1948	Existencialismo, filosofía y poesía: Ensayo de sintesis	
1951	Studies at St. Albert in Europe	
1955	Ordained to priesthood	First General Conference of Latin American Bishops, Rio de Janeiro Teilhard de Chardin's Le Phénomene Humain (ET: 1955)
1956	Licentiate in theology, Eegenhoven Louvain, Belgium	
1959	Returns to reside in Montevideo	Castro seizes control of Cuba
1960		Church in Cuba opposes Castro's regime
1962	Función de la Iglesia en la realidad rioplatense and Etapas precristianas de la fe: Evolución de la idea de Dios en el Antiguo Testamento	Vatican II begins
1963	Doctorate in Letters, University of Paris Berdiaeff: Une réflexion chrétienne sur la personne	Kennedy assassinated
1964	La cristiandad, ¿una utopia? I. Los hechos; II. Los principios and Concepción cristiana del hombre	*Coup d'etat* in Brazil Civil Rights Act in U.S.
1965	Peter Faber Center founded in Montevideo	Vatican II ends Moltmann's Theologie der Hoffnung (ET: 1967)

YEAR	EVENTS IN LIFE OF SEGUNDO	MAJOR HISTORICAL EVENTS
1966	Begins publication of monthly Perspectivas de Diálogo	Death of Camilo Torres in Columbia *Coup d'etat* in Argentina
1967		Death of Che Guevera in Bolivia
1968	Esa comunidad llamada Iglesia (ET: 1973) and Gracia y condición humana (ET: 1973)	Second General Conference of Latin American Bishops (CELAM), Medellín "Priests for the Third World" discussion of Gaudium et Spes Martin Luther King, Jr., assassinated Rise of feminist theology
1969		*Coup d'etat* in Peru Lessened tension between episcopacy and government in Cuba
1970	De la sociedad a la teología and Nuestra idea de Dios (ET: 1973)	Allende elected president in Chile
1971	Los sacramentos hoy (ET: 1974) and Que es un cristiano	Gutiérrez's Teología de la liberación (ET: 1973) Opposition of Chilean episcopacy to Allende Vekemans and Bishop Trujillo's attack on liberation theology and publication of Tierra Nueva *Coup d'etat* in Bolivia

YEAR	EVENTS IN LIFE OF SEGUNDO	MAJOR HISTORICAL EVENTS
1972	Evolución y culpa (ET: 1974) and Acción pastoral latinoamericana: sus motivos ocultos (ET: 1978)	"Christians for Socialism" in Santiago, Chile Third General Conference of Latin American Bishops, Sucre, Bolivia Trujillo elected secretary-general of CELAM, collapses CELAM
1973	Masas y minorías en la dialéctica divina de la liberación	Pinochet *coup d'etat* in Chile (Allende assassinated)
1974	"Capitalism-Socialism: A Theological Crux" Lectures at Harvard Divinity School	*Coup d'etat* in Uruguay
1975	Liberación de la teología (ET: 1976) Uruguayan government suppresses publication of Perspectivas de Diálogo; Ecclesiastical superiors close Peter Faber Center	Right-wing government in Peru
1976		Right-wing government in Ecuador *Coup d'etat* in Argentina
1978	Lectures at University of Chicago Divinity School	
1979		Bishops gather in Puebla Pope John Paul II visits Mexico
1980		Assassination of Oscar Romero in El Salvador Sandanista government in Nicaragua

YEAR	EVENTS IN LIFE OF SEGUNDO	MAJOR HISTORICAL EVENTS
1982	El hombre de hoy ante Jesús de Nazarét, I. Fe e ideología (ET: 1984); II/1. Historia y actualidad: Sinópticos y Pablo (ET: 1985, 1986); II/2. Historia y actualidad: Las cristologías en la espiritualidad (ET: 1987, 1988)	
1983	Teología abierta: I. Iglesia-Gracia; II. Dios-Sacramentos-Culpa	John Paul II visits Central America Ratzinger letter attacking Gutiérrez's theology
1984	Teología abierta: III. Reflexiones críticas	Vatican Congregation for the Doctrine of Faith issues "Instruction on Certain Aspects of the 'Theology of Liberation'"
1985	Theology and the Church: A Response to Cardinal Ratzinger and a Warning to the Whole Church	Silencing of Leonardo Boff John Paul II visits Andean countries Return to civilian rule in Brazil, Argentina, Uruguay, Peru, Bolivia, Ecuador, Honduras, El Salvador
1989	El Dogma que libera (ET: 1992)	Assassination of Jesuit priests in El Salvador U.S. invasion of Panama
1990		Return to civilian rule in Nicaragua
1992		Clinton elected president in U.S.
1993	Signs of the Times	

Notes

Preface

1. Bertram's essay would later be published under the title, "Liberation by Faith: Segundo and Luther in Mutual Criticism," dialog 27:4 (Fall, 1988): 268-276.
2. El Dogma que libera: Fe, revelación y magisterio dogmático (Santander, Spain: Editorial Sal Terrae, 1989). ET: The Liberation of Dogma: Faith, Revelation, and Dogmatic Teaching Authority (Maryknoll, N.Y.: Orbis Books, 1992).
3. Signs of the Times: Theological Reflections, edited by Alfred T. Hennelly, S.J., translated by Robert R. Barr (Maryknoll, N.Y.: Orbis Books, 1993).
4. Sinópticos y Pablo, 557-558. ET: Paul, 157.

Introduction

5. Edward LeRoy Long, Jr., A Survey of Recent Christian Ethics (New York: Oxford University Press, 1982), 156-174.
6. James H. Cone, "Black Theology," in The Westminster Dictionary of Christian Theology, ed. Alan Richardson and John Bowden (Philadelphia: The Westminster Press, 1983), 72.
7. Ibid.
8. Ibid.
9. Ibid., 73. See Joseph Washington, Black Religion (Boston: Beacon Press, 1964).
10. Cone, "Black Theology," 74.
11. Ibid. See James H. Cone, Black Theology and Black Power (New York: Seabury Press, 1969); A Black Theology of Liberation (Philadelphia: J.B. Lippincott Company, 1970).
12. Cone, "Black Theology," 74-75.

13. Kari Elizabeth Børrensen, Subordination et equivalence, nature et role de la femme d'aprés Augustin et Thomas Aquin (Oslo: Universitetsforlaget, 1968). ET: Subordination and Equivalence: The Nature and Role of Woman in Augustine and Thomas Aquinas (Washington, D.C.: University Press of America, 1981); Mary Daly, The Church and the Second Sex (New York: Harper and Row, 1968) and Beyond God the Father (Boston: Beacon Press, 1973); Rosemary Radford Ruether, Religion and Sexism: Images of Woman in Jewish and Christian Traditions (New York: Simon and Schuster, 1974).

14. Rosemary Radford Ruether, "Feminist Theology," in The Westminster Dictionary of Christian Theology, 210. The text of Margaret Fell is reprinted in Mary Waite, A Warning to All Friends (Los Angeles: William Andrews Clark Memorial Library, University of California, 1979).

15. Ruether, "Feminist Theology," 210.

16. Ibid., 211.

17. Ibid., 211-212.

18. Ibid., 210; cf. Alistair Kee, "Liberation Theology," in The Westminster Dictionary of Christian Theology, 329-330. See also Elsa Tamez, Against Machismo (Oak Park, IL: Meyer-Stone, 1987). Tamez has interviewed several male Latin American liberation theologians, including Juan Luis Segundo (pp. 3-10), about the role of women in Latin America. A second volume is intended to be published by Tamez on the responses of women theologians to what the "male" theologians have written.

19. Deane William Ferm, Third World Liberation Theologies: An Introductory Survey (Maryknoll, N.Y.: Orbis Books, 1986), 1; see also Ferm's companion volume, Third World Liberation Theologies: A Reader (Maryknoll, N.Y.: Orbis Books, 1986).

20. Ferm, Third World Liberation Theologies: An Introductory Survey, 1, 4; see also Kee, "Liberation Theology," 328.

21. Ferm, Third World Liberation Theologies: An Introductory Survey, 1.

22. Ibid.

23. Ibid., 2.

24. Ibid., 16. See Gustavo Gutiérrez, Teología de la liberación, Perspectivas (Lima: CEP, 1971). ET: A Theology of Liberation (Maryknoll, N.Y.: Orbis Books, 1973).

25. Theology and the Church, 74.

26. See Harvey Cox, The Silencing of Leonardo Boff: The Vatican and the Future of World Christianity (Oak Park, IL: Meyer-Stone Books, 1988), 7-8.

27. For a more complete survey of historical events in Segundo's life, see Alfred T. Hennelly, Theologies in Conflict: The Challenge of Juan Luis Segundo (Orbis Books: Maryknoll, N.Y., 1979), 50-51; Signs of the Times, 1-2. See also the "Appendix" in this book, pp. 175-179.

28. Alfred T. Hennelly, "The Search for a Liberating Christology," Religious Studies Review 15, no. 1 (January 1989): 45. Hennelly made this same claim at the American Academy of Religion in a presentation entitled, "Steps to a Theology of Mind," Currents in Contemporary Christology Group, Newsletter VIII, no. 2 (November 1988): 24.

29. Teófilo Cabestrero, Faith: Conversations with Contemporary Theologians, trans. Donald D. Walsh (Maryknoll, N.Y.: Orbis Books, 1980), 172.

30. Ibid.

31. Liberación, 13. ET: Liberation, 9.

32. Gutiérrez, A Theology of Liberation, 15.

33. "Statement by Juan Luis Segundo," in Theology in the Americas, ed. Sergio Torres and John Eagleson (Maryknoll, N.Y.: Orbis Books, 1976), 280.

34. "Has Latin America a Choice?" America 120, no. 8 (22 February 1969): 215.

35. Vivian Lindermayer, "Liberation theology here and now: Where is it going? For whom does it speak?" Christianity and Crisis 49, no. 9 (12 June 1989): 181.

36. Liberación, 7-10. ET: Liberation, 3-6.

37. Sinópticos y Pablo, 300. ET: Paul, 9.

38. See Carl E. Braaten, The Apostolic Imperative: Nature and Aim of the Church's Mission and Ministry (Minneapolis: Augsburg Publishing House, 1985), 92-114; see also Joseph Cardinal Ratzinger and the Congregation for the Doctrine of the Faith, "Instruction on Certain Aspects of the Theology of Liberation," VII, reprinted in Segundo, Theology and the Church, 176-179. On the relationship of Marxism and biblical hermeneutics in liberation theology, see Dennis P. McCann, "Liberation Theology," The Westminster Dictionary of Christian Ethics, ed. James F. Childress and John Macquarrie (Philadelphia: The Westminster Press, 1986), 349-350.

39. Braaten, The Apostolic Imperative, 98. Cf. Carl Braaten, "Liberation Theology Coming of Age," dialog 27:4 (Fall, 1988), 242.

40. Ibid.

41. Alfred T. Hennelly, Theologies in Conflict, 157-175.

42. "Capitalism-Socialism: A Theological Crux," in Concilium, Vol. 96, ed. Claude Geffré and Gustavo Gutiérrez (New York: Herder and Herder, 1974), 123.

43. Ibid.

44. Theology and the Church, 91.

45. Ferm, Third World Liberation Theologies: An Introductory Survey, 36. See also José Porfirio Miranda, Marx and the Bible: A Critique of the Philosophy of Oppression (Maryknoll, N.Y.: Orbis Books, 1974).

46. Michael Novak, Will it Liberate? Questions About Liberation Theology (New York: Paulist Press, 1986), 15. See also Phillip Berryman, Liberation Theology: Essential Facts About the Revolutionary Movement in Latin America and Beyond (Philadelphia: Temple University Press, 1987), 194.

47. Craig Nessan, "Liberation Praxis: Challenge to Lutheran Theology," dialog 25, no. 2 (Spring, 1986): 126.

48. See e.g. Etapas precristianas de la fe: Evolución de la idea de Dios en el Antiguo Testamento (Montevideo: Cursos de Complementación Cristiana, 1962); Evolución y culpa (Buenos Aires: Ediciones Carlos Lohlé, 1972). ET: Evolution and Guilt, trans. John Drury (Maryknoll, N.Y.: Orbis Books, 1974); El hombre de hoy ante Jesús de Nazarét, II/2, Historia y actualidad: Las cristologías en la espiritualidad (Madrid: Ediciones cristiandad, 1982). ET: An Evolutionary Approach to Jesus of Nazareth, trans. John Drury (Maryknoll, N.Y.: Orbis Books, 1988). Segundo also gave a lecture on "Teilhard de Chardin" at a conference in Montevideo in 1975.

49. Nessan, "Liberation Praxis," 126.

50. Hennelly, "Steps to a Theology of Mind," 30.

51. Ibid.

52. Hennelly, "The Search for a Liberating Christology," 45. See also El hombre de hoy ante Jesús de Nazarét, I, Fe e ideología (Madrid: Ediciones cristiandad, 1982). ET: Faith and Ideologies (Maryknoll, N.Y.: Orbis Books, 1984).

53. Hennelly, "The Search for a Liberating Christology," 45.

54. Hennelly, Theologies in Conflict, 51.

55. Ibid., 52-175. Each of these themes are explored in separate chapters in Hennelly's tome.

56. Ibid., 52.

57. Hennelly, "The Search for a Liberating Christology," 45.

58. "Preface," in Theologies in Conflict, xiii-xviii.

59. Ibid., xiv. The italics are mine.

60. This series is three-volumes in Spanish (1982); five volumes in English translation (1984-1988).

61. Hennelly calls Segundo's attempt a "failure." Hennelly, "The Search for a Liberating Christology," 47.

62. See Iglesia, 7. ET: Church, vii.

63. Segundo, interview with Teófilo Cabestrero, Faith, 174. The italics are mine.

64. Ibid.

65. Hidden Motives, 84.

66. Ibid., 84-88.

67. Ibid., 88-92.

68. Ibid., 92-106.

69. Ibid., 110-111.

70. Ibid., 111-113.
71. Ibid., 113.
72. Ibid., 114. The conforms especially to the third feature of Pope Paul VI's *Evangelii Nuntiandi* on evangelism: (1) "verbal proclamation of the Good News"; (2) "a life of personal witness to the Good News"; and (3) "transforming social praxis in accordance with the Good News." Hennelly, Theologies in Conflict, 82.
73. Hidden Motives, 115.
74. Ibid. See also interview with Cabestrero, in Faith, 175.
75. Iglesia, 91. ET: Church, 57; Sinópticos y Pablo, 416. ET: Paul, 80.
76. Hidden Motives, 115.
77. Ibid., 115-116.
78. Ibid., 120.
79. Hennelly, Theologies in Conflict, 51. The italics are mine.
80. "Capitalism-Socialism: A Theological Crux," 119-121; De la sociedad a la teología (Buenos Aires: Ediciones Carlos Lohlé, 1970), 80-94.
81. Hennelly, Theologies in Conflict, 14.
82. Interview with Cabestrero, in Faith, 173.

Chapter 1

83. Función de la Iglesia en la realidad rioplatense (Montevideo: Barriero y Ramos, 1962).
84. Hennelly, Theologies in Conflict, 74. The dissertation volumes were entitled, La cristiandad ¿una utopia? I. Los hechos. II. Los principios (Montevideo: Mimeográfica "Luz," 1964).
85. The five volume series produced by Segundo and the Peter Faber Center were entitled, Teología abierta para el laico adulto. The other faculty and staff members of the Center were Andrés Assandri, Ricardo Cetrulo, Orlando Costa, Darío Ubilla, Roberto Viola, Mario Kaplún, and Carlos Rojf. The volumes in this series were based on actual classes held for adult laity in Uruguay, and sought to provide education in human sciences (anthropology, sociology, economics, etc.) and theology. Iglesia, jacket, and pp. 12-14; also Hennelly, Theologies in Conflict, 51. Segundo himself indicates, "Christian liberty and its involvement in history . . . has been the central concern of the works in this collection." Los sacramentos hoy (Buenos Aires: Ediciones Carlos Lohlé, 1971), 89. ET: The Sacraments Today (Maryknoll, N.Y.: Orbis Books, 1974), 65. This is also reflected in the English title for this particular series-- "A Theology for Artisans for a New Humanity." That phrase is borrowed from the conclusion of Vatican II's Gaudium et Spes. See Vatican Council II: The Conciliar and Post Conciliar Documents, Volume 1, edited by Austin Flannery (Collegeville, MN: Liturgical Press, 1975), 999-1001.

86. Esa comunidad llamada Iglesia (Buenos Aires: Ediciones Carlos Lohlé, 1968). ET: The Community Called Church, trans. John Drury (Maryknoll, N.Y.: Orbis Books, 1973).

87. Acción pastoral latinoamericana: sus mótivos ocultos (Buenos Aires: Ediciones Carlos Lohlé, 1972). ET: The Hidden Motives of Pastoral Action, trans. John Drury (Maryknoll, N.Y.: Orbis Books, 1978).

88. Hennelly, Theologies in Conflict, 69. Hennelly wrote this in 1979, prior to Segundo's major christological works.

89. Masas y minorías, 94-110.

90. "Fe e ideología," Perspectivas de Diálogo 9 (November, 1974): 227-233. Hennelly notes that Perspectivas de Diálogo was "an official organ of the Center. The periodical was abruptly suppressed by the Uruguayan government in 1975, and soon afterward the Center was closed by Segundo's religious superiors." Hennelly, Theologies in Conflict, 51. The last issue of Perspectivas before its suppression was "devoted . . . entirely to the subject of prayer. The issue (August 1975) was entitled 'Oración y praxis,' and included articles by José Gómez Caffarena, Luis María Pérez Aguirre, and Andrés Assandri as well as an editorial on "¿Crisis de oración o desencuentro con Dios?" [A Crisis of Prayer, or an Uncenteredness with God?] References in the issue to prayer at moments of arrest and imprisonment were cited as the cause for the suppression of the periodical." Hennelly, Theologies in Conflict, 153, n. 17.

91. Liberación de la teología (Buenos Aires: Ediciones Carlos Lohlé, 1975). ET: The Liberation of Theology, trans. John Drury (Maryknoll, N.Y.: Orbis Books, 1976). Alfred Hennelly has noted that "the relation of faith and ideology throughout The Liberation of Theology . . . could be designated as the dominant theme of that entire volume." Hennelly, Theologies in Conflict, 134.

92. El hombre de hoy ante Jesús de Nazarét. I. Fe e ideología. II. Historia y actualidad: Sinópticos y Pablo. III. Historia y actualidad: Las cristologías en la espiritualidad (Madrid: Ediciones Christiandad, 1982). This work was translated into five volumes in English by John Drury, and published by Orbis Books in Maryknoll, N.Y., in 1984-1988.

93. Hennelly, "The Search for a Liberating Christology," 45, refers to the faith/ideology dialectic as Segundo's "overarching and unifying vision" in this series.

94. Dennis P. McCann, "Political Ideologies and Practical Theology: Is There a Difference?" Union Seminary Quarterly Review 36, no. 4 (Summer 1981): 247.

95. Fe e ideología, 13. ET: Faith and Ideologies, 3. Segundo adds, "This is to say nothing about those who do not seem to adhere to either group and who exist in a manner that cannot be classified." Segundo is not very specific about who he had in mind for each of these groups. However, he writes in an

earlier source: "'Faith is not an ideology': that is a frequent statement from the [*ecclesiastical*] *hierarchy* when it launches an attack on liberation theology. 'Faith is not an ideology--and what we need now is an ideology': that is the frequent complaint of *younger Christians*, who are told to go back to the gospel message but who do not find in it sufficient direction for making a sound political commitment vis-à-vis liberation. 'Faith is not an ideology--that is why we hold a Christian faith but a Marxist ideology': that is the attitude of *growing numbers of Christians who have moved or been pushed towards the margins of Latin American life.*" Liberación, 117. ET: Liberation, 102-103. The italics are mine.

96. Masas y minorías, 94-95.
97. Fe e ideología, 13-14. ET: Faith and Ideologies, 4. The italics are mine.
98. Fe e ideología, 14. ET: Faith and Ideologies, 4.
99. Fe e ideología, 15. ET: Faith and Ideologies, 4. Elsewhere, Segundo phrases it more graphically: "He drops his friends, passes over his rights, and does not vacillate in killing his mother whom he loves, etc., not to be cruel but in order to be free." "Fe e ideología," 227.
100. Fe e ideología, 15. ET: Faith and Ideologies, 4.
101. Segundo writes, "to choose one path is to close ourselves off to others." Fe e ideología, 15. ET: Faith and Ideologies, 5.
102. Fe e ideología, 17. ET: Faith and Ideologies, 6. In Masas y minorías, 96, Segundo has this more detailed parallel: "The revolutionary and the conservative, the Christian and the atheist, the laborer and the professional--no one can go to the end of the journey and return with the certitude (*certidumbre*) that it is worth the trouble (*vale la pena*) to travel it the whole life long." Segundo argued for the same point in his Harvard lectures: "No human being can have the lived experience of his life, and [therefore know] that life is worth the trouble [*vale la pena*] of being lived. In other words, no one can take an exploratory journey toward the realization of a human ideal, to see if it is satisfactory, and then begin the real journey toward it." Liberación, 118. ET: Liberation, 103-104.
103. Segundo, "Fe e ideología," 228.
104. Fe e ideología, 18-19. ET: Faith and Ideologies, 6.
105. Ibid. See also Masas y minorías, 98.
106. "Fe e ideología," 228.
107. Fe e ideología, 24. ET: Faith and Ideologies, 10-11.
108. Fe e ideología, 24. ET: Faith and Ideologies, 11.
109. Ibid.
110. Fe e ideología, 25. ET: Faith and Ideologies, 11.
111. Fe e ideología, 24-25. ET: Faith and Ideologies, 11.
112. Fe e ideología, 25. ET: Faith and Ideologies, 11.

113. Fe e ideología, 28. ET: Faith and Ideologies, 14. Segundo adds: "For example, those who 'believe' in Jesus Christ may now ask who he was, and what he really said historically, and what criteria they can or should use to determine that. The important point here is that this new emphasis on 'orthodoxy,' on the objective Jesus--whether it is used to accept or reject faith in him--leaves intact the phenomenon of 'faith' as an anthropological dimension."

114. Fe e ideología, 20-21. ET: Faith and Ideologies, 7-8.

115. Liberación, 116. ET: Liberation, 102.

116. Fe e ideología, 21. ET: Faith and Ideologies, 8.

117. Fe e ideología, 22. ET: Faith and Ideologies, 9.

118. Fe e ideología, 23. ET: Faith and Ideologies, 9-10.

119. Liberación, 122. ET: Liberation, 106-107.

120. Segundo, "Fe e ideología," 233.

121. Fe e ideología, 41. ET: Faith and Ideologies, 26.

122. Fe e ideología, 25. ET: Faith and Ideologies, 12. The italics are mine.

123. Fe e ideología, 27. ET: Faith and Ideologies, 13.

124. Fe e ideología, 28. ET: Faith and Ideologies, 14.

125. Fe e ideología, 46. ET: Faith and Ideologies, 32.

126. Fe e ideología, 46-47. ET: Faith and Ideologies, 32-33. Segundo quotes this passage from the Spanish edition of Pannenberg's The Faith of the Apostles, entitled, La fe de los apóstles (Salamanca: Ed. Sígueme, 1974). The italics are mine.

127. Fe e ideología, 47. ET: Faith and Ideologies, 33.

128. Fe e ideología, 49. ET: Faith and Ideologies, 34.

129. Fe e ideología, 47, n. 1. ET: Faith and Ideologies, 55, n. 1. We might also note that, in Pannenberg's text, the concept of "ultimate concern" is employed, a concept that is usually associated with Paul Tillich. Alfred Hennelly believes that there is a proximate understanding between Segundo's concept of "faith" and Tillich's understanding of "ultimate concern." See Hennelly, Theologies in Conflict, 171, n. 8. However, Segundo himself contends that Tillich's concept of "ultimate concern" restricts "faith" to Christian categories of thought, and "makes a 'Christian' value, such as love, an absolute in the midst of relative realities." Liberación, 202, 202-203, n. 12. ET: Liberation, 178, 181-182, n. 12.

130. David Tracy, Blessed Rage for Order: The New Pluralism in Theology (New York: Seabury Press, 1975), 93. Quoted in Segundo, Fe e ideología, 51. ET: Faith and Ideologies, 35-36. The italics are mine.

131. Fe e ideología, 51-52. ET: Faith and Ideologies, 36.

132. Fe e ideología, 54-55. ET: Faith and Ideologies, 37-38.

133. Fe e ideología, 57-73. ET: Faith and Ideologies, 40-50.

134. Fe e ideología, 112-113. ET: Faith and Ideologies, 87.

135. Fe e ideología, 112. ET: Faith and Ideologies, 88. The italics are mine. Segundo quotes from *Jesús para ateos* (Ed. Sígueme, Salamanca 1974), pp. 28-29. For an English translation of Machovec̆'s work, see A Marxist Looks at Jesus (Philadelphia: Fortress Press, 1976), 25. Segundo describes the goal of Machovec̆'s classic text as follows: "Machovec̆ is trying to spell out, as carefully as he can, how and why an atheistic Marxist can be interested in the life and teaching of Jesus of Nazareth while still remaining consistent with his own ideology." Fe e ideología, 112. ET: Faith and Ideologies, 88.
136. Fe e ideología, 112. ET: Faith and Ideologies, 88.
137. Fe e ideología, 116. ET: Faith and Ideologies, 90-91.
138. Fe e ideología, 117. ET: Faith and Ideologies, 92. The quote is from Gregory Bateson, Steps to an Ecology of Mind (New York: Ballantine Books, 1972), 314.
139. Fe e ideología, 119. ET: Faith and Ideologies, 93.
140. Fe e ideología, 121. ET: Faith and Ideologies, 94. The italics are mine.
141. Fe e ideología, 133. ET: Faith and Ideologies, 95.
142. Fe e ideología, 122-123. ET: Faith and Ideologies, 95. The italics are Segundo's.
143. Fe e ideología, 123. ET: Faith and Ideologies, 96.
144. Fe e ideología, 123-124. ET: Faith and Ideologies, 96.
145. Fe e ideología, 124-125. ET: Faith and Ideologies, 96-97.
146. Fe e ideología, 125. ET: Faith and Ideologies, 97. The use of the term "ideology" in the thought of Marx, Mannheim, etc., may be more complex than Segundo presents for his readers. Whether there is even a "neutral" sense is debatable, and Segundo himself notes: "To what extent can we really talk about a neutral use of the term 'ideology' by Marx? Some Marxists do find such a use; others deny it." Fe e ideología, 124. ET: Faith and Ideologies, 96. For a brief synopsis of the various understandings of "ideology," see Daniel Bell, "Ideology," in The Harper Dictionary of Modern Thought, edited by Alan Bullock and Stephen Trombley (New York: Harper & Row, 1977), 404-405. Segundo has one other detailed reference on the subject of "ideology" and its current usages. In examining the thought of Karl Mannheim's Ideology and Utopia (New York: Harcourt, Brace, Jovanovich, Harvest Books, 1936), 192-195, Segundo writes: "Using the terminological distinction made by Mannheim, we can say that the praxis of Christians should be 'utopian' rather than 'ideological.' Segundo then quotes Mannheim's distinction: "A state of mind is utopian when it is incongruous with the state of reality within which it occurs. . . . Only those orientations transcending reality will be referred to by us as utopian which, when they pass over into conduct, tend to shatter, either partially or wholly, the order of things prevailing at the time. . . . Ideologies are the situationally transcendent ideas which *never succeed de facto* in the realization of their projected contents. . .

The idea of Christian brotherly love, for instance, in a society founded on serfdom remains an unrealizable and, in this sense, ideological idea, even when the intended meaning is, in good faith, a motive in the conduct of the individual." Liberación, 114-115. ET: Liberation, 100. Even here, therefore, "ideology" carries a negative connotation.

147. This is an important, even if fine, point. Other scholarly works of Segundo's writings prior to Fe e ideología were not able to make this clear distinction. Hennelly, in Theologies in Conflict, 123, distinguished between a "negative" and "neutral" use of ideology in Segundo, and ascribed the latter to Segundo's understanding of the term. Anthony Tambasco, in The Bible for Ethics (Lanham, MD: University Press of America, 1981), 91-106, likewise makes a distinction between "negative" and "positive" uses of the term ideology, ascribing the latter to Segundo. While both of these scholars were essentially close to Segundo's understanding, Segundo has since provided further elaboration on the common uses of the term "ideology" and has distinguished these understandings from his own.

148. Fe e ideología, 135. ET: Faith and Ideologies, 104. The italics are Segundo's.

149. Fe e ideología, 111. ET: Faith and Ideologies, 87.

150. Liberación, 121, n. 5. ET: Liberation, 123, n. 5. The italics are Segundo's.

151. Phillip Berryman, Liberation Theology: Essential Facts about the Revolutionary Movement in Latin America and Beyond (Philadelphia: Temple University Press, 1987), 63-79.

152. Specifically, I am referring here to Función de la Iglesia en la realidad rioplatense (see note 83). Segundo's first major work, Existencialismo, filosofía y poesía, Ensayo de sintesis (Mexico: Espasa-Calpe, 1948), was an attempt to show the interrelationship of existentialism and poetry, which would also find place in some of Segundo's later writings. See Hennelly, "The Search for a Liberating Christology," 45.

153. Función, 8.

154. Ibid., 9.

155. Ibid.

156. Ibid., 6.

157. Ibid., 9-10.

158. Ibid., 10.

159. Ibid., 11.

160. Ibid., 13-19.

161. Ibid., 19-23.

162. Ibid., 23-27. Segundo's analysis of the Church's mission vis-à-vis these three sectors is furthered in his later work. See, for example, chapters 2, 4, and 5 of Hidden Motives.

163. Función, 11-12.

164. Ibid., 30.
165. Iglesia, 15. ET: Church, 3.
166. Función, 30.
167. Ibid., 31.
168. Ibid.
169. Ibid., 32.
170. Ibid.
171. Ibid. See also Iglesia, 48. ET: Church, 26.
172. Función, 32.
173. Ibid., 33.
174. Ibid. The italics are mine.
175. Ibid., 34.
176. Ibid., 35.
177. Ibid. The italics are mine.
178. Ibid.
179. Ibid., 35-36.
180. Ibid., 36.
181. Iglesia, 46. ET: Church, 25.
182. Ibid.
183. Iglesia, 27. ET: Church, 11.
184. Iglesia, 85-86. ET: Church, 53. The italics are Segundo's (in the Spanish original). Quoted from Karl Rahner, Theological Investigations, II, Man in the Church (London: Darton, Longman & Todd; Baltimore: Helicon, 1963), 129-130.
185. Iglesia, 86. ET: Church, 53-54.
186. Iglesia, 86. ET: Church, 54.
187. Iglesia, 86. ET: Church, 54. The italics are mine.
188. Iglesia, 30. ET: Church, 14. We might note a similar expression in The Epistle of Mathetes to Diognetus (130 C.E.): "what the soul is in the body, that are Christians in the world." See The Ante Nicene Fathers, Vol. 1, edited by Alexander Roberts and James Donaldson (Grand Rapids, Mich.: Wm B. Eerdmans, 1987), 27.
189. Función, 45. Matthew L. Lamb, in Solidarity with Victims: Toward a Theology of Social Transformation (New York: Crossroad, 1982), xiii, writes similarly: "Faith as genuine is a knowledge born of love, and the agapic praxis, or love lived in solidarity with victims struggling to overcome their suffering, is the heart of liberation theologies."
190. For the full discussion of this connection in Segundo's thought, see Evolución y culpa, 31-43, 161-168. ET: Evolution and Guilt, 21-30, 126-131; see also Liberación, 248-257. ET: Liberation, 221-228.
191. De la sociedad a la teología (Buenos Aires: Ediciones Carlos Lohlé, 1970), 157. Hennelly, in Theologies in Conflict, 82, notes that Teilhard's evolutionary perspective influenced not only Segundo's ecclesiology, but also

the ecclesiology of Vatican II.
192. Función, 68. New Testament texts cited as support for this understanding include John 1:8-17; 12:32; I Corinthians 15:28; II Corinthians 5:17; Colossians 1:15-20; Ephesians 1:9-10, 19-23; and Romans 8:19, 22. See Función, 64-69.
193. Liberación, 238. ET: Liberation, 212.
194. Liberación, 257. ET: Liberation, 228. The italics are Segundo's.
195. Función, 70.
196. Ibid., 72-73. See also Liberación, 245. ET: Liberation, 218.
197. Función, 72.
198. Ibid.
199. Liberación, 255, 257. ET: Liberation, 226, 228.
200. "Education, Communication, and Liberation: A Christian Vision," IDOC International--North American Edition, no. 35 (13 November 1971): 72.
201. Iglesia, 125. ET: Church, 81. The italics are in the Spanish text.
202. "The Church: A New Direction in Latin America," Catholic Mind 65, no. 1 (March 1967): 46, 47; Hidden Motives, 72.
203. Función, 75.
204. Ibid., 76.
205. Hidden Motives, 53-54.
206. Fe e ideología, 73. ET: Faith and Ideologies, 50.
207. Fe e ideología, 96. ET: Faith and Ideologies, 73.
208. Ibid.
209. Fe e ideología, 97-98. ET: Faith and Ideologies, 73-74.
210. Fe e ideología, 101. ET: Faith and Ideologies, 76.
211. Fe e ideología, 101-102. ET: Faith and Ideologies, 76-77.
212. Fe e ideología, 101. ET: Faith and Ideologies, 76.
213. Vatican Council II: The Conciliar and Post Conciliar Documents, Vol. 1, 367-368.
214. Iglesia, 89-90. ET: Church, 56. The italics are Segundo's.
215. Iglesia, 90. ET: Church, 56.
216. Ibid. The italics are in the Spanish text.
217. Iglesia, 91. ET: Church, 56.
218. Iglesia, 91. ET: Church, 56-57.
219. Iglesia, 91. ET: Church, 57.
220. Ibid.
221. Iglesia, 91-92. ET: Church, 57. The italics are Segundo's.
222. Nuestra idea de Dios (Buenos Aires: Ediciones Carlos Lohlé, 1970), 62. ET: Our Idea of God, translated by John Drury (Maryknoll, N.Y.: Orbis Books, 1973), 44.
223. Iglesia, 91. ET: Church, 56.
224. Iglesia, 92. ET: Church, 57.
225. Iglesia, 92-93. ET: Church, 58.

226. Iglesia, 93-94. ET: Church, 58.
227. Iglesia, 94. ET: Church, 58.
228. Iglesia, 95. ET: Church, 59.
229. Ibid.
230. Iglesia, 96. ET: Church, 59. Segundo has based this point in the teachings of Gaudium et Spes, the Pastoral Constitution on the Church in the Modern World. See Flannery, Vatican Council II: The Conciliar and Post Conciliar Documents, Vol. 1, 905, 912. The concept of the "signs of the times" was elaborated with relevance to the Latin American situation in an essay delivered at CELAM II in Medellín by Bishop Marcos McGrath, entitled, "The Signs of the Times in Latin America Today." See The Church in the Present-Day Transformation of Latin America in Light of the Council, Vol. 1, Position Papers (Bogota: Latin American Bureau, CELAM, 1970), 79-106.
231. Paul Tillich, "Rechtfertigung und Zweifel," Offenbarung und Glaube, Band 8, Gesammelte Werke (Stuttgart: Evangelisches Verlagswerk, 1970), 85-100.

Chapter 2

232. Liberación, 14. ET: Liberation, 9.
233. In Concepción cristiana del hombre, Segundo notes, and apparently accepts, the premise of Bultmann that "the letters of St. John and St. Paul" are the "primary phenomenology of Christian existence." See Segundo, Qué es un cristiano (Montevideo: Mosca Hnos., 1971), 94. Throughout Segundo's text, it is quite evident that the bulk of biblical references are from the writings of St. John and St. Paul. However, here, as in other places, Segundo does not think of these two writers as theologically discrepant. See Segundo, De la sociedad a la teología (Buenos Aires: Ediciones Carlos Lohlé, 1970), 84. See also Hennelly, Theologies in Conflict, 93, and 100, n. 29. One might also consider that in the first, second, and fifth volumes of Segundo's Artisans for a New Humanity series, there is a predominance of Pauline texts and thought cited throughout the "Biblical Tapestry" appendices. See Segundo, Church, 150-168; Grace, 194-208; and Evolution and Guilt, 140-148.
234. Sinópticos y Pablo, 287-599. ET: Paul.
235. Liberación, 11. ET: Liberation, 7.
236. Ibid.
237. Ibid.
238. Liberación, 12. ET: Liberation, 8.
239. Ibid.
240. Ibid.
241. Ibid.
242. Liberación, 13. ET: Liberation, 8.
243. Liberación, 13. ET: Liberation, 9.

244. Liberación, 14. ET: Liberation, 9.
245. Liberación, 12. ET: Liberation, 8.
246. Hennelly, Theologies in Conflict, 109.
247. Hennelly, "Introduction," in Signs of the Times, 3. The italics are
Hennelly's.   See also Theology and the Church, 3, where Segundo writes:
"there is nothing further from that [Latin American] context than the
Bultmannian methodology and agenda.   One needs only to think of
'demythologization,' born of the 'death of God' and proper to the 'developed'
mentality of the modern world; the rejection of the search for the historical
Jesus and of the historical causes of his death; the purely eschatological,
ahistorical idea of the coming of the kingdom of God supposedly preached by
Jesus; the method of personalistic, existential biblical interpretation, without
any depth or social analysis; and so on."
   Cf. Winston D. Persaud, "The Article of Justification and the Theology
of Liberation," Currents in Theology and Mission 16, no. 5 (October, 1989):
363, n. 6. Persaud implies that Segundo's concept of the "hermeneutic circle"
is indebted to the influence of Marx.   Segundo certainly does admit "the
influence of Marxist thought on the creation of a theology of liberation in Latin
America." But he adds in defense, "there are problems connected in applying
the label 'Marxist' to a line of thought or a source of influence. First of all,
those who identify themselves with Marx and his thinking have a thousand
different ways of conceiving and interpreting 'Marxist' thought. Aside from
that fact, the point is that the great thinkers of history do not replace each
other; rather, they compliment and enrich each other.   Philosophic thought
would never be the same after Aristotle as it was before him. In that sense all
Westerners who philosophize now are Aristotelians. *After Marx, our way of
conceiving and posing the problems of society will never be the same again.
Whether everything Marx said is accepted or not, and in whatever way one may
conceive his 'essential' thinking, there can be no doubt that present-day social
thought will be 'Marxist' to some extent: that is, profoundly indebted to Marx.
In that sense Latin American theology is certainly Marxist. I know my remark
will be taken out of context, but one cannot go on trying to forestall every
partisan or stupid misunderstanding forever.*" Liberación, 19, n. 10. ET:
Liberation, 35, n. 10. The italics are mine. Persaud might be partially correct
in his assessment of Segundo's "hermeneutic circle" given that the problems
recognized may well be influence by Marxist thought. But Segundo could
rebut, and not without reason, that Persaud is taking the Marxist emphasis out
of context. Nowhere in Segundo's elaboration of the "hermeneutic circle" does
Marx explicitly enter the picture. Furthermore, the footnote cited above is in
a section that criticizes Marx himself for never completing the "hermeneutic
circle" (obviously, because Marx failed to consider the Scriptures and religion
as a legitimate source).

248. See "America hoy," Vispera (August 1967): 53-57, as a critique of Protestant theology (including that of José Míguez Bonino); see "Teología: Mensaje y proceso," Perspectivas de Diálogo 9 (December 1974): 259-270, as a critique of Catholic theology (particularly that of José Luis Carvias). Segundo commends the positive advances of Vatican II for a more dynamic exegesis in "Hacia una exégesis dinámica," Vispera (October 1967): 77-84. However, Segundo regards the recent direction of the Vatican to be a dangerous return to more static formulations of revealed "dogma." See Liberation of Dogma, (Maryknoll, NY: Orbis Books, 1992), 1-15.
249. Liberación, 127. ET: Liberation, 110.
250. Liberación, 127. ET: Liberation, 111.
251. Ibid.
252. Ibid. Segundo is referring specifically to Cullman, Gutiérrez, and Ignacio Ellacuría. See also Sinópticos y Pablo, 577, n. 12. ET: Paul, 223, n. 248.
253. Liberación, 128. ET: Liberation, 112. The italics are Segundo's.
254. Liberación, 129. ET: Liberation, 113. Segundo addresses the issue of the ongoing educational process in the history of Israel in his early tome, Etapas precristianas de al fe (Montevideo: Cursos de Complementación Cristiana, 1962), reproduced in Qué es un cristiano, 5-85. Segundo depicts four predominant stages in the history of Israel's faith and understanding of God. The first stage is that of the Yahwist and Elohist writers, who understood God as a deity whose power is limited to the territory of Israel, in conjunction with other deities who control other lands (Qué, 27-28). God is "encountered in the terrible and in the inexplicable" through "an intermediary"--whether a person like Moses, or a purification ritual, or a sacred place like Jerusalem, or a sacred object like the ark (Qué, 28-34). The positive contribution of this stage, according to Segundo, is the appreciation of the absolute through ritual; negatively, it gives rise to superstition, handed down to the sacramental practices of the church today (Qué, 34-37). The second stage is associated with the early and latter prophets and the deuteronomic source. God is now understood as being in alliance with the people of Israel through "covenant." Consequently, the history of the people of Israel plays a more prominent role. The "equality of relationship with the Absolute" for all the people of Israel is clearly the positive aspect of this stage; the negative aspect is that there is disguised aggressiveness toward those who do not "belong to our clan" (Qué, 39-50). The third stage is the stage of "God, transcendent and creator." Principal writers of this stage include the exilic and post-exilic prophets and writings (Second Isaiah, Priestly source, Ezekiel, Job). As a result of the exilic experience, God is regarded as the *only* God, creator of heaven and earth and "all flesh." The creature relates to God as the transcendent Holy One through "adoration and terror" (Qué, 68). While the behavior is positively appropriate for creatureliness, the negative corollary is

"passivity" before an all-powerful deity (Qué, 70-71). The fourth, and final, stage of Israel's biblical history understands God as the "legislator of the universe." Here, Segundo focuses on one text only: the Book of Wisdom (175 B.C.E.). In all of the previous stages, God moves progressively closer relationship with the people. In this stage, the transcendent God oversees the just direction of agents of transcendent freedom (Qué, 73-79). There is a positive regard for "justice in the afterlife," the value of "personal liberty," and a "connection between external event and internal liberty" (Qué, 79-80). But this is not yet Christianity; and life is negatively regarded as a testing ground for righteousness (Qué, 80-81). For a further exposition, see Hennelly, Theologies in Conflict, 53-59.

255. Liberación, 130. ET: Liberation, 113.
256. Ibid.
257. Liberación, 130-131. ET: Liberation, 114.
258. Liberación, 131. ET: Liberation, 114.
259. Liberación, 131. ET: Liberation, 114-115. The italics in the Matthean text are Segundo's.
260. Liberación, 132. ET: Liberation, 115.
261. Liberación, 132, 137. ET: Liberation, 116, 120.
262. Liberación, 133. ET: Liberation, 116. This would also seem to imply that Segundo's understanding of the *etapas precristianas de la fe* (see note 254) is that these stages were really part and parcel of one faith seeking new answers about the deity in new historical situations. Segundo, however, is less explicit about this connection in his earlier work.
263. Hennelly, Theologies in Conflict, 126.
264. Liberación, 134. ET: Liberation, 117.
265. Liberación, 136, 138. ET: Liberation, 119, 121.
266. Liberación, 137. ET: Liberation, 120.
267. Liberación, 138. ET: Liberation, 121.
268. Liberación, 139. ET: Liberation, 121.
269. Liberación, 139-140. ET: Liberation, 121-122. The italics are Segundo's.
270. Liberación, 140. ET: Liberation, 122.
271. Liberación, 124. ET: Liberation, 109.
272. Liberación, 125. ET: Liberation, 110. The italics are Segundo's.
273. Liberación, 126. ET: Liberation, 110. The italics are Segundo's.
274. Liberación, 125. ET: Liberation, 109.
275. Ibid.
276. Fe e ideología, 152. ET: Faith and Ideologies, 123.
277. Fe e ideología, 155-156. ET: Faith and Ideologies, 126.
278. Hennelly, Theologies in Conflict, 92-96.

279. For a fuller treatment of these four themes of Christian morality, see Iglesia, 157-171. ET: Church, 103-112. See also De la sociedad a la teología, 95-104.

280. These four themes correspond to the four chapters of Gracia (ET: Grace). See also the following articles by Segundo, all published in Perspectivas de Diálogo: "¿Que nombre dar a la existencia cristiana?" (1967): 3-9; "La condición humana" (1967): 30-35, 55-61, 67; "La vida eterna" (1967): 83-89, 109-115; "Profundidad de la gracia" (1967): 235-240, 249-255.

281. Masas y minorías, 7-10. See also Liberación, 236-239. ET: Liberation, 211-213.

282. Sinópticos y Pablo, 11-14. ET: The Historical Jesus of the Synoptics, (Maryknoll, NY: Orbis Books, 1985), 3-7. Boff's text may also be found in Leonardo Boff, Passion of Christ, Passion of the World, translated by Robert R. Barr, (Maryknoll, NY: Orbis Books, 1987), 130-133.

283. Sinópticos y Pablo, 17. ET: The Historical Jesus of the Synoptics, 8.

284. Sinópticos y Pablo, 29. ET: The Historical Jesus of the Synoptics, 16.

285. Sinópticos y Pablo, 63. ET: The Historical Jesus of the Synoptics, 38-39. The italics are Segundo's.

286. Sinópticos y Pablo, 33. ET: The Historical Jesus of the Synoptics, 18. The question surfaces in Augustine's In Ioannis Evangelium Tractatus, tract. XIX, 14.

287. Sinópticos y Pablo, 49. ET: The Historical Jesus of the Synoptics, 29. Segundo is sharply critical of Wolfhart Pannenberg's Jesus--God and Man (Philadelphia: Westminster Press, 1977), 38-49. Segundo perceives that Pannenberg has divided christology from soteriology. While Segundo would agree with Pannenberg that christology should start "from below," because this is the most soteriologically promising, he claims that Pannenberg actually starts his christology "from above," arguing first for the divinity of Christ. There may be some validity in Segundo's argument here, but his further attempt to equate Pannenberg's theology with the "'signs from heaven'. . . theology of the Pharisees and Sadducees" is unwarranted. Sinópticos y Pablo, 49-50. ET: The Historical Jesus of the Synoptics, 30.

288. Sinópticos y Pablo, 65. ET: The Historical Jesus of the Synoptics, 40. The italics are Segundo's.

289. Sinópticos y Pablo, 66. ET: The Historical Jesus of the Synoptics, 41.

290. Sinópticos y Pablo, 289. ET: Paul, 2. See also how Anders Nygren has developed this theme of the "Gospel of Paul" in his Commentary on Romans (Philadelphia: Fortress Press, 1949), 1-3. Segundo views Pauline theology as having three "stages" of christological development. The first stage would include the writing to the Thessalonians (circa 50 C.E.), in which Paul relied heavily upon Jewish imagery. In order for Paul to bring the gospel to the "pagans," there was a need to make the transition beyond the "cultural barriers" between Jewish and Gentile (Greek) culture. The second stage (circa

57 C.E.) includes Paul's correspondence with the Corinthians, Galatians, and Romans. Here, and especially in Romans, Paul has reached a major landmark in his christology: "the possibility of employing *one single* (hence *new*) idiom to speak to Jews and pagans (i.e., humanity as a whole) about the significance of the Christ, Jesus of Nazareth." The third stage (circa 61-63 C.E.) includes the correspondence to the Colossians and Philemon. These epistles are largely exhortatory; but, christologically speaking, "they present highly structured, brief compositions about Jesus of Nazareth: who he is, what he means and, in particular, what his relationship is to God and God's universal plan." Sinópticos y Pablo, 289-295. ET: Paul, 2-6.

Segundo does not say exactly where he discovered this three-stage development of Pauline christology; but there is exegetical evidence for development in Paul's theology. See J.C. Hurd, "Paul the Apostle," in The Interpreter's Dictionary of the Bible, Supplementary Volume, (Nashville: Abingdon Press, 1976), 648-651. Segundo offers more detailed exegesis for the "occasion" of Romans. While Paul was well aware of problems in the churches of Galatia and Corinth, there is some question about how much Paul knew about the situation in Rome. Segundo claims that Paul wrote his letter "to a community he did not yet know personally, because he had neither founded it nor visited it." Segundo adds: "We should not, however, underestimate Paul's possible knowledge of the Roman community and its problems. . . . The Christian community of Rome was undoubtedly made up of both converted Jews and converted pagans. In all likelihood Paul's protestations of personal unfamiliarity with the community were largely a rhetorical device to win their good will [*captatio benevolentiae*]. He was trying to suggest his own impartiality toward the conflicts that may have already existed in the community, or that may have arisen in connection with his projected visit to it." Sinópticos y Pablo, 294-295. ET: Paul, 5-6. Exegetes have held wide-ranging viewpoints on this issue. The older viewpoint (e.g., that of Bernhard Weiss) regards Romans strictly as a treatise, with little direct understanding of the problems in Rome. See William Sanday and Arthur Headlam, The International Critical Commentary: The Epistle to the Romans, (Edinburgh: T. & T. Clark, 1895), xl. Paul S. Minear, in The Obedience of Faith: The Purpose of Paul in the Epistle to the Romans, (London: SCM Press Ltd., 1971), argues that the problems in Rome and their resolution are central to Paul's writing. For a survey of responses to this issue, see Günter Klein, "Romans, Letter to the," in The Interpreter's Dictionary of the Bible, Supplementary Volume, 753-754.

291. Sinópticos y Pablo, 301. ET: Paul, 10. The italics are Segundo's. Segundo's "anthropological" key may be close to Rudolf Bultmann's analysis of Paul. Bultmann writes: "Therefore, Pauline theology is not a speculative system. It deals with God not as He is in Himself but only with God as He is significant for man, for man's responsibility and man's salvation.

Correspondingly, it does not deal with the world and man as they are in themselves, but constantly sees the world and man in their relation to God. Every assertion about God is simultaneously an assertion about man and vice versa. For this reason and in this sense, *Paul's theology is, at the same time, anthropology.*" Bultmann, Theology of the New Testament, Volume 1, translated by Kendrick Grobel (New York: Charles Scribners' Sons, 1951), 190-191. The italics are mine. However, Segundo distances himself from Bultmann's strictly existential focus. Sinópticos y Pablo, 430, n. 18. ET: Paul, 205, n. 135.

292. Sinópticos y Pablo, 303. ET: Paul, 11.

293. Sinópticos y Pablo, 369. ET: Paul, 50.

294. In essence, Segundo addresses all of Romans 1-8, with the exception of the introduction in 1:1-15. In Segundo's text, 2:28 includes 2:28-29; and 5:20 includes 5:20-21. Segundo offers his own translation of the Romans text at the beginning of each chapter. One can find this translation reproduced in its entirety in the beginning of an article entitled, "Christ and the Human Being," Cross Currents 36, no. 1 (Spring 1986):39-67. The article itself is the basis of Segundo's ninth chapter ("Conclusions") in Sinópticos y Pablo, 535-563. ET: Paul, 143-160.

295. Sinópticos y Pablo, 308. ET: Paul, 15.

296. Sinópticos y Pablo, 316. ET: Paul, 18. The italics are Segundo's.

297. Sinópticos y Pablo, 321. ET: Paul, 21. The italics are mine.

298. Sinópticos y Pablo, 318. ET: Paul, 19. The italics are Segundo's (in the Spanish original).

299. Sinópticos y Pablo, 347, n. 14. ET: Paul, 193, n. 69. The italics are Segundo's. It might have been helpful had Segundo said more about the exact kinship he perceives between Sigmund Freud's concept of "instinct" and Paul's concept of "concupiscence." For Freud's concept of "instincts," see his Civilization and Its Discontents, translated and edited by James Strachey (New York: W W Norton & Company, 1961), 64-69, in which "instincts" which emanate from the "libido" conflict with ego-instincts. Ernest Becker's description of human activity resulting from the fear of death in The Denial of Death (New York: Free Press, 1973) might be a contemporary neo-Freudian parallel to Paul's concept of concupiscence.

300. Gracia, 37-41. ET: Grace, 23-25.

301. Karl Rahner, "The Theological Concept of Concupiscentia," in Theological Investigations, Volume I (New York: Crossroad, 1961, 1982), 369. Cf. Gracia, 40. ET: Grace, 24.

302. Sinópticos y Pablo, 321. ET: Paul, 21. The italics are mine.

303. Sinópticos y Pablo, 310. ET: Paul, 16.

304. Gracia, 38-39. ET: Grace, 23. The italics are mine.

305. Sinópticos y Pablo, 320. ET: Paul, 20. One may wonder how much Segundo's concept of "sin" has really made a theological advance beyond the Thomistic/Aristotelian understanding of human nature needing to be properly aligned by reason. See The Encyclopedia of Philosophy, Volume 8 (New York: Macmillan, 1967), 105-114. This seems especially apparent when Segundo expresses his incredulity vis-à-vis the Augustinian position that "even children *without the use of reason*" could be characterized as "sinners." Sinópticos y Pablo, 419. ET: Paul, 82.

306. Sinópticos y Pablo, 339. ET: Paul, 33.

307. Sinópticos y Pablo, 340. ET: Paul, 34.

308. Sinópticos y Pablo, 342. ET: Paul, 35. The italics are Segundo's.

309. Sinópticos y Pablo, 343. ET: Paul, 36.

310. Sinópticos y Pablo, 353. ET: Paul, 43. The italics are Segundo's (in the Spanish original). The new theme here corresponds to the Pauline thesis in Romans 1:16-17.

311. Sinópticos y Pablo, 302. ET: Paul, 11. The two expressions are not antithetical, according to Segundo: "this assimilation of justification and salvation is currently disputed (without foundation, in my opinion)."

312. Sinópticos y Pablo, 361. ET: Paul, 46-47. Elsewhere, Segundo will speak of how "*it suited God*" to abandon the approach of the second stage of the moral Law in order to incorporate the third stage of "faith." Sinópticos y Pablo, 371. ET: Paul, 52. The italics are Segundo's.

313. Sinópticos y Pablo, 462. ET: Paul, 106. The italics are Segundo's.

314. Sinópticos y Pablo, 462. ET: Paul, 106-107.

315. Sinópticos y Pablo, 462. ET: Paul, 107.

316. Sinópticos y Pablo, 361. ET: Paul, 47.

317. Sinópticos y Pablo, 302. ET: Paul, 11. The italics are Segundo's. Segundo does not seem at all interested in getting into an exegetical debate here. He certainly does not leave himself open to the charge of "legal fiction," however, as in Sanday and Headlam, The International Critical Commentary: The Epistle to the Romans (Edinburgh: T. & T. Clark, 1895), 36. He is unambiguously affirming a forensic/juridical sense for the meaning of *dikaioō*.

318. Sinópticos y Pablo, 364. ET: Paul, 48. The italics are Segundo's.

319. Sinópticos y Pablo, 367. ET: Paul, 49.

320. Sinópticos y Pablo, 368-369. ET: Paul, 50.

321. Sinópticos y Pablo, 367-368. ET: Paul, 49-50.

322. Sinópticos y Pablo, 355. ET: Paul, 44. The italics are Segundo's.

323. Fe e ideología, 153. ET: Faith and Ideologies, 124. The italics are Segundo's (in the Spanish original).

324. Sinópticos y Pablo, 536. ET: Paul, 145-146. The italics are Segundo's.

325. Sinópticos y Pablo, 383. ET: Paul, 60. The italics are Segundo's.

326. Sinópticos y Pablo, 383-384. ET: Paul, 60-61. The italics are Segundo's.

327. Sinópticos y Pablo, 386-388. ET: Paul, 62-63. Segundo cites Abraham's lie about his relationship to his wife, Sarah, as an example of Abraham's sinfulness. Segundo also charitably describes Abraham as one "in perpetual motion to carry out the will of Yahweh." Sinópticos y Pablo, 387, 392. ET: Paul, 62, 65.

328. Sinópticos y Pablo, 388-389. ET: Paul, 63-64. The italics are Segundo's.

329. Sinópticos y Pablo, 401. ET: Paul, 71. The italics are Segundo's.

330. Sinópticos y Pablo, 396. ET: Paul, 67.

331. Sinópticos y Pablo, 394, 396. ET: Paul, 66, 67.

332. Sinópticos y Pablo, 395. ET: Paul, 67. The italics are Segundo's.

333. Sinópticos y Pablo, 406. ET: Paul, 74.

334. Sinópticos y Pablo, 397, 366. ET: Paul, 68, 49. The italics are mine.

335. Sinópticos y Pablo, 396-397. ET: Paul, 68. The italics are Segundo's. The translation by John Drury corrects Segundo's error (in the Spanish) in referring to Abraham as "Adam."

336. Sinópticos y Pablo, 397. ET: Paul, 68.

337. Sinópticos y Pablo, 397-398. ET: Paul, 68. The italics are mine.

338. Sinópticos y Pablo, 399. ET: Paul, 69. The italics are mine.

339. Sinópticos y Pablo, 411. ET: Paul, 78. The italics are Segundo's.

340. Sinópticos y Pablo, 410. ET: Paul, 77. The italics are Segundo's.

341. Sinópticos y Pablo, 412-413. ET: Paul, 79. The italics are Segundo's.

342. Sinópticos y Pablo, 413-414. ET: Paul, 79. The italics are Segundo's.

343. Masas y minorías, 8-9. See also Liberación, 238. ET: Liberation, 213. Segundo does not document his reference to Barth, but the context of the argument seems to refer to Barth's charge against the Reformers who "wildly estimated" the value of faith. See Karl Barth, Church Dogmatics, Volume IV/1, The Doctrine of Reconciliation, translated by G.W. Bromiley (Edinburgh: T. & T. Clark, 1956), 617.

344. Sinópticos y Pablo, 414. ET: Paul, 79. The italics are Segundo's.

345. Ibid. The italics are Segundo's.

346. Sinópticos y Pablo, 415. ET: Paul, 79. The italics are mine.

347. Sinópticos y Pablo, 415. ET: Paul, 80.

348. Ibid. The italics are mine.

349. Ibid. The italics are Segundo's.

350. Sinópticos y Pablo, 416. ET: Paul, 80. The italics are Segundo's.

351. Ibid. The italics are mine.

352. Sinópticos y Pablo, 416. ET: Paul, 80-81. The italics are Segundo's.

353. Sinópticos y Pablo, 548. ET: Paul, 152. The italics are Segundo's.

354. Sinópticos y Pablo, 417. ET: Paul, 81.

355. Sinópticos y Pablo, 418. ET: Paul, 81.

356. Sinópticos y Pablo, 418. ET: Paul, 82. The italics are Segundo's.

357. Sinópticos y Pablo, 420-421. ET: Paul, 82-83.

358. Sinópticos y Pablo, 525. ET: Paul, 140. The italics are mine.
359. Sinópticos y Pablo, 421. ET: Paul, 83.
360. Ibid.
361. Sinópticos y Pablo, 422, n. 10. ET: Paul, 204, n. 127. The italics are mine.
362. Ibid. The italics are Segundo's.
363. Sinópticos y Pablo, 422. ET: Paul, 83.
364. Ibid.
365. Sinópticos y Pablo, 427-428. ET: Paul, 86. The italics are Segundo's.
366. Sinópticos y Pablo, 424, 427. ET: Paul, 84, 86.
367. Sinópticos y Pablo, 426-427. ET: Paul, 85-86. The italics are Segundo's.
368. Sinópticos y Pablo, 429. Paul, 87. The italics are Segundo's.
369. Sinópticos y Pablo, 451. ET: Paul, 100-101.
370. Sinópticos y Pablo, 477. ET: Paul, 114. Segundo takes this to be the meaning of Paul's phrase, "from faith to faith" (Romans 1:17).
371. Sinópticos y Pablo, 452. ET: Paul, 101. Drury's translation mistakenly attributes Romans 7:1-13 as liberation for "pagan" converts.
372. Ibid. The italics are mine.
373. Sinópticos y Pablo, 452-453. ET: Paul, 101.
374. Sinópticos y Pablo, 453. ET: Paul, 101-102. The italics are Segundo's.
375. Sinópticos y Pablo, 452. ET: Paul, 101.
376. Sinópticos y Pablo, 454. ET: Paul, 102.
377. Ibid.
378. Sinópticos y Pablo, 455. ET: Paul, 103.
379. Sinópticos y Pablo, 455. ET: Paul, 102.
380. Ibid. The italics are Segundo's.
381. Sinópticos y Pablo, 457. ET: Paul, 104. The italics are Segundo's.
382. Ibid. The italics are Segundo's.
383. Sinópticos y Pablo, 373. ET: Paul, 53.
384. Sinópticos y Pablo, 467. ET: Paul, 109.
385. Sinópticos y Pablo, 463. ET: Paul, 107.
386. Sinópticos y Pablo, 466. ET: Paul, 108.
387. Sinópticos y Pablo, 467. ET: Paul, 109.
388. Ibid. The italics are Segundo's.
389. Ibid.
390. Sinópticos y Pablo, 472-473. ET: Paul, 111.
391. Sinópticos y Pablo, 473. ET: Paul, 111. The italics are Segundo's.
392. Sinópticos y Pablo, 479. ET: Paul, 114. The italics are Segundo's.
393. Sinópticos y Pablo, 476. ET: Paul, 113-114.
394. Sinópticos y Pablo, 481. ET: Paul, 115. The italics are Segundo's.
395. Sinópticos y Pablo, 484. ET: Paul, 116-117.
396. Sinópticos y Pablo, 496. ET: Paul, 123. The italics are Segundo's.

397. Sinópticos y Pablo, 496-498. ET: Paul, 123-125. The italics are Segundo's. For an early article on Pauline eschatology, see "Reconciliación y conflicto," Perspectivas de Diálogo 9 (September 1974): 172-178.
398. Sinópticos y Pablo, 494. ET: Paul, 122. The italics are Segundo's.
399. Sinópticos y Pablo, 502. ET: Paul, 128. The italics are Segundo's.
400. Sinópticos y Pablo, 504. ET: Paul, 129. The italics are Segundo's.
401. Sinópticos y Pablo, 504. ET: Paul, 130. The italics are mine.
402. The translation is Segundo's in Sinópticos y Pablo, 505. ET: Paul, 130.
403. Ibid.
404. Ibid.
405. Sinópticos y Pablo, 506. ET: Paul, 131. The italics are Segundo's.
406. Sinópticos y Pablo, 507. ET: Paul, 131. The italics are Segundo's.
407. Ibid.
408. Sinópticos y Pablo, 478. The italics are Segundo's. This is my translation. The text, in addition to almost an entire page of the Spanish edition, was paraphrased but never translated by John Drury (cf. Paul, 114).
409. Sinópticos y Pablo, 546, n. 9. ET: Paul, 218, n. 223. The italics are Segundo's.
410. Sinópticos y Pablo, 507. ET: Paul, 131. The italics are Segundo's.
411. Sinópticos y Pablo, 508. ET: Paul, 131. The italics are Segundo's.
412. Ibid.
413. Ibid.
414. Sinópticos y Pablo, 508. ET: Paul, 132.
415. Sinópticos y Pablo, 509. ET: Paul, 132. The italics are Segundo's.
416. Sinópticos y Pablo, 510. ET: Paul, 132. The italics are Segundo's.
417. Sinópticos y Pablo, 511. ET: Paul, 133. The italics are mine.
418. Ibid.
419. Sinópticos y Pablo, 515. ET: Paul, 134.
420. Sinópticos y Pablo, 517. ET: Paul, 135. The italics are Segundo's.
421. Sinópticos y Pablo, 518. ET: Paul, 135. The italics are Segundo's.
422. Sinópticos y Pablo, 518-519. ET: Paul, 136-137. The italics are Segundo's.
423. Sinópticos y Pablo, 520. ET: Paul, 137. The italics are Segundo's.
424. Sinópticos y Pablo, 522. ET: Paul, 138. The italics are Segundo's.
425. Sinópticos y Pablo, 524. ET: Paul, 139.
426. Ibid. The italics are Segundo's.
427. Sinópticos y Pablo, 528. ET: Paul, 141. The italics are Segundo's.
428. Sinópticos y Pablo, 528. ET: Paul, 142.
429. Sinópticos y Pablo, 527. ET: Paul, 141.
430. Sinópticos y Pablo, 533. ET: Paul, 144. The italics are Segundo's.
431. Sinópticos y Pablo, 535-536. ET: Paul, 145. The italics are Segundo's.
432. Sinópticos y Pablo, 536. ET: Paul, 146.
433. Sinópticos y Pablo, 546. ET: Paul, 151. The italics are Segundo's.

204 *The Faith that Works*

434. Sinópticos y Pablo, 548. ET: Paul, 152. The italics are Segundo's.
435. Sinópticos y Pablo, 557-558. ET: Paul, 157.
436. Sinópticos y Pablo, 303, n. 22; 304, n. 24. ET: Paul, 185, n. 22 and n. 24. Segundo is referring to the International Critical Commentary: A Critical and Exegetical Commentary on the Epistle to the Romans (Edinburgh: T. & T. Clark). The first edition was published by W. Sanday and A.C. Headlam in 1895; the later edition was published by C.E.B. Cranfield in 1975.
437. "I have nothing whatever to say against historical criticism. I recognize it, and once more state quite definitely that it is both necessary and justified. My complaint is that recent commentators confine themselves to an interpretation of the text which seems to me to be no commentary at all, but merely the first step towards a commentary. Recent commentaries contain no more than a reconstruction of the text, a rendering of the Greek words and phrases by their precise equivalents, a number of additional notes in which archaeological and philological material is gathered together, and a more or less plausible arrangement of the subject-matter in such a manner that it may be made historically and psychologically intelligible from the standpoint of pure pragmatism." Karl Barth, "Preface to the Second Edition," The Epistle to the Romans, translated from the Sixth Edition by Edwyn C. Hoskyns (London: Oxford University Press, 1933, 1968), 6.
438. Günther Bornkamm, Paul, translated by D.M.G. Stalker (New York: Harper & Row, 1971), 115. The italics are Bornkamm's.
439. Rudolf Bultmann, "*pisteuō, ktl.*," in Theological Dictionary of the New Testament, Volume VI, edited by Gerhard Friedrich, translated by Geoffrey W. Bromiley (Grand Rapids, Mich.: Wm. B. Eerdmans Publishing Company, 1968), 219.
440. C.K. Barrett, A Commentary on the Epistle to the Romans (New York: Harper & Row, 1957), 17, 30. The italics are Barrett's.
441. Ernst Käsemann, Perspectives on Paul, translated by Margaret Kohl (Philadelphia: Fortress Press, 1971), 74.
442. Krister Stendahl, Paul Among Jews and Gentiles (Philadelphia: Fortress Press, 1976), 27. The italics are Stendahl's. Stendahl is not the first to argue against the centrality of "justification" in Paul's theology. John Reumann notes (and rejects) the argument of some that "Paul came to use this vocabulary [*dikaiosynē*] and to make justification prominent only when he encountered 'the Judaizers' in Galatia (and elsewhere). . . . On this view, justification cannot be his chief theme, but merely one forced on him for a brief period of his ministry, in a polemical situation." Reumann, Righteousness in the New Testament (Philadelphia: Fortress Press, 1982), 41-42. Käsemann, in an essay entitled, "Justification and Salvation History in the Epistle to the Romans" places Stendahl's position in a trajectory of thought along with William Wrede, Albert Schweitzer, and F.C. Baur. Käsemann, Perspectives on Paul, 61.
443. Stendahl, Paul Among Jews and Gentiles, 27-28.

444. Käsemann, Perspectives on Paul, 75.
445. Stendahl, Paul Among Jews and Gentiles, 129-132.
446. Sinópticos y Pablo, 364, n. 11. ET: Paul, 196, n. 83.
447. Sinópticos y Pablo, 358, n. 6. ET: Paul, 195, n. 78. Cf. Stendahl, Paul Among Jews and Gentiles, 80, 14.
448. Sinópticos y Pablo, 473, n. 17. ET: Paul, 210, n. 167.
449. Sinópticos y Pablo, 364, n. 11. ET: Paul, 196, n. 83. Cf. Stendahl, Paul Among Jews and Gentiles, 16.
450. Sinópticos y Pablo, 546, n. 9. ET: Paul, 218, n. 223. The italics are Segundo's. It should be noted here that Stendahl's exegesis receives extensive recognition by Segundo, second only to the ICC commentators. Stendahl is also acknowledged for having provided "warm and affectionate help" during Segundo's stay as visiting professor at Harvard Divinity School. Liberación, 10. ET: Liberation, vii.
451. Manfred T. Brauch, "Perspectives on 'God's righteousness' in recent German discussion", in E.P. Sanders, Paul and Palestinian Judaism (Philadelphia: Fortress Press, 1977), 523-542. See also Günther Klein, "Righteousness in the New Testament", in Interpreter's Dictionary of the New Testament, Supplementary Volume (Nashville: Abingdon Press, 1976), 750-752.
452. Brauch, "Perspectives on 'God's righteousness'", 542.
453. See the chapter headings in the Contents of Käsemann's Commentary on Romans, translated by Geoffrey W. Bromiley (Grand Rapids, Mich.: Wm. B. Eerdmans Publishing Company, 1980), ix-xi.
454. Brauch, "Perspectives on 'God's righteousness'", 526-527.
455. Rudolf Bultmann, Theology of the New Testament, Volume 1 (New York: Charles Scribners' Sons, 1951), 314. The italics are Bultmann's.
456. Bornkamm, Paul, 136. The italics are Bornkamm's. For Bornkamm's discussion of "faith," see Ibid., 141-146.
457. Barrett, Romans, 74.
458. Karl Barth, Romans, 41-42, 91, et passim.
459. Ibid., 28.
460. Ibid., 38-39. See also Karl Barth, Church Dogmatics, IV/1, 620, where "faith" is defined as "humble obedience."
461. Karl Barth, Church Dogmatics, IV/1, 527.
462. Karl Barth, Church Dogmatics, Volume 2/1, The Doctrine of God (Edinburgh: T. & T. Clark, 1957), 148-149.
463. Markus Barth, Justification: Pauline Texts Interpreted in the Light of the Old and New Testaments, translated by A.M. Woodruff III (Grand Rapids, Mich.: Wm. B. Eerdmans Publishing Company, 1971), 12.
464. Ibid., 38-39, 53.
465. Ibid., 65.
466. Ibid., 68.

467. Käsemann, Romans, 93.
468. Ibid., 94.
469. Bornkamm, Paul, 147.
470. Käsemann, Romans, 95-96.
471. Käsemann, Perspectives on Paul, 83.
472. Ibid., 84.
473. Käsemann, Romans, 109.
474. Bultmann, Theology of the New Testament, Vol. 1, 283-284, 315-317. Bultmann is somewhat ambiguous, however, with regard to the relationship of grace and faith. On the one hand, Bultmann claims that Paul "never describes faith as inspired. Though the Spirit is given to the believer, *pistis* is not a gift of the Spirit." On the other hand, Bultmann notes that "Paul can certainly regard it as a gift (of God) that a congregation has come to believe;" and the discussion of "faith" properly follows the discussion of "grace." Bultmann, "*pisteuō, ktl.*", in Theological Dictionary of the New Testament, Volume VI, 219. Cf. also Bultmann, Theology of the New Testament, 288-314.
475. Käsemann, Romans, 111, 113. The italics are mine.
476. Käsemann, Perspectives on Paul, 89.
477. Ibid., 82. Käsemann is reluctant to speak of an "object" or "content" of faith here, "because the Lord who acts is here forced into a neutral category and thus into the dimension of what is at our disposal and can be replaced by something else." Ibid., 83.
478. Reumann, Righteousness in the New Testament, 55. Romans 3:21 and Galatians 2:16 use the phrase *dia pisteōs Iesou Christou.*
479. Karl Barth, Church Dogmatics, IV/1, 627-628. See also Hans Küng, Justification: The Doctrine of Karl Barth and a Catholic Reflection (Philadelphia: The Westminster Press, 1957, 1981), 79-81.
480. Karl Barth, Romans, 61-62. The italics are Barth's.
481. Markus Barth, Justification, 39. The italics are mine.
482. Ibid., 69-70.
483. Bultmann, Theology of the New Testament, Volume 1, 324.
484. Bultmann, "*pisteuō, ktl.*", in Theological Dictionary of the New Testament, Volume VI, 219.
485. Ibid., 225, 228.
486. Bornkamm, Paul, 153.
487. Ibid.
488. E.C. Blackman, "Faith, Faithfulness", in Interpreter's Dictionary of the Bible, Volume 2 (Nashville: Abingdon Press, 1962), 232.
489. Käsemann, Perspectives on Paul, 89.
490. Brauch, "Perspectives on 'God's righteousness'", 527.
491. Käsemann, Romans, 172, 175.

492. Georg Bertram, "*synergos, ktl.*", in Theological Dictionary of the New Testament, Volume VII, edited by Gerhard Kittel and Gerhard Friedrich, translated by Geoffrey W. Bromiley (Grand Rapids, Mich.: Wm. B. Eerdmans Publishing Company, 1971), 874-875. The noun is used thirteen times in the New Testament, twelve of them by Paul; the verb is used five times, three of them by Paul.

493. Georg Bertram, "*ergon*", in Theological Dictionary of the New Testament, Volume II, edited by Gerhard Kittel, translated by Geoffrey W. Bromiley (Grand Rapids, Mich.: Wm. B. Eerdmans Publishing Company, 1964), 649.

494. Reumann, Righteousness in the New Testament, 69-70. The italics are mine. The quoted text is from Käsemann, Romans, 56-57.

495. Reumann, Righteousness in the New Testament, 72. The italics are Reumann's.

496. Sanday and Headlam, Romans, 57.

497. Ibid. The italics are in the original text.

498. Käsemann, Romans, 57.

499. Ibid., 58.

500. Cranfield, Romans, 151. See also Reumann, Righteousness in the New Testament, 70.

501. Cranfield, Romans, 95.

502. Ibid. The italics are mine.

503. Sanday and Headlam, Romans, 38. The italics are mine.

504. Cranfield, Romans, 152.

Chapter 3

505. "Evangelio, política y socialismos: Documento de trabajo propuesto por los Obispos de Chile," in Documentos del episcopado: Chile 1970-1973 (Santiago: Mundo, 1974), 58-100. The English title here is by John Drury in Liberation, 130.

506. "Christian Faith and Political Activity: Declaration of the Chilean Bishops," in John Eagleson, translator and editor, Christians and Socialism: Documentation of the Christians For Socialism Movement in Latin America (Maryknoll, N.Y.: Orbis Books, 1975), 179-228.

507. Ibid., 183. The italics are mine.

508. Ibid., 216-217. The italics are in the text.

509. Ibid., 217. The italics are mine.

510. Segundo notes, "it is sad and almost embarrassing to find that the last document in that anthology was finally approved by the Chilean episcopate on September 13, 1973, *two days after* the military coup and Allende's own death. When their partisans were being persecuted and sometimes killed in the streets, the Chilean bishops were meeting to make some final observations on the

"Christians For Socialism" movement and to condemn them." Liberación, 148, n. 2. ET: Liberation, 152, n. 2. The italics are Segundo's.

Cardinal Raúl Silva Henríquez, the principal leader of the Catholic Church in Chile at this time, refused to condemn the hostile military takeover by the Junta and appeased the Junta on a number of occasions so that the Church might enjoy its benefits under the state with the hope of a quick return to civilian rule (which, of course, never happened). He was severely criticized for this position by several bishops in North America and Europe. Nevertheless, one of the persons who would speak a kind word in Cardinal Silva's defense was ironically Mrs. Allende, the President's widow: "Cardinal Silva Henríquez devoted himself constantly--just as Salvador Allende did--to avoiding civil war, and we all know how much he did to prevent it." Gary MacEoin, No Peaceful Way: Chile's Struggle For Dignity (New York: Sheed and Ward, Inc., 1974), 174-175.

Jürgen Moltmann notes, with disdain, the reaction of Protestant leaders who celebrated the overthrow of Allende as a victory over "satanic Marxism" in favor of the rule of the military junta. Moltmann, "An Open Letter to José Míguez Bonino," Christianity and Crisis 36, no. 5 (29 March 1976):62-63.
511. MacEoin, No Peaceful Way, 21.
512. Enrique Dussel, History and the Theology of Liberation: A Latin American Perspective, translated by John Drury (Maryknoll, N.Y.: Orbis Books, 1976), 106. In Chile, the Christian Democratic Party was formed in 1936. Ibid., 122.
513. Liberación, 106. ET: Liberation, 91.
514. Ibid.
515. *Rerum novarum* ("On the Condition of the Working Classes") became an official pronouncement by Leo XIII on May 15, 1891.
516. Liberación, 106-107. ET: Liberation, 92.
517. Liberación, 107. ET: Liberation, 92. The italics are mine.
518. Ibid.
519. Liberación, 107-108. ET: Liberation, 92-93.
520. Liberación, 108. ET: Liberation, 93.
521. Ibid.
522. Liberación, 109. ET: Liberation, 94.
523. Liberación, 109, 146. ET: Liberation, 94, 130.
524. MacEoin, No Peaceful Way, 58-76.
525. Liberación, 146-147. ET: Liberation, 130.
526. Liberación, 147. ET: Liberation, 130. The italics are mine.
527. For a more detailed critique of "third-way" approaches, see Liberación, 104-106. ET: Liberation, 90-91. See also Fe e ideología, 338-340. ET: Faith and Ideologies, 278-280, and 302, n. 3.
528. MacEoin, No Peaceful Way, 142-143, 156, 163, 172-173.

529. See MacEoin, <u>No Peaceful Way</u>; Paul M. Sweezy and Harry Magdorff, editors, <u>Revolution and Counter-Revolution in Chile</u> (New York: Monthly Review Press, 1974); and Lawrence Birns, editor, <u>The End of Chilean Democracy: An IDOC Dossier on the Coup and Its Aftermath</u> (New York: Seabury Press, 1974).

530. <u>Liberación</u>, 109. ET: <u>Liberation</u>, 94.

531. <u>Liberación</u>, 147. ET: <u>Liberation</u>, 130.

532. Ibid.

533. Ibid.

534. Segundo criticizes the bishops' document in three sources. His earliest, and most thorough, critique is the three-part series of articles entitled, "La iglesia chilena ante el socialismo," <u>Marcha</u> nos. 1558-1560 (27 August 1971 to 10 September 1971). His second critique is offered in "Capitalism-Socialism: A Theological Crux," <u>Concilium</u>, Vol. 96 (New York: Herder and Herder, 1974), 107-110. The third critique is in <u>Liberación</u>, 147-150. ET: <u>Liberation</u>, 130-133. While the critical approach is different in each source, the conclusions are consistent.

535. "Evangelio, política y socialismos," 65, 67, *et passim*.

536. Ibid., 65, *et passim*. The italics are in the text.

537. Ibid., 82. The italics are in the text.

538. <u>Liberación</u>, 147. ET: <u>Liberation</u>, 130.

539. In response to youth questioning the need for the Church "to speak, to define itself, to opt" in difficult socio-economic times, the bishops answer: "The Church is the people who have opted *absolutely* and *for all time* for the Gospel of the risen Christ: that is our *unique*, official and fundamental option, which conditions all the rest." "Evangelio, política y socialismos," 65. In response to questions raised about the Church's role in the face of poverty, the bishops answer: "The response of the Church in this matter is, at base, the same as always: she opts for the risen Christ, and therefore invites Christians to struggle for those socio-economic structures which will allow for making more effective all those *values* of personal and social liberation, of justice and love, contained in the Gospel." "Evangelio, política y socialismos," 67. The italics are theirs. For other references to this "unique option" of the Church, see "Evangelio, política y socialismos," 69, 71.

540. "La iglesia chilena ante el socialismo III," <u>Marcha</u> no. 1560 (10 September 1971): 19. The italics are Segundo's. Segundo is quoting from "Evangelio, política y socialismos," 61-62.

541. "La iglesia chilena ante el socialismo III," 19.

542. Ibid. Segundo is referring to the bishops' claim that "no option can be absolutized, intending to identify it--in a false messianic rage--with the full liberation of the human being which only Jesus Christ can promise and work." "Evangelio, política y socialismos," 70.

543. "La iglesia chilena ante socialismo III," 19. The italics are Segundo's.

544. "La iglesia chilena ante el socialismo I," Marcha no. 1558 (27 August 1971): 14. Segundo quotes the following text from the bishops' document: "It is not the Church but technology . . . which ought to determine the opportunity of a system and the guarantees of good use for Chile today." "Evangelio, política y socialismos," 65. Cf. also "La iglesia chilena ante el socialismo III," 19.

545. "La iglesia chilena ante el socialismo III," 19. Segundo quotes the bishops' text ("Evangelio, política y socialismos," 69): "We Christians have an obligation to conform to the Gospel as our supreme criterion and *common* option. . . . Therefore, remaining *united in our absolute and fundamental option* for the risen Christ, we can, in practice, arrive at different positions." Ibid. The italics are Segundo's.

546. "La iglesia chilena ante el socialismo III," 19.

547. Ibid.

548. Ibid. The italics are mine.

549. Liberación, 154-156. ET: Liberation, 136-137. The italics are Segundo's. See also C. Peter Wagner, Latin American Theology: Radical or Evangelical? (Grand Rapids, Mich.: Wm. B. Eerdmans Publishing Company, 1970), 21-66.

550. Liberación, 157. ET: Liberation, 138.

551. "Capitalism--Socialism: A Theological Crux," 108.

552. Ibid., 110. The italics are mine.

553. "La iglesia chilena ante el socialismo III," 19. Segundo cites the following as further evidence for his claim: "[In Vatican II,] faith in the Gospel does not carry an other-worldly focus toward salvation, but orients 'the mind toward *fully human* solutions' (Gaudium et Spes, para. 11). . . . For the [bishops'] document, the Church has the purpose of identifying itself with 'all the people of Chile;' for the Council, by contrast, the purpose of the Church is that of acting as a ferment in the mass of humanity (Gaudium et Spes, para. 40). . . . The possibility of opening oneself to the divine life, to the liberty of love, does not come precisely from the Gospel, but it is given by Christ 'to all human beings of good will,' *even though they may not be Christians* (Gaudium et Spes, para. 22); the Gospel does not call to some (those who believe it) to be something more than human, but from the beginning 'the supreme destiny of all human beings is one only, that is, divine' (Gaudium et Spes, para. 22)." Ibid. The italics are Segundo's.

554. Liberación, 151. ET: Liberation, 134.

555. Liberación, 152. ET: Liberation, 134.

556. Ibid. The italics are Segundo's.

557. "Evangelización y humanización: ¿progreso del reino y progreso temporal?", Perspectivas de Diálogo 5 (March 1970): 9-17.

558. Ibid., 9.

559. Ibid., 10.

560. Ibid., 12.
561. Ibid., 13-15.
562. Ibid., 16.
563. "La iglesia chilena ante el socialismo III," 19. See also "La iglesia chilena ante el socialismo II," Marcha no. 1559 (4 September 1971): 15; Liberación, 169. ET: Liberation, 148.
564. "La iglesia chilena ante el socialismo II," 15. The italics are Segundo's. Segundo is quoting from "Evangelio, política y socialismos," 65.
565. Eagleson, Christians and Socialism, 199. The italics are mine.
566. Liberación, 148. ET: Liberation, 131. The italics are mine.
567. Ibid. An example of this fear of threat to faith is evident in the critical remarks which the bishops made to "The Eighty," a group of priests committed to socialist ideology and the predecessor group to "Christians For Socialism." The priests affirmed: "The underlying reason for our commitment is our faith in Jesus Christ, which takes on depth and vitality and concrete shape in accordance with historical circumstances." The bishops responded: "We have always insisted, and we will continue to insist, that our priest abstain from taking partisan political positions in public. To act otherwise would be to revert to an outdated clericalism. . . ." Eagleson, Christians and Socialism, 3-4, 14.
568. "La iglesia chilena ante el socialismo II," 15.
569. Ibid.
570. Ibid. The italics are Segundo's. Segundo is quoting from "Evangelio, política y socialismos," 66.
571. Ibid.
572. Ibid. The italics are question marks are Segundo's. Segundo is quoting from "Evangelio, política y socialismos," 69.
573. Ibid. Cf. "Evangelio, política y socialismos," 69-70.
574. Ibid. Cf. also the support Segundo has for this concern in The Church in the Present-Day Transformation of Latin America in the Light of the Council, Vol. 2, Conclusions (Washington, D.C.: Division for Latin America, 1975), 61.
575. Liberación, 52. ET: Liberation, 43.
576. "La iglesia chilena ante el socialismo III," 24.
577. "La iglesia chilena ante el socialismo II," 15. Segundo cites the following biblical references: Matthew 23:1, 4, 13; Mark 4:10-12, *et passim*; and Matthew 10:34-36.
578. "Capitalism--Socialism: A Theological Crux," 110.
579. Liberación, 150. ET: Liberation, 133.
580. "La iglesia chilena ante el socialismo I," 12. The italics are Segundo's. Segundo is quoting from "Evangelio, política y socialismos," 74.

212   *The Faith that Works*

581. "La iglesia chilena ante el socialism I," 12. Segundo's reference to the "rich and happy" is taken from the bishops' document: "capitalism . . . has defined itself . . . as a method full of good intentions and promises, and [as] that [which] will make human beings richer and happier." "Evangelio, política y socialismos," 81.
582. "La iglesia chilena ante el socialismo I," 12.
583. Ibid.
584. Ibid.
585. Eagleson, Christians and Socialism, 96, 190-191, 227, n. 3. The bishops claimed that Segundo was a "spokesman for Christians For Socialism" (Christians and Socialism, 190). But Segundo declined the invitation to attend the "Christians For Socialism" convention. "Although he was sympathetic to the movement politically, Segundo judged that its theological foundations were deficient (via oral communication)." Alfred T. Hennelly, Theologies in Conflict, 174, n. 2.
586. "La iglesia chilena ante el socialismo I," 12. See "Evangelio, política y socialismos," 73. As it turned out, Allende would not be the "dehumanizing State" figure commonly associated with socialism by the Church. The Declaration of the Bishops in 1971 publicly acknowledges Allende's assurances "to respect and safeguard the rights of the religious conscience" even though they demonstrate a luke-warm reception: "We thank him for this cordial and considerate attitude, and we offer the same considerateness and cordiality in return." But these pronouncements appear hypocritical in light of the bishops' further declarations that caution against the evils of a Marxist socialism and chastise the early movements of what would eventually become "Christians For Socialism." Eagleson, Christians and Socialism, 12-15.
587. "La iglesia chilena ante el socialismo I," 12.
588. Ibid. The italics are Segundo's. The bishops' document is quoted by Segundo: "The influence of Marxism in Chilean socialism ought to be carefully taken into account to clear up in some measure the unknown [reality] . . . of the future development." See "Evangelio, política y socialismos," 73-74.
589. "La iglesia chilena ante el socialismo I," 12.
590. Ibid., 13.
591. Ibid. The italics are Segundo's. Segundo is quoting from "Evangelio, política y socialismos," 79. For the actual text of Marx, see his Critique of Political Economy (New York: International Publishers, 1970), 20-21.
592. "La iglesia chilena ante el socialismo I," 13.
593. Ibid. The quotation is from "Evangelio, política y socialismos," 79.
594. Ibid.
595. Liberación, 150. ET: Liberation, 133.
596. "La iglesia chilena ante el socialismo I," 13. The italics are Segundo's.

597. Ibid. The italics are Segundo's. Segundo is quoting from "Evangelio, política y socialismos," 76.

598. Ibid. Segundo is quoting from "Evangelio, política y socialismos," 77.

599. Liberación, 150. ET: Liberation, 133.

600. Ibid. The italics are mine.

601. Ibid. The translation is mine.

602. Liberación, 147. ET: Liberation, 130-131. The actual bishops' text is as follows: "the human being [in Marxist socialism] . . . is entirely subordinated to the necessity or conveniences of the process of production, reduced to the condition of means, turned into a slave of mass production and deprived of his dignity and of his full liberty as a person. . . . It is for this reason that concrete realizations of existing Marxist socialism up to now cannot be accepted as a *true alternative* before capitalism, since they remain exactly in the same materialist and economic sphere." "Evangelio, política y socialimos," 82. Segundo is aware of the abuses of Marxism, but he is more intent on exposing the bishops' underlying ideological preferences: "Suppose someone were to ask me, 'Are you totally in accord with Marxist thought?' I would answer, 'Certainly not.' 'Do you believe that the substance of this disagreement has grave importance?' 'Yes.' 'Do you not recognize in the experiences of Marxist socialism inhuman deviations?' 'Yes.' 'Then where is your problem with the document?' 'The most important differences have to do with the nuances, the accents, the universal attitude, for which all that interrogatory flows in the document, and in its conclusion, so clear, for those who read between the lines or for those who simply read with attention. Its message is: we should remain like we are.'" "La iglesia chilena ante el socialismo I," 14.

603. "La iglesia chilena ante el socialismo I," 14. See also "La iglesia chilena ante el socialismo II," 15.

604. Liberación, 149. ET: Liberation, 132.

605. Liberación, 150. ET: Liberation, 132.

606. "Christian Faith and Political Activity," in Eagleson, Christians and Socialism, 183.

607. Liberación, 143-144, 151. ET: Liberation, 126-127, 134. See also Eagleson, Christians and Socialism, 29.

608. The "Open Letter" appeared in Christianity and Crisis 36, no. 5 (29 March 1976):57-63. See note 6 above.

609. The key texts to which Moltmann specifically refers are those of Rubem Alves, A Theology of Human Hope (Washington, D.C.: Corpus Books, 1969), 55-68; Segundo, "Capitalism--Socialism: A Theological Crux;" José Míguez Bonino, Doing Theology in A Revolutionary Situation (Philadelphia: Fortress Press, 1975), 132-153; and Gustavo Gutiérrez, A Theology of Liberation (Maryknoll, N.Y.: Orbis Books, 1973), 213-250. Moltmann's references to Hugo Assmann (in "Open Letter," 57) concern Assman's

presentation at the Geneva conference of 1973, in which Assmann called for "incommunication" between Latin American Liberation Theology and European theology. Assmann did not mean to break off existing dialogue, but to emphatically challenge European theology to stop abusing Latin American theology by misunderstanding or down-playing its significance. See Archie LeMone, "When Traditional Theology Meets Black and Liberation Theology," Christianity and Crisis (17 September 1973):177-178.

610. Moltmann, "Open Letter," 58-59.

611. Ibid., 60.

6﹢2. Ibid.

613. Ibid.

614. Ibid. It is worth observing that a major difference between Alves' A Theology of Human Hope and Míguez Bonino's Doing Theology in A Revolutionary Situation is that the former is pre-Medellín and the latter is post-Medellín. However, this may still not address the larger substance of Moltmann's criticism.

615. Ibid., 60-61.

616. Ibid., 61.

617. Ibid.

618. Ibid., 61-62. Cf. also Arthur F. McGovern and Thomas L. Schubeck, "Updating Liberation Theology," America 159, no. 2 (16 July 1988): 33. Contrary to Moltmann's insinuation, Ismael Garcia maintains that Latin American theories of justice favor democratic socialism. See Ismael Garcia, Justice in Latin American Theology of Liberation (Atlanta: John Knox Press, 1987).

619. Ibid., 62.

620. The lecture was delivered in English to an audience at Regis College, Toronto, and was originally published in French in the French Jesuit review Etudes (September, 1984). It was later published in English in two other sources: under the title, "Two Theologies of Liberation," The Monthe (October, 1984): 321-327; and under the title, "The Shift Within Latin American Theology," Journal of Theology for Southern Africa 52, no. 3 (September, 1985): 17-29. An excellent summary of the article is provided by Phillip Berryman, Liberation Theology, 86-87.

621. "Two Theologies of Liberation," 321-323; "The Shift Within Latin American Theology," 17-22.

622. See Gustavo Gutiérrez, A Theology of Liberation (1973) and The Power of the Poor in History (Maryknoll, N.Y.: Orbis Books, 1983); Leonardo Boff, Jesus Christ Liberator (Maryknoll, N.Y.: Orbis Books, 1978) and Ecclesiogenesis (Maryknoll, N.Y.: Orbis Books, 1986); and Jon Sobrino, Christology at the Crossroads (Maryknoll, N.Y.: Orbis Books, 1978) and The True Church and the Poor (Maryknoll, N.Y.: Orbis Books, 1984).

623. "Two Theologies of Liberation," 321; "The Shift Within Latin American Theology," 17.

624. "Two Theologies of Liberation," 321; "The Shift Within Latin American Theology," 18.

625. Ibid.

626. Theology and the Church, 3, 74-75.

627. McGovern and Schubeck, "Updating Liberation Theology," 33. See also Peter Steinfels, "New Liberation Faith: Social Conflict is Muted," New York Times (27 July 1988): 2. The point is also conceded in part by Michael Novak, Will It Liberate?, 15.

628. "Two Theologies of Liberation," 324; "The Shift Within Latin American Theology," 23.

629. "Two Theologies of Liberation," 325, 323; "The Shift Within Latin American Theology," 25, 21.

630. Joel Zimbelman, "Theology, Christology and Ethics in the thought of Juan Luis Segundo, S.J.," unpublished presentation at the Society for Christian Ethics, Chicago, 1989.

631. "Two Theologies of Liberation," 325; "The Shift Within Latin American Liberation Theology," 24-26.

632. "Two Theologies of Liberation," 323; "The Shift Within Latin American Theology," 21-22. The italics are mine. See also the interesting accounts about Segundo in Phillip Berryman, Liberation Theology, 86-87, and Harvey Cox, Religion in the Secular City: Toward a Post-Modern Theology (New York: Simon and Schuster, 1984), 243-245.

633. Theology and the Church, 140.

634. Carl Braaten, for example, following Moltmann's lead, writes in The Apostolic Imperative, 32: "When Latin American theologians shift their attention from intellectual alliance with Marxist ideology to the popular religion of the poor, in order to work with the poor to motivate and structure their understanding of their faith and life, they will find their most useful point of contact in a theology of the cross. Perhaps then too they will find in Luther an ally, and therewith feel less the need to impose the rhetoric and slogans of Marxist ideology, which is an ideology made in Europe just as alien to the poor and oppressed peoples of Latin America as any other since colonial times."

635. Liberación, 158. ET: Liberation, 139. The italics are Segundo's. The German original of this statement may be found in an article by Moltmann entitled, "Gott in der Revolution," in Diskussion zur "Theologie der Revolution", edited by Ernst Feil and Rudolf Weth (München: Chr. Kaiser Verlag, 1969), 77.

636. "Capitalism--Socialism: A Theological Crux," 111. The italics are mine.

637. Ibid.

638. Liberación, 158. ET: Liberation, 139. Segundo adds: "All Christian churches contain an eschatological element, since our faith 'gives substance' to the things for which we hope (Heb. 11:1). And what we look forward to is the kingdom, or reign, of God." Ibid. Hennelly has noted definite similarities between Segundo and Moltmann in their understandings of ecclesiology, ideology, the Bible as a book in favor of the oppressed, and socialism as a "symbol of the liberation of man from the vicious circle of poverty." See Hennelly, Theologies in Conflict, 82, 84, 171, 172.

639. Liberación, 158, 161. ET: Liberation, 139, 142.

640. Liberación, 161. ET: Liberation, 141.

641. Iglesia, 33-37. ET: Church, 16-19.

642. Liberación, 161, 163, 164. ET: Liberation, 142, 143, 144. See also "Capitalism--Socialism: A Theological Crux," 113.

643. Liberación, 161. ET: Liberation, 142. The italics are Segundo's.

644. Ibid.

645. Liberación, 164, n. 22. ET: Liberation, 153, n. 22. See also "Capitalism--Socialism: A Theological Crux," 113. Segundo is not very specific here, but he may have the theology of Johann Baptist Metz and the early theology of Joseph Ratzinger. See "Capitalism--Socialism: A Theological Crux," 110-111, 112 and Masas y minorías, 55-56.

646. See, for example, Douglas Sturm's article on "Political Theology" in The Westminster Dictionary of Christian Ethics, 481-482, where he writes, "political theology is critical of other forms of theological method: traditional Thomism, with its doctrine of nature and natural law, is ahistorical; transcendental Thomism (Karl Rahner), with its turn toward the subject, is apolitical; *Lutheranism, with its two-kingdom theory and orders of creation, is dualistic and static*; modern Protestantism (Rudolf Bultmann), with its existential commitment, is individualistic." Sturm adds that the presuppositions of political theology find a basis in the Frankfurt School (Block, Adorno, Habermas).

647. Liberación, 163-164. ET: Liberation, 143-144. See also "Capitalism--Socialism: A Theological Crux," 113; Masas y minorías, 69.

648. Rudolf Weth, "'Theologie der Revolution' im Horizont von Rechtfertigung und Reich," in Diskussion zur "Theologie der Revolution", 94.

649. "Capitalism--Socialism: A Theological Crux," 112. The italics are Segundo's.

650. Liberación, 163. ET: Liberation, 143. The italics are Segundo's.

651. Liberación, 164, 158. ET: Liberation, 144, 139. See also "Capitalism--Socialism: A Theological Crux," 112. The italics are mine. Segundo is quoting from Moltmann, "Gott in der Revolution," 77. In the German original, the word translated "anticipation" is "*Vorwegnahme.*"

652. Jürgen Moltmann, Theology of Hope, trans. by James W. Leitch (New York: Harper and Row, 1965), 17-18. See also the following: "Faith, as an *anticipation* of the salvation of the whole, thus opens a future for the moral body, for society, and for nature--in short, for everything which still lies in anguish." Jürgen Moltmann, "Toward a Political Hermeneutics of the Gospel," in New Theology, No. 6, edited by Martin E. Marty and Dean G. Peerman (London: The Macmillan Company, 1969), 76. The italics are mine.

653. Ibid. The italics are Segundo's.

654. Masas y minorías, 67. The italics are Segundo's. Segundo is quoting from Weth, "'Theologie der Revolution' in Horizont von Rechtfertigung und Reich," 94-95. Cf. also Liberación, 164. ET: Liberation, 144. "Capitalism--Socialism: A Theological Crux," 112. The German words here for "analogy" and "analogical image" are *"Entsprechungen"* and *"gleichnisbedürftig,"* respectively.

655. Liberación, 164. ET: Liberation, 144. See also "Capitalism--Socialism: A Theological Crux," 112.

656. "Capitalism--Socialism: A Theological Crux," 110. Segundo is quoting from Metz, L'homme, Anthropocentrique chrétienne (Paris, 1971), 111. The italics are Segundo's from a citation of the text in Masas y minorías, 63-64.

657. Masas y minorías, 64. The italics are mine. Henri de Lavalette's quote (undocumented here by Segundo) is from his article, "La 'théologie politique' de Jean-Baptiste Metz," in Recherches de Sciences Religieuses 58, no. 3 (July-August, 1970), 340-341. The French word for "outline" here is *ébauche*.

658. "Capitalism--Socialism: A Theological Crux," 112.

659. Liberación, 164. ET: Liberation, 144. "Capitalism--Socialism: A Theological Crux," 112.

660. Moltmann, "Open Letter," 58.

661. Ibid.

662. Liberación, 166. ET: Liberation, 146.

663. Sinópticos y Pablo, 596, n. 5. ET: Paul, 213, n. 184. The italics are mine.

664. Carl E. Braaten, Justification: The Article on Which the Church Stands or Falls (Minneapolis: Augsburg/Fortress Press, 1990), 121.

665. "Capitalism--Socialism: A Theological Crux," 123. See Moltmann, "Open Letter," 58. The italics are mine.

666. Moltmann, "Open Letter," 58.

667. Liberación, 122-123. ET: Liberation, 106-107.

668. Liberación, 175. ET: Liberation, 154.

669. Ibid.

670. "Capitalism--Socialism: A Theological Crux," 118-119. The italics are mine.

671. Ibid., 120-121.

672. Ibid., 112.

673. Moltmann, "Open Letter," 58.
674. "Capitalism--Socialism: A Theological Crux," 123.
675. Liberación, 165. ET: Liberation, 145.
676. Liberación, 142. ET: Liberation, 126.
677. Ibid.
678. Liberación, 166. ET: Liberation, 145.
679. Liberación, 168. ET: Liberation, 147. The italics are mine.
680. "Capitalism--Socialism: A Theological Crux," 123. The italics are
mine.
681. Enrique Dussel, "Sobre la historia de la teología en América Latina," in
Liberación y cautiverio: Debates en torno al metodo de la teología en América
Latina, edited by E. Dussel (Mexico City: Comité Organizador, 1975), 58.
The period to which Dussel refers was the present period at the time of
Dussel's writing. It is distinguished from two earlier periods, identified as "the
period of preparation (1962-1968)" and the period of "the formulation of
'liberation theology' (1968-1972)." Ibid.
   Segundo also contributed to "Liberation and Captivity" conference at the
Latin American Center of Theology in Mexico, held in August, 1975.
Segundo contrasts the kind of theological reflection which took place in Latin
America prior to and during Medellín with the kind of theological reflection
in the more oppressive period after Medellín. See "Condicionamientos actuales
de la reflexión teológia en Latinoamérica," in Liberación y cautiverio, 91-101,
561-563. In later reflection, Segundo speaks of "three successive crises" in
Latin America between 1950-1975. "It was an intense and wide-ranging
experience, and the common denominator in the crises might well be described
as desperation or despair. In the first stage desperation surfaced and grew, in
the second stage it led to desperate actions, and in the third stage it gave way
to despairing passivity." Fe e ideología, 335. ET: Faith and Ideologies, 276.
682. Berryman, Liberation Theology, 97.
683. Ibid., 98-99.
684. Signs of the Times, 2. In this source, Hennelly claims these events took
place in 1971. However, in Theologies in Conflict, 51, Hennelly states that
1975 was the year of their suppression, and claims that "the Center was closed
by Segundo's religious superiors."
685. Signs of the Times, 62. This is from Hennelly's translation of Segundo's
"Derechos humanos, evangelización e ideología," Christus (November 1978):
29-35. See also Berryman, Liberation Theology, 117.
686. "Camilo Torres, sacerdocio y violencia," Vispera (May 1967): 71-75.
687. Fe e ideología, 348-352. ET: Faith and Ideologies, 285-289. This
position is reaffirmed in Theology and the Church, 130.
688. "Christianity and Violence in Latin America," Christianity and Crisis 28,
no. 3 (March 1968): 34.

689. Berryman, Liberation Theology, 1-3. We might add to that list the internationally-publicized slaying of Jesuit priests by right-winged military forces in El Salvador in November, 1989.

690. Norbert Greinacher, "'Liberation' from Liberation Theology? Motives and Aims of the Antagonists and Defamers of Liberation Theology," in The Church in Anguish: Has the Vatican Betrayed Vatican II?, edited by Hans Küng and Leonard Swidler (New York: Harper and Row, 1987), 146. Cf. also Berryman, Liberation Theology, 3-4.

691. Berryman, Liberation Theology, 1-3, 108.

692. Greinacher, "'Liberation' from Liberation Theology," in The Church in Anguish, 145. Cf. also the following articles from that anthology: Hans Küng, "Cardinal Ratzinger, Pope Wojtyla, and Fear at the Vatican: An Open Word after a Long Silence," 58-74; Hermann Häring, "Joseph Ratzinger's 'Nightmare Theology,'" 75-90. For a more sympathetic treatment of Ratzinger's theology, see Aidan Nichols, The Theology of Joseph Ratzinger: An Introductory Study (Edinburgh: T. & T. Clark, 1988), especially 241-291.

693. Greinacher, "'Liberation' from Liberation Theology," in The Church in Anguish, 145.

694. Joseph Cardinal Ratzinger with Vittorio Messori, The Ratzinger Report: An Exclusive Interview on the State of the Church, translated by Salvator Attanasio and Graham Harrison (San Francisco: Ignatius Press, 1985), 169. The text of the Instruction is reprinted by Segundo in Theology and the Church, 169-188.

695. Harvey Cox, The Silencing of Leonardo Boff: The Vatican and the Future of World Christianity (Oak Park, IL: Meyer-Stone Books, 1988), 3.

696. Ibid., 6; Berryman, Liberation Theology, 106-110.

697. The quote is by Vittorio Messori, the journalist who interviewed Cardinal Ratzinger in The Ratzinger Report, 17.

698. Messori, The Ratzinger Report, 17-18. Cox, in The Silencing of Leonardo Boff, 29-30, recounts Ratzinger's "spectacular accent: a noted scholar; a *peritus* at Vatican II; a founder of Concilium, the organ of the postconciliar 'progressives'; a respected professor of theology at Münster, Tübingen, and Regensburg; an editor of Communio, the 'rival' of Concilium; the bishop of Munich; and now the cardinal-prefect of the Congregation for the Doctrine of the Faith."

699. Messori, The Ratzinger Report, 30-31. The italics are in the text. For the entire discussion of Ratzinger's opinion of Vatican II, see The Ratzinger Report, 27-44.

700. Messori, The Ratzinger Report, 45. Cox also notes this introductory statement by Ratzinger to the section of The Ratzinger Report entitled, "At the Root of the Crisis: The Idea of the Church," and comments: "Both phrases in this sentence are crucial for understanding Ratzinger's diagnosis and the treatment he prescribes (and intends to administer). It is a false 'conception'

or 'model' of the church that is spreading. But the insidious part, he feels, is that the authentic and classical Catholic idea is not 'expressly rejected.' Herein lies the cunning of the disease germ and the difficulty of the prophylactic." Cox, The Silencing of Leonardo Boff, 84.

701. Messori, The Ratzinger Report, 49. The italics are mine. Cf. also J.K.S. Reid, "The Ratzinger Report," Scottish Journal of Theology 40, no. 1 (1987): 125-133.

702. Messori, The Ratzinger Report, 158.

703. Ibid., 169-190.

704. Ibid., 175. The italics are mine.

705. Ibid., 177. The italics are mine.

706. "Instruction," introduction, in Theology and the Church, 169.

707. Messori, The Ratzinger Report, 172.

708. Ibid., 177-182. These same two elements would surface in the "Instruction," VI, 10, in Theology and the Church, 176.

709. Ibid., 179, 180.

710. Ibid., 185-186.

711. Berryman, Liberation Theology, 188.

712. Theology and the Church, 8, 10, 13-14, 136.

713. Ibid., 15.

714. Ibid., 14.

715. Ibid., 21. The italics are Segundo's.

716. Ibid., 65.

717. Ibid., 22.

718. Ibid., 22-23.

719. Ibid., 23.

720. Ibid., 24.

721. "Instruction" VI, 10, in Ibid., 176.

722. Ibid.

723. "Instruction" VIII, 6, *et passim*, in Ibid., 179.

724. Segundo writes, "I do not feel that the second half of the document alludes to me." Ibid., 65.

725. Ibid., 96. The italics are Segundo's. See Segundo's very critical analysis of Marxism in Fe e ideología, 217-301. ET: Faith and Ideologies, 177-247; also Theology and the Church, 14-15.

726. Ibid., 98-105.

727. Ibid., 160-161, n. 22.

728. Messori, The Ratzinger Report, 177, 179-180; see also "Instruction," X, 8, in Theology and the Church, 183.

729. Theology and the Church, 3.

730. Ibid., 108-109.

731. Ibid., 110-118.

732. Ibid., 118-132.

733. Ibid., 132-137. Segundo discusses the issue of violence further in other writings. See especially Liberación, 177-205. ET: Liberation, 156-182; Fe e ideología, 343-352. ET: Faith and Ideologies, 282-289.
734. Ibid., 106.
735. Ibid., 91.
736. "Instruction," VI, 5 and IX, 3, in Theology and the Church, 176, 180. The italics are mine.
737. Ibid., 54. The italics are Segundo's.
738. Ibid., 66-67. The italics are Segundo's.
739. Ibid., 68. The italics are mine.
740. Ibid., 68-69. The italics are mine.
741. Ibid., 70. The italics are Segundo's.
742. Ibid., 70-71. The italics are Segundo's.
743. Ibid., 67.
744. "Instruction," Introduction, in Ibid., 169.
745. Ibid., 27-28.
746. Ibid., 28.
747. Ibid.
748. Ibid.; cf. also Ibid., 38.
749. Ibid., 29.
750. "Instruction," I, 1, in Ibid., 170.
751. Ibid., 31.
752. Messori, The Ratzinger Report, 177. The italics are mine.
753. Theology and the Church, 32.
754. Ibid., 46.
755. "Instruction," IV, 5, in Ibid., 173.
756. Ibid., 52.
757. Ibid., 53.
758. Ibid., 81, 136.
759. Ibid., 82.
760. Berryman, Liberation Theology, 193. The italics are mine.
761. Theology and the Church, 152-156.
762. Ibid., 156.

Chapter 4

763. Gracia, 204-207. ET: Grace, 142-144; Teología abierta, III: Reflexiones críticas (Madrid: Ediciones cristiandad, 1984), 225.
764. Iglesia, 9. ET: Church, ix.
765. Liberación, 9. ET: Liberation, 5.
766. Iglesia, 9. ET: Church, ix.
767. Liberación, 143. ET: Liberation, 127.
768. Gracia, 202. ET: Grace, 141.

769. Gracia, 200. ET: Grace, 140.
770. Ibid. The italics are Segundo's.
771. Gracia, 201. ET: Grace, 141.
772. Ibid.
773. Gracia, 202. ET: Grace, 141.
774. Ibid. The italics are mine.
775. Ibid.
776. Sinópticos y Pablo, 556, n. 18. ET: Paul, 221, n. 232.
777. Fe e ideología, 153. ET: Faith and Ideologies, 123; Sinópticos y Pablo, 385, n. 4. ET: Paul, 198, n. 96.
778. Gracia, 203. ET: Grace, 142.
779. Liberación, 172. ET: Liberation, 150. The translation and italics are mine.
780. Gracia, 204-205. ET: Grace, 142-143. The italics are Segundo's.
781. Gracia, 206. ET: Grace, 143-144. The italics are Segundo's.
782. Gracia, 206. ET: Grace, 144. Segundo may be thinking here of Hans Küng, Justification: The Doctrine of Karl Barth and a Catholic Reflection (Philadelphia: The Westminster Press, 1957, 1981). Interestingly, Segundo would have support for his contention in Barth's response to Küng (p. xl). See also El dogma que libera, 304, n. 18. ET: The Liberation of Dogma, 292, n. 18.
783. Gracia, 216. ET: Grace, 150.
784. Reflexiones críticas, 225, 227.
785. Gracia, 209. ET: Grace, 145-146. The italics are mine.
786. Gracia, 204, n. 2. ET: Grace, 150, n. 2. The italics are mine.
787. Gracia, 204, n. 3. ET: Grace, 150, n. 3. The italics are mine.
788. Gracia, 205, n. 4. ET: Grace, 151, n. 4.
789. Gracia, 205, n. 6. ET: Grace, 151, n. 6. The italics are mine.
790. Gracia, 204, n. 2. ET: Grace, 150, n. 2. The text of Bouillard in Karl Barth: Parole de Dieu et existence humaine (Paris: Aubier, 1957).
791. Liberación, 158. ET: Liberation, 139.
792. Gracia, 212-213, n. 12. ET: Grace, 151, n. 12.
793. Liberación, 159. ET: Liberation, 139-140.
794. Liberación, 159. ET: Liberation, 140.
795. Ibid.
796. Ibid. Segundo notes here the critical argument of Gustavo Gutiérrez, A Theology of Liberation, 63-77.
797. Ibid. The italics are Segundo's.
798. Ibid.
799. Liberación, 159-160. ET: Liberation, 140-141. The italics are Segundo's.
800. Liberación, 161. ET: Liberation, 141.
801. Gutiérrez, A Theology of Liberation, 69.

802. Liberación, 161. ET: Liberation, 141-142.
803. Liberación, 161. ET: Liberation, 142.
804. Ibid.
805. Ibid. Segundo borrows the concept of a "theology of history" from Harvey Cox, The Secular City, revised edition (New York: Macmillan, 1966), 91-95.
806. Liberación, 162. ET: Liberation, 142. The connection of "two kingdoms" and "two planes" is more explicit in the Spanish text.
807. "El possible aporte de la teología a protestante para el cristianismo latinoamericano en el futuro," Cristianismo y sociedad 8, no. 22 (1 October 1970): 41-49; "The Possible Contribution of Protestant Theology to Latin American Christianity in the Future," Lutheran Quarterly 22, no. 1 (February 1970): 60-69. See also El Dogma que libera, 301-307. ET: The Liberation of Dogma, 196-201.
808. Liberación, 162-163. ET: Liberation, 142-143. See also the critique of "two kingdoms" by José Míguez Bonino, Toward a Christian Political Ethics (Philadelphia: Fortress Press, 1983), 22-25.
809. Reflexiones críticas, 228, n. 2.
810. Liberación, 163. ET: Liberation, 143.
811. Masas y minorías, 9.
812. Karl Barth, Church Dogmatics, IV/1, The Doctrine of Reconciliation, 617.
813. Masas y minorías, 9.
814. Sinópticos y Pablo, 418. ET: Paul, 82.
815. Sinópticos y Pablo, 418, n. 5. ET: Paul, 202, n. 122. The italics are mine.
816. Sinópticos y Pablo, 418, 421. ET: Paul, 82, 83. The concept of "essential disproportion" is evident in rudimentary form in Gracia, 213. ET: Grace, 148.
817. Reflexiones críticas, 228.
818. Sinópticos y Pablo, 416. ET: Paul, 80-81. The italics are Segundo's.
819. Sinópticos y Pablo, 438. ET: Paul, 92. The italics are Segundo's.
820. Sinópticos y Pablo, 440. ET: Paul, 93.
821. Sinópticos y Pablo, 440-441. ET: Paul, 93.
822. Sinópticos y Pablo, 442, n. 27. ET: Paul, 206, n. 144. My translation.
823. Liberación, 161, n. 18. ET: Liberation, 153, n. 18.
824. Sinópticos y Pablo, 441, n. 26. ET: Paul, 206, n. 143. My translation. Segundo is quoting from the Spanish edition of Emile G. Léonard's Historie Générale du Protestantisme. Translation edition: Historia general del protestantismo (trad. cast. Ed. Península, Madrid, 1967), I, 161. In a later writing, Segundo refers to the translation as "deplorable." El Dogma que libera, 300, n. 14. ET: The Liberation of Dogma, 291, n. 14.
825. "Capitalism-Socialism: A Theological Crux," 122. The italics are mine.

826. Liberación, 163. ET: Liberation, 143. The italics are mine.
827. Ibid. The italics are mine.
828. "Capitalism-Socialism: A Theological Crux," 113.
829. Ibid., 122. The italics are mine.
830. Liberación, 172. ET: Liberation, 150. The italics are Segundo's. Segundo's is borrowing Erich Fromm's distinction of "freedom *from*" and "freedom *to*." See Erich Fromm, Escape from Freedom (New York: Avon, 1969), 56-156.
831. Sinópticos y Pablo, 507, n. 5. ET: Paul, 213, n. 184. The italics are mine.
832. Sinópticos y Pablo, 557, n. 19. ET: Paul, 221, n. 233. The italics are Segundo's. The reference is to Bultmann's Theology of the New Testament, Vol. I (New York: Charles Scribners', 1951), 4.
833. Sinópticos y Pablo, 506-507, n. 5. ET: Paul, 213, n. 184. Segundo's reference here is to Moltmann's "Open Letter to José Míguez Bonino," 57-63.
834. See El Dogma que libera, 301-307. ET: The Liberation of Dogma, 196-201. The Reformation is examined through the lens of Emile Léonard, Paul Tillich, Yves Congar and John A.T. Robinson.
835. "Capitalism--Socialism: A Theological Crux," 113; Masas y minorías, 69; Liberación, 164. ET: Liberation, 144.
836. Rudolf Weth, "'Theologie der Revolution' in Horizont von Rechtfertigung und Reich," 94.
837. See Ibid., 94, n. 30.
838. "Capitalism--Socialism: A Theological Crux," 113, n. 10; Masas y minorías, 68-69; Liberación, 164, n. 21. ET: Liberation, 153, n. 21.
839. On the theological differences between Barth and Luther, see Werner Elert, Law and Gospel, trans. Edward H. Schroeder (Philadelphia: Fortress Press, 1967); Robert W. Bertram, The Human Subject as the Object of Theology: Luther by Way of Barth, Ph.D. dissertation, University of Chicago, 1964; Alister E. McGrath, Iustitia Dei: A History of the Christian Doctrine of Justification, Volume II (London: Cambridge University Press, 1986), 170-184.
840. Christopher Morse, "Jürgen Moltmann," in A Handbook of Christian Theologians, enlarged edition, ed. Martin E. Marty and Dean G. Peerman (Nashville: Abingdon Press, 1984), 662.
841. Rubem Alves, A Theology of Human Hope (Washington, D.C.: Corpus Books, 1969), 61. See also Liberación, 165-166. ET: Liberation, 145.
842. The concepts of "strict" and "loose" here may come from Gregory Bateson. See Las cristologías, 849. ET: Evolutionary Approach, 38.
843. Karl H. Hertz, ed., Two Kingdoms and One World: A Sourcebook in Christian Social Ethics (Minneapolis: Augsburg Publishing House, 1976), 68-69, 160-163.

844. James S. Preus, "The Political Function of Luther's <u>Doctrina</u>," <u>Concordia Theological Monthly</u> 43, no. 9 (October 1972): 595-598.
845. Luther's treatise "Against the Robbing and Murdering Hordes of Peasants (1525)" is frequently quoted as evidence against Luther. But this needs to be read in the context of Luther's earlier treatise, "Admonition to Peace (1525)," and the treatise which followed, "An Open Letter on the Harsh Book Against the Peasants" (1525). <u>LW</u> 46, 3-85. See also Eric W. Gritsch, <u>Martin--God's Court Jester: Luther in Retrospect</u> (Philadelphia: Fortress Press, 1983), 59-60, 118; Hubert Kirchner, <u>Luther and the Peasants' War</u> (Philadelphia: Fortress Press, 1972); Mark U. Edwards, Jr., <u>Luther's Last Battles: Politics and Polemics, 1531-1546</u> (Ithica: Cornell University Press, 1983), 20-37.
846. Eric W. Gritsch and Robert W. Jenson, <u>Lutheranism: The Theological Movement and Its Confessional Writings</u> (Philadelphia: Fortress Press, 1976), 36. The phrase "the *article* by which the church stands or falls" is traced to Valentin E. Löscher's <u>Timotheus Verinus</u> (1712, 1718). Friedrich Loofs, "Der *articulus stantis et cadentis ecclesiae*," <u>Theologische Studien und Kritiken</u> 90 (1917): 344-345. Interestingly, Segundo also makes use of a variation of this phrase in reference to the gospel: "At first the cross seemed to be the most radical lie that history could give to the pretensions of a small community deprived of its leaders and defender. By the same token, the experiences of the risen Jesus constituted the most powerful confirmation that reality could offer a seemingly defeated and disrupted community. Here was a decisive article (*stantis aut cadentis ecclesiae*) if there ever was one in history. And whether we approve or disapprove, it was only natural that it would center the attention and preaching of the Christian community on a point other than the one that was central for Jesus himself." <u>Sinópticos y Pablo</u>, 280. ET: <u>The Historical Jesus of the Synoptics</u>, 185.
847. Robert W. Bertram, "Recent Lutheran Theologies on Justification by Faith: A Sampling," in <u>Justification by Faith, Lutherans and Catholics in Dialogue VII</u>, ed. H. George Anderson, T. Austin Murphy, and Joseph A. Burgess (Minneapolis: Augsburg Publishing House, 1985), 245.
848. <u>BoC</u>, 30, 48ff.
849. <u>BoC</u>, AC IV, 30.
850. J. M. Reu, <u>The Augsburg Confession, A Collection of Sources</u> (St. Louis: Concordia Seminary Press, 1966), 350-353, 359-360.
851. Robert Stupperich, "Die Rechtfertigungslehre bei Luther und Melanchthon 1530-1536," in <u>Luther and Melanchthon in the Theology of the Reformation</u>, ed. Vilmos Vatja (Göttingen: Vandenhoeck & Ruprecht, 1961), 79-81.
852. <u>BoC</u>, 107:2. The italics are mine. These two themes--the necessity of the crucified and risen Christ and the comforting of Christian consciences--are repeatedly echoed throughout the "Augsburg Confession" and the "Apology."
853. <u>BoC</u>, 292:1, 4. The italics are mine.

854. E. Gordon Rupp and Philip S. Watson, ed., Luther and Erasmus: Free Will and Salvation (Philadelphia: The Westminster Press, 1969), 51.
855. Ibid., 52-53.
856. Ibid., 25.
857. Ibid.
858. LW 33, 35. WA XVIII, 614:1ff. Weimar Edition citations from Luther's De servo arbitrio are provided because this is the one Luther source to which Segundo refers.
859. LW 33, 234-241. WA XVIII, 748-753.
860. LW 33, 164-206. WA XVIII, 702-730.
861. LW 33, 206-212. WA XVIII, 730-733.
862. LW 33, 186. WA XVIII, 716:25.
863. LW 33, 162. WA XVIII, 700:16f.
864. LW 33, 268. WA XVIII, 770:20f.
865. BoC, 150:287; 109:17ff.
866. LW 31, 53. The italics are mine.
867. LW 33, 237. WA XVIII, 750:5ff.
868. LW 33, 238. WA XVIII, 750:34f.
869. LW 33, 239. WA XVIII, 751:29f.
870. LW 33, 138. WA XVIII, 684:27f.
871. LW 33, 287. WA XVIII, 728:30ff. The italics are mine.
872. LW 45, 91.
873. LW 33, 139. WA XVIII, 685:5f. The concept of the "hidden God" is traced throughout Luther's theology by Walther von Loewenlich, Luther's Theology of the Cross, trans. Herbert J. A. Bouman (Minneapolis: Augsburg Publishing House, 1976), 27-49.
874. LW 33, 139. WA XVIII, 685:7ff.
875. LW 33, 39. WA XVIII, 616, n. 1.
876. LW 33, 190. WA XVIII, 719:4ff.
877. LW 33, 43. WA XVIII, 619:16ff.
878. LW 33, 292. WA XVIII, 785:28f.
879. LW 33, 291. WA XVIII, 784:36ff.
880. LW 33, 291-292. WA XVIII, 785:17ff. The italics are mine.
881. LW 33, 292. WA XVIII, 785:30f.
882. LW 33, 292. WA XVIII, 785:31ff.
883. LW 33, 292. WA 785:35ff. The italics are in the English translation.
884. LW 33, 289. WA XVIII, 783:17ff.
885. LW 33, 247. WA XVIII, 757:10ff.
886. LW 26, 6.
887. LW 33, 270. WA XVIII, 771:38.
888. LW 26, 6.
889. LW 26, 8. The italics are mine.
890. LW 26, 11. The italics are mine.

891. LW 33, 270. WA XVIII, 771:37f.
892. BoC 132:183; Concordia Triglotta (St. Louis: Concordia Publishing House, 1921), II, 172:62.
893. McGrath, Iustitia Dei, II, 17. McGrath quotes from WA 39, I:208.9-10: "*Duplex in scripturis traditur iustificatio, altera fidei coram Deo, altera operum coram mundo.*"
894. LW 26, 10.
895. LW, 26, 9.
896. LW 31, 298.
897. LW 26, 9.
898. LW 26, 277-278.
899. LW 26, 278.
900. LW 26, 280. Cf. LW 33, 290. WA XVIII, 784:14ff.
901. LW 26, 280. The italics are mine.
902. Ibid.
903. LW 26, 281.
904. LW 26, 281.
905. LW 26, 281.
906. LW 26, 281.
907. LW 26, 284, 278.
908. LW 26, 177.
909. LW 26, 288-289. The italics are mine.
910. LW 26, 288.
911. LW 26, 284.
912. LW 26, 284, 280, 278.
913. McGrath, Iustitia Dei, II, 12-13.
914. LW 26, 284.
915. McGrath, Iustitia Dei, II, 14.
916. Concordia Triglotta, II, 44:1; McGrath, Iustitia Dei, 24-25.
917. Robert W. Bertram, "'Faith Alone Justifies: Luther on *Iustitia Dei*," in Justification by Faith, 177.
918. LW 26, 227.
919. LW 26, 228. See also von Loewenlich, Luther's Theology of the Cross, 52-92. Loewenlich addresses the critical relationship of faith vis-à-vis all the human "points of contact" known to Luther: *synteresis* (conscience), understanding, reason, experience, and perception.
920. LW 26, 229.
921. LW 44, 23.
922. LW 26, 229. The italics are mine. See also BoC, 117:72.
923. Ibid.
924. LW 26, 230.
925. Ibid.
926. Ibid.

927. Ibid.

928. Ibid.

929. Ibid.

930. LW 26, 232.

931. LW 31, 298, 300.

932. LW 34, 176. The italics are mine.

933. LW 26, 11.

934. LW 35, 370-371. The italics are mine.

935. LW 26, 154-155.

936. LW 26, 284-285.

937. LW 26, 266.

938. LW 27, 29.

939. LW 31, 371. See also Sinópticos y Pablo, 441, n. 26. ET: Paul, 206, n. 143. Drury's translation notes that Bucer received the idea from Luther, but the Spanish text is not as clear on this point.

940. LW 26, 88.

941. BoC, 146:265. Concordia Triglotta, II, 196:144.

942. BoC, 112:35, 147:269.

943. BoC, 149:278.

944. LW 26, 155.

945. Ibid.

946. For an insightful discussion of Luther's struggle with the value of the book of James, see Johann Heinz, Justification and Merit: Luther vs. Catholicism (Berrien Springs, Mich.: Andrews University Press, 1981), 234-235.

947. BoC, 142:248.

948. BoC, 142:249.

949. BoC, 143:250. The italics are mine.

950.   Gritsch, Martin--God's Court Jester, 76; Stupperich, "Die Rechtfertigungslehre bei Luther und Melanchthon 1530-1536," 74, 76.

951. BoC, 107:1.

952. BoC, 117:73.

953. BoC, 126:136.

954. BoC, 132:184.

955. McGrath, Iustitia Dei, II, 58.

956. Ibid., 58-59.

957. Ibid., 61.

958. LW 33, 147-155. WA XVIII, 690-696. Luther also briefly addresses this subject matter in LW 33, 242. WA XVIII, 753:25ff.

959. LW 33, 150. WA XVIII, 692:20ff.

960. LW 33, 151. WA XVIII, 693:13ff.

961. LW 33, 152. WA XVIII, 693:38ff.

962. LW 33, 152. WA XVIII, 694:9ff.

Notes229

963. LW 33, 152-153. WA XVIII, 694:15ff.
964. LW 33, 153. WA XVIII, 694:17ff.
965. LW 33, 153. WA XVIII, 694:22ff.
966. LW 33, 154. WA XVIII, 695:9ff. The italics are mine.
967. LW 33, 154. WA XVIII, 695:11ff.
968. LW 33, 154. WA XVIII, 695:22ff.
969. LW 33, 155. WA XVIII, 695:28ff. The italics are mine.
970. LW 33, 242, WA XVIII, 753:23ff.
971. LW 33, 242. WA XVIII, 753:32f.
972. LW 33, 242. WA XVIII, 753:34f.
973. BoC, 536:77.
974. BoC, 534:65. The italics are mine.
975. This same point has also been made by Gerhard O. Forde, "The Viability of Luther Today: A North American Perspective," Word and World 7, no. 1 (Winter 1987): 22-31.

Chapter 5

976. Theology and the Church, 74-75. The italics are Segundo's. Segundo also expresses his gratitude for the "undeserved friendship" with his former professor Malevez.
977. Ibid., 75. The italics are mine.
978. Ibid. The italics are Segundo's. George H. Tavard refers to the Second Council of Orange as having adopted a position of "strict Augustinianism. According to canon 5, even the first movement of faith results from the Holy Spirit. There is an 'inspiration. . . which makes our will pass from infidelity to faith and from impiety to piety.'" Tavard, Justification: An Ecumenical Study (New York: Paulist Press, 1983), 24.
979. Theology and the Church, 75.
980. Ibid., 76. The italics are Segundo's.
981. Ibid.
982. Ibid.
983. Ibid. The italics are Segundo's.
984. Ibid., 162, n. 28.
985. Ibid., 76.
986. See Karl Rahner, Theological Investigations, Vol. 1, God, Christ, Mary and Grace (New York: Crossroad, 1961, 1982), 297-317. See also Iglesia, 35. ET: Church, 18.
987. Ibid., 75. The italics are Segundo's.
988. Karl Rahner and Herbert Vorgrimler, "Revelation," Dictionary of Theology, second edition (New York: Crossroad, 1981), 445.
989. Karl Rahner, Foundations of Christian Faith: An Introduction to the Idea of Christianity, trans. William V. Dych (New York: Crossroad, 1987), 126.

990. Iglesia, 36. ET: Church, 18. The italics are Segundo's.

991. Theology and the Church, 76. The italics are mine.

992. Segundo cites "Pertinent Conciliar Texts" as an Appendix in three of the Volumes in his early series on "An Open Theology for the Adult Laity." Gaudium et spes is cited 99 times (para. 22, twelve times; para. 39, 10 times); Lumen Gentium is cited 31 times; all other conciliar texts, 20 times. See Iglesia, 205-221. ET: Church, 139-149; Gracia, 249-275. ET: Grace, 176-193; and Los sacramentos hoy, 163-179. ET: The Sacraments Today, 124-137. See also Theology and the Church, 68, 74, 76-77, and 161, ns. 24 and 25. The Conciliar texts are reprinted in Flannery, Vatican Council II, Vol. 1, 350-426, 903-1001.

993. Flannery, Vatican Council II, 367.

994. Ibid.

995. Ibid., 367-368. The italics are mine.

996. Timothy F. Lull, "Anonymous Christianity," in The Westminster Dictionary of Christian Theology, ed. Alan Richardson and John Bowden (Philadelphia: The Westminster Press, 1983), 22-23.

997. Theology and the Church, 77.

998. Flannery, Vatican Council II, 918-922. This is a major theme for Segundo in Nuestra idea de Dios, 7-13, 225-230. ET: Our Idea of God, 3-11, 178-182.

999. Flannery, Vatican Council II, 922. The italics are mine.

1000. Ibid., 923-924. The italics are mine.

1001. Ibid., 924. The italics are mine.

1002. Gracia, 26. ET: Grace, 14. See also Gracia, 145-165. ET: Grace, 100-114.

1003. Gracia, 38-41. ET: Grace, 23-25. Segundo appeals here to Rahner's "The Theological Concept of Concupiscentia," Theological Investigations, Vol. 1, 347-382.

1004. Gracia, 44. ET: Grace, 27.

1005. Gracia, 39. ET: Grace, 23. The italics are mine.

1006. Gracia, 35, 98. ET: Grace, 21, 65.

1007. Gracia, 44-45. ET: Grace, 27.

1008. Gracia, 37. ET: Grace, 22.

1009. Ibid.

1010. Evolución y culpa, 11. ET: Evolution and Guilt, 6. The italics are mine.

1011. Flannery, Vatican Council II, 937-938. The italics are mine.

1012. See, e.g., Evolución y culpa, 20, 21, 36, et passim. ET: Evolution and Guilt, 15, 30, et passim. Of special importance to Segundo is Teilhard de Chardin's The Phenomenon of Man (New York: Harper and Row, 1959, 1975).

1013. Las cristologías, 936-943. ET: Evolutionary Approach, 93-98. Cf. also Hennelly, "Steps to a Theology of Mind," 30. Segundo, particularly in this later work, draws on the insights of Gregory Bateson as the necessary corrective to Teilhard de Chardin.

1014. Evolución y culpa, 32. ET: Evolution and Guilt, 22. The italics are Segundo's.

1015. Ibid. The italics are Segundo's.

1016. Ibid.

1017. Evolución y culpa, 33. ET: Evolution and Guilt, 22.

1018. Evolución y culpa, 33. ET: Evolution and Guilt, 23.

1019. Evolución y culpa, 34. ET: Evolution and Guilt, 23.

1020. Ibid. The italics are Segundo's.

1021. Ibid. The italics are Segundo's.

1022. Evolución y culpa, 36. ET: Evolution and Guilt, 24-25. The italics are mine.

1023. Evolución y culpa, 40. ET: Evolution and Guilt, 28.

1024. Evolución y culpa, 37-39. ET: Evolution and Guilt, 26-27.

1025. Evolución y culpa, 161-162. ET: Evolution and Guilt, 126.

1026. Evolución y culpa, 161. ET: Evolution and Guilt, 126.

1027. Sinópticos y Pablo, 416. ET: Paul, 80-81.

1028. Iglesia, 89-91. ET: Church, 56-57. The italics are Segundo's.

1029. Las cristologías, 806. ET: Evolutionary Approach, 12. The italics are Segundo's.

1030. Las cristologías, 806-807. ET: Evolutionary Approach, 12.

1031. Las cristologías, 807-808. Evolutionary Approach, 12-13.

1032. Las cristologías, 811-815. ET: Evolutionary Approach, 15-18.

1033. Las cristologías, 816. ET: Evolutionary Approach, 18.

1034. Iglesia, 90. ET: Church, 56. The italics are mine.

1035. Iglesia, 27. ET: Church, 11.

1036. Sinópticos y Pablo, 533, n. 35. ET: Paul, 216, n. 213. The italics are mine.

1037. Evolución y culpa, 161. ET: Evolution and Guilt, 126. The italics are mine.

1038. Las cristologías, 821-822. ET: Evolutionary Approach, 21-22. The italics are mine. The text is from Teilhard de Chardin, L'activation de l'energie (Paris: Ed. du Seuil, 1963), 80.

1039. Las cristologías, 826. ET: Evolutionary Approach, 24.

1040. Las cristologías, 829-830. ET: Evolutionary Approach, 26. The italics are Segundo's.

1041. Las cristologías, 854. ET: Evolutionary Approach, 41.

1042. Las cristologías, 887. ET: Evolutionary Approach, 62.

1043. Las cristologías, 892. ET: Evolutionary Approach, 65. The italics are Segundo's.

1044. Las cristologías, 803. ET: Evolutionary Approach, 10. The italics are Segundo's.
1045. Las cristologías, 892. ET: Evolutionary Approach, 66.
1046. Las cristologías, 854, *et passim*. ET: Evolutionary Approach, 41, *et passim*. The italics are Segundo's. The quote is from Teilhard de Chardin, The Phenomenon of Man, 71.
1047. Las cristologías, 895. ET: Evolutionary Approach, 67.
1048. Las cristologías, 933. ET: Evolutionary Approach, 91.
1049. Las cristologías, 933-934. ET: Evolutionary Approach, 91.
1050. Las cristologías, 934. ET: Evolutionary Approach, 91.
1051. Evolución y culpa, 167. ET: Evolution and Guilt, 131.
1052. Las cristologías, 957. ET: Evolution and Guilt, 107. The italics are mine.
1053. Las cristologías, 953, 956. ET: Evolutionary Approach, 104, 106. Segundo prefers the concept of "recapitulation" as more expressive of his point here than other New Testament concepts ("resurrection," "regeneration," "restoration").
1054. Hidden Motives, 115. See also Segundo, interview with Cabestrero, in Faith, 175-176.
1055. Hidden Motives, 115.
1056. See, e.g., 1 Cor. 15:58.
1057. Sinópticos y Pablo, 556. ET: Paul, 156.
1058. Las cristologías, 964. ET: Evolutionary Approach, 111. The italics are mine.
1059. Las cristologías, 966. ET: Evolutionary Approach, 112.
1060. Ibid.
1061. Ibid. The italics are Segundo's.
1062. Las cristologías, 967. ET: Evolutionary Approach, 113.
1063. Las cristologías, 969. ET: Evolutionary Approach, 114.
1064. Ibid.
1065. Las cristologías, 969-970. ET: Evolutionary Approach, 114. The italics are Segundo's.
1066. Las cristologías, 970. ET: Evolutionary Approach, 114. The italics are Segundo's.
1067. Las cristologías, 970. ET: Evolutionary Approach, 115.
1068. Ibid. The italics are Segundo's.
1069. Las cristologías, 973. ET: Evolutionary Approach, 117.
1070. Ibid. The italics are Segundo's.
1071. Las cristologías, 974. ET: Evolutionary Approach, 117.
1072. Las cristologías, 973. ET: Evolutionary Approach, 117.
1073. Las cristologías, 974. ET: Evolutionary Approach, 117.
1074. Las cristologías, 974. ET: Evolutionary Approach, 117-118.
1075. Las cristologías, 978. ET: Evolutionary Approach, 120.

1076. Sinópticos y Pablo, 310. ET: Paul, 16.
1077. Käsemann, Commentary on Romans, 38. The italics are mine.
1078. Barrett, The Epistle to the Romans, 36. The italics are mine.
1079. Bornkamm, Paul, 120. The italics are mine.
1080. Käsemann, Commentary on Romans, 38.
1081. Sinópticos y Pablo, 314. ET: Paul, 17.
1082. Sinópticos y Pablo, 314-315. ET: Paul, 18.
1083. Sinópticos y Pablo, 314, 321. ET: Paul, 18, 21.
1084. Sinópticos y Pablo, 314-315. ET: Paul, 18.
1085. Sinópticos y Pablo, 529. ET: Paul, 142.
1086. Käsemann, Commentary on Romans, 199; Barrett, The Epistle to the Romans, 150.
1087. Sinópticos y Pablo, 314, n. 8. ET: Paul, 187, n. 32.
1088. Gracia, 174. ET: Grace, 120.
1089. Sinópticos y Pablo, 393, n. 15. ET: Paul, 200, n. 107.
1090. Sinópticos y Pablo, 401. ET: Paul, 70.
1091. Sinópticos y Pablo, 394, 397. ET: Paul, 66, 68. The italics are Segundo's.
1092. Käsemann, Commentary on Romans, 118.
1093. Käsemann, Perspectives on Paul, 79. The italics are mine.
1094. See Käsemann, Commentary on Romans, 120.
1095. Käsemann, Perspectives on Paul, 84.
1096. Ibid., 89.
1097. Käsemann, Commentary on Romans, 294.
1098. Barrett, Epistle to the Romans, 204.
1099. Sinópticos y Pablo, 397-398. ET: Paul, 68.
1100. Sinópticos y Pablo, 418. ET: Paul, 82.
1101. Sinópticos y Pablo, 416, 548. ET: Paul, 80-81, 152.
1102. See Deuteronomy 5:1-21; 6:5; Luke 10:25-29; Matthew 19:16-22; Romans 7:4-6; 13:9-10.
1103. Barrett, The Epistle to the Romans, 114.
1104. Nygren, Commentary on Romans, 206.
1105. Käsemann, Commentary on Romans, 142-143.
1106. Ibid., 131.
1107. Sinópticos y Pablo, 421. ET: Paul, 83. The italics are mine.
1108. Sinópticos y Pablo, 422, n. 10. ET: Paul, 204, n. 127.
1109. Cranfield, The Epistle to the Romans, Volume 1, 269. See Sinópticos y Pablo, 412, n. 1. ET: Paul, 201, n. 118.
1110. Käsemann, Commentary on Romans, 141.
1111. Sinópticos y Pablo, 529. ET: Paul, 142.
1112. Sinópticos y Pablo, 529. ET: Paul, 142-143.
1113. Sinópticos y Pablo, 529. ET: Paul, 143.
1114. Sinópticos y Pablo, 530-531. ET: Paul, 143.

1115. Theology and the Church, 78.
1116. Ibid.
1117. Sinópticos y Pablo, 529. ET: Paul, 142.
1118. Iglesia, 115-119. ET: Church, 73-76. See also Liberación, 230-232. ET: Liberation, 203-205.
1119. Función, 5-27.
1120. Iglesia, 45-46. ET: Church, 24.
1121. Iglesia, 87. ET: Church, 53.
1122. Iglesia, 27. ET: Church, 11.
1123. Iglesia, 27. ET: Church, 11. The italics are Segundo's.
1124. Ibid. The italics are mine.
1125. Iglesia, 23-26. ET: Church, 8-10.
1126. Iglesia, 26. ET: Church, 10-11.
1127. See also David Hill, The Gospel of Matthew (London: Marshall, Morgan and Scott, 1972), 330.
1128. Hidden Motives, 140. The italics are mine.
1129. Berryman, Liberation Theology, 188. The italics are Berryman's.
1130. Moltmann, "An Open Letter to José Míguez Bonino," 58.
1131. Messori, The Ratzinger Report, 175.
1132. "Instruction," in Theology and the Church, 180.
1133. Theology and the Church, 67-68.
1134. "Evangelio, política y socialismos," 65, et passim.
1135. Función, 45.
1136. LW 33, 150. WA XVIII, 692:20ff. A noted homiletician has also warned of the dangers of "presupposing" the gospel in exhortation. See Richard R. Caemmerer, Preaching for the Church (St. Louis: Concordia Publishing House, 1959), 179-180, 185-189.
1137. BoC, "Apology," Article IV, 107:3. Concordia Triglotta, 120:3.
1138. "Fe e ideología," 228; Sinópticos y Pablo, 396. ET: Paul, 67; Fe e ideología, 15, 21. ET: Faith and Ideologies, 5, 8.
1139. Fe e ideología, 92-104. ET: Faith and Ideologies, 70-86.
1140. Fe e ideología, 15-19. ET: Faith and Ideologies, 5-7.
1141. Las cristologías, 854. ET: Evolutionary Approach, 41.
1142. Liberación, 118. ET: Liberation, 103.
1143. Sinópticos y Pablo, 416. ET: Paul, 80.
1144. Fe e ideología, 13-15. ET: Faith and Ideologies, 3-4; Liberación, 118. ET: Liberation, 103; "Fe e ideología," 227-228.
1145. Frederick A. Olafson, "Camus, Albert," in The Encyclopedia of Philosophy, Vol. 2, ed. Paul Edwards (New York: Macmillan, 1967), 16.
1146. Ibid.
1147. Fe e ideología, 169-177. ET: Faith and Ideologies, 136-142. Cf. also Jürgen Moltmann, Trinity and the Kingdom: The Doctrine of God, trans. Margaret Kohl (New York: Harper and Row, 1981), 191-222.

1148. Liberación, 14. ET: Liberation, 9.
1149. Liberación, 133. ET: Liberation, 116.
1150. Ibid.
1151. Liberación, 126. ET: Liberation, 110.
1152. Liberación, 139. ET: Liberation, 121.
1153. Liberación, 124. ET: Liberation, 108. The italics are mine.
1154. Liberación, 140. ET: Liberation, 122.
1155. Richard John Neuhaus, The Naked Public Square: Religion and Democracy in America, (Grand Rapids, Mich.: William B. Eerdmans Publishing Company, 1984), 228, 273-274, n. 2. While the point which Neuhaus makes is accurate, his posturing of the point is seriously weakened by his own failure to engage in any kind of "ideological suspicion."
1156. Hidden Motives, 115.

Conclusion

1157. Liberación, 171-173, 164, n. 22. ET: Liberation, 149-151, 153, n. 22.
1158. See Karl Rahner, "The Question of Justification Today," in his own work, Grace in Freedom (New York: Herder and Herder, 1969), 95-111. See also Anderson, et al., Justification by Faith: Lutherans and Catholics in Dialogue VII.
1159. Gerhard Ebeling, Luther: An Introduction to His Thought (Philadelphia: Fortress Press, 1972), 173-174.
1160. Gritsch and Jenson, Lutheranism, 179-180.
1161. Mark Thompson, "On Relating Justification and Justice," Word and World 7, no. 1 (Winter 1987): 10. The italics are mine.
1162. Richard Shaull, The Reformation and Liberation of Theology: Insights for the Challenge of Today (Louisville, Kentucky: Westminster/John Knox Press, 1991), 12.
1163. Walter Altmann, Luther and Liberation: A Latin American Perspective, trans. by Mary M. Solberg (Minneapolis: Fortress Press, 1992), ix.
1164. Elsa Tamez, The Amnesty of Grace: Justification by Faith from a Latin American Perspective, trans. by Sharon H. Ringe, (Nashville: Abingdon Press, 1993), 42.
1165. Michael Hoy, "The Courage to be Liberated," in A Crossings Celebration: Ed Schroeder and His Ministry (St. Louis: Greenhorn Productions and HomeLee Press, 1993), 53-64.
1166. On the identification of "love" with "justice," see Ismael Garcia, Justice in Latin American Theology of Liberation (Atlanta: John Knox Press, 1987), 99-102.
1167. Liberación, 171. ET: Liberation, 149-150.

Bibliography

I. Works by Segundo

Books

Segundo, Juan Luis, S.J. Acción pastoral latinoamericana: sus motivos ocultos. Buenos Aires: Búsqueda, 1972. ET: The Hidden Motives of Pastoral Action: Latin American Reflections. Translated by John Drury. Maryknoll, N.Y.: Orbis Books, 1978.

_____. Berdiaeff: Une réflexion chrétienne sur la personne. Paris: Motaigne, 1963.

_____. Concepción cristiana del hombre. Montevideo: Mimeográfica "Luz," 1964.

_____. La cristiandad, ¿una utopia? I. Los hechos. Montevideo: Mimeográfica "Luz," 1964.

_____. La cristiandad, ¿una utopia? II. Los principios. Montevideo: Mimeográfica "Luz," 1964.

_____. De la sociedad a la teología. Buenos Aires: Carlos Lohlé, 1970.

_____. El Dogma que libera: Fe, revelación y magisterio dogmático. Santander, Spain: Editorial Sal Terrae, 1989. ET: The Liberation of Dogma: Faith, Revelation, and Dogmatic Teaching Authority. Translated by Phillip Berryman. Maryknoll, N.Y.: Orbis Books, 1992.

_____. Esa comunidad llamada Iglesia. Buenos Aires: Carlos Lohlé, 1968. ET: The Community Called Church. Translated by John Drury. Maryknoll, N.Y.: Orbis Books, 1973.

_____. Etapas precristianas de la fe: Evolución de la idea de Dios en el Antiguo Testamento. Montevideo: Cursos de Complementación Cristiana, 1962.

_____. Evolución y culpa. Buenos Aires: Carlos Lohlé, 1972. ET: Evolution and Guilt. Translated by John Drury. Maryknoll, N.Y.: Orbis Books, 1974.

_____. Existencialismo, filosofía y poesía: Ensayo de sintesis. Buenos Aires: Espasa-Calpe, 1948.

_____. Función de la Iglesia en la realidad rioplatense. Montevideo: Barreiro y Ramos, 1962.

_____. Gracia y condición humana. Buenos Aires: Carlos Lohlé, 1968. ET: Grace and the Human Condition. Translated by John Drury. Maryknoll, N.Y.: Orbis Books, 1973.

_____. El hombre de hoy ante Jesús de Nazarét, Tomo I, Fe e Ideología. Madrid: Ediciones cristiandad, 1982. ET: Faith and Ideologies. Translated by John Drury. Maryknoll, N.Y.: Orbis Books, 1984.

_____. El hombre de hoy ante Jesús de Nazarét, Tomo II/1, Historía y actualidad: Sinópticos y Pablo. Madrid: Ediciones cristiandad, 1982. ET: The Historical Jesus of the Synoptics. Translated by John Drury. Maryknoll, N.Y.: Orbis Books, 1985. The Humanist Christology of Paul. Translated by John Drury. Maryknoll, N.Y.: Orbis Books, 1986.

_____. El hombre de hoy ante Jesús de Nazarét, Tomo II/2, Historía y actualidad: Las cristologías en la espiritualidad. Madrid: Ediciones cristiandad, 1982. ET: The Christ of the Ignatian Exercises. Translated by John Drury. Maryknoll, N.Y.: Orbis Books, 1987. An Evolutionary Approach to Jesus of Nazareth. Translated by John Drury. Maryknoll, N.Y.: Orbis Books, 1988.

_____. Liberación de la teología. Buenos Aires: Carlos Lohlé, 1975. ET: The Liberation of Theology. Translated by John Drury. Maryknoll, N.Y.: Orbis Books, 1976.

_____. Masas y minorías en la dialéctica divina de la liberación. Buenos Aires: La Aurora, 1973.

_____. Nuestra idea de Dios. Buenos Aires: Carlos Lohlé,

1970. ET: <u>Our Idea of God</u>. Translated by John Drury.
Maryknoll, N.Y.: Orbis Books, 1973.
_____. <u>Que es un cristiano</u>. Montevideo: Mosca Hnos. S.A.
Editores, 1971.
_____. <u>Los sacramentos hoy</u>. Buenos Aires: Carlos Lohlé,
1971. ET: <u>The Sacraments Today</u>. Translated by John Drury.
Maryknoll, N.Y.: Orbis Books, 1974.
_____. <u>Signs of the Times</u>. Edited by Alfred T. Hennelly, S.J.
Translated by Robert R. Barr. Maryknoll, N.Y.: Orbis Books,
1993.
_____. <u>Teología abierta</u>. I. <u>Iglesia-Gracia</u>. Madrid:
Ediciones cristiandad, 1983.
_____. <u>Teología abierta</u>. II. <u>Dios-Sacramentos-Culpa</u>.
Madrid: Ediciones cristiandad, 1983.
_____. <u>Teología abierta</u>. III. <u>Reflexiones críticas</u>. Madrid:
Ediciones cristiandad, 1984.
_____. <u>Theology and the Church: A Response to Cardinal
Ratzinger and a Warning to the Whole Church</u>. Translated by
John W. Diercksmeier. Minneapolis: Winston Press, 1985.

Articles and Public Addresses

Segundo, Juan Luis, S.J. "América hoy." <u>Vispera</u> 1 (October
1967): 53-57.
_____. "¿Autoridad o que?" <u>Perspectivas de Diálogo</u> 4
(December 1969): 270-272.
_____. "Camilo Torres, sacerdocio y violencia." Vispera 1
(May 1967): 71-75.
_____. "Capitalism-Socialism: A Theological Crux." In
<u>Concilium</u>, Vol. 96, <u>The Mystical and Political Dimension of the
Christian Faith</u>, ed. Claude Geffre and Gustavo Gutiérrez, 105-
123. New York: Herder and Herder, 1974.
_____. "Christ and the Human Being," <u>Cross Currents</u> 36
(Spring 1986): 39-67.
_____. "Christianity and Violence in Latin America."
<u>Christianity and Crisis</u> 28:3 (4 March 1968): 31-34.
_____. "The Church: A New Direction in Latin America."
<u>Catholic Mind</u> 65 (March 1967): 43-47.
_____. "La condición humana I." <u>Perspectivas de Diálogo</u> 2
(1967): 30-35.

_____. "La condición humana II." Perspectivas de Diálogo 2 (1967): 55-61.

_____. "Condicionamientos actuales de la reflexión teológica en latinoamerica." In Liberación y cautiverio: debates en torno al metodo de la teología en América Latina, 99-101. Mexico City: Comité Organizador, 1975.

_____. "A Conversation with Juan Luis Segundo, S.J." Interview with Teófilo Cabestrero. In Faith: Conversations with Contemporary Theologians, trans. Donald D. Walsh, 172-180. Maryknoll, N.Y.: Orbis Books, 1980.

_____. "Conversión y reconciliación en la perspectiva de la moderna teología de la liberación." Cristianismo y sociedad 13 (1975): 17-25.

_____. "Del ateísmo a la fe." Perspectivas de Diálogo 3 (April 1968): 44-47.

_____. "Derechos humanos, evangelización e ideología." Christus (November 1978): 29-35.

_____. "Desarrollo y subdesarrollo: Polos teológicos." Perspectivas de Diálogo 5 (May 1970): 76-80.

_____. "¿Un Dios a nuestra imagen?" Perspectivas de Diálogo 4 (March 1969): 14-18.

_____. "¿Dios nos interesa o no?" Perspectivas de Diálogo 3 (March 1968): 13-16.

_____. "Education, Communication, and Liberation: A Christian Vision." IDOC International: North American Edition, (13 November 1971): 63-96.

_____. "Las élites latinoamericanas: problemática humana y cristiana ante el cambio social." In Fe cristiana y cambio social en América Latina: Encuentro de El Escorial, 1972, 203-212. Salamanca: Sigueme, 1973.

_____. "Evangelización y humanización: ¿Progreso del reino y progreso temporal?" Perspectivas de Diálogo 5 (March 1970): 9-17.

_____. "Fe e ideología." Perspectivas de Diálogo 9 (November 1974): 227-233.

_____. "Hacia una exégesis dinámica." Vispera 1 (October 1967): 77-84.

_____. "¿Hacia una Iglesia de izquierda?" Perspectivas de Diálogo 4 (April 1969): 35-39.

_____. "Has Latin America a Choice?" America 120 (22

February 1969): 213-216.

_____. "Hipótesis sobre la situación de Uruguay: Algunas posibilidades de investigación." In Uruguay 67: Una interpretación, 11-32. Montevideo: Alfa, 1967.

_____. "La ideología de un diario católica." Perspectivas de Diálogo 5 (June-July 1970): 136-144.

_____. "La iglesia chilena ante el socialismo I." Marcha no. 1558 (27 August 1971): 12-14.

_____. "La iglesia chilena ante el socialismo II." Marcha no. 1559 (4 September 1971): 13.

_____. "La iglesia chilena ante el socialismo III." Marcha no. 1560 (11 September 1971): 19, 24.

_____. "Intellecto y salvación." In Salvación y construcción del mundo, 77-86. Barcelona: Editorial Nova Terra, 1967.

_____. "Interview with Juan Luis Segundo." Interview by Elsa Tamez. In Against Machismo, 3-10. Oak Park, IL.: Meyer-Stone Books, 1987.

_____. "Introducción." In Iglesia latinoamerica ¿protesta o profecia?, 8-17. Buenos Aires: Búsqueda, 1969.

_____. "El legado de Colón y la jerarquía de verdades cristianas." Miscelanea Comillas, Vol. 46, (1988): 107-127.

_____. "Un nuevo comienzo." Vispera 1 (August 1967): 39-43.

_____. "On a Missionary Awareness of One's Own Culture." Jesuit Missions Newsletter, (May 1974): 1-6.

_____. "Padre, Hijo, Espíritu: Una historia." Perspectivas de Diálogo 3 (May 1968): 71-76.

_____. "Padre, Hijo, Espíritu: Una libertad I." Perspectivas de Diálogo 3 (July 1968): 142-148.

_____. "Padre, Hijo, Espíritu: Una libertad II." Perspectivas de Diálogo 3 (August 1968): 183-188.

_____. "Padre, Hijo, Espíritu: Una sociedad." Perspectivas de Diálogo 3 (June 1968): 103-109.

_____. "Perspectivas para una teología latinoamericana." Perspectiva Teológica (January-June 1977): 9-25.

_____. "El poder del habito." Perspectivas de Diálogo 3 (May 1968): 90-92.

_____. "El posible aporte de la teología protestante para el cristianismo latinoamericano en el futuro." Cristianismo y Sociedad 8 (1970): 41-49.

_____. "The Possible Contribution of Protestant Theology to Latin American Christianity in the Future." Lutheran Quarterly 22 (February 1970): 60-69.

_____. "Preface." In Theologies in Conflict: The Challenge of Juan Luis Segundo, by Alfred T. Hennelly, xiii-xviii. Maryknoll, N.Y.: Orbis Books, 1979.

_____. "Profundidad de la gracia I." Perspectivas de Diálogo 2 (1967): 235-240.

_____. "Profundidad de la gracia II." Perspectivas de Diálogo 2 (1967): 249-255.

_____. "¿Que nombre dar a la existencia cristiana?" Perspectivas de Diálogo 2 (1967): 3-9.

_____. "Reconciliación y conflicto." Perspectivas de Diálogo 9 (September 1974): 172-178.

_____. "La revancha eclesiastica del Parido Nacional I." Marcha no. 1519 (13 November 1970): 7.

_____. "La revancha eclesiastica del Parido Nacional II." Marcha no. 1520 (20 November 1970): 12-13, 18.

_____. "Riqueza y pobreza como obstáculos al desarrollo." Perspectivas de Diálogo 4 (April 1969): 54-56.

_____. "Ritmos de cambio y pastoral de conjunto." Perspectivas de Diálogo 4 (July 1969): 131-137.

_____. "The Shift Within Latin American Theology." Journal of Theology for Southern Africa 52 (September 1985): 17-29.

_____. "Social Justice and Revolution." America 118 (27 April 1968): 574-577.

_____. "Statement by Juan Luis Segundo." In Theology in the Americas, ed. Sergio Torres and John Eagleson, 280-283. Maryknoll, N.Y.: Orbis Books, 1976.

_____. "Teilhard de Chardin." Unpublished paper. Montevideo: Uruguay (1975).

_____. "Teología: Mensaje y proceso." Perspectivas de Diálogo 9 (December 1974): 259-270.

_____. "Teología y ciencias sociales." In Fe cristiana y cambio social en América Latina: Encuentro de El Escorial, 1972, 285-295. Salamanca: Sigueme, 1973.

_____. "Theological Response to Talk on Evangelization and Development." Studies in the International Apostolate of Jesuits (November 1974): 79-82.

_____. "Two Theologies of Liberation." The Monthe

(October 1984): 321-327.

_____. "La vida eterna I." <u>Perspectivas de Diálogo</u> 2 (1967): 83-89.

_____. "La vida eterna II." <u>Perspectivas de Diálogo</u> 2 (1967): 109-110.

_____. "Wealth and Poverty as Obstacles to Development." In <u>Human Rights and the Liberation of Man</u>, ed. Louis M. Colonnese, 12-31. South Bend, Ind.: University of Notre Dame Press, 1970.

_____. "What Kind of Politics, if Any, Did Jesus Teach?" Unpublished presentation at University of Chicago (September 1978).

II. Additional Resources

Alves, Rubem. <u>A Theology of Human Hope</u>. Washington: Corpus Books, 1969.

Altmann, Walter. <u>Luther and Liberation</u>. Translated by Mary Solberg. Minneapolis: Augsburg Fortress, 1992.

Anderson, H. George, Murphy, T. Austin, and Burgess, Joseph A., ed. <u>Justification by Faith: Lutherans and Catholics in Dialogue VII</u>. Minneapolis: Augsburg Publishing House, 1985.

Barrett, C.K. <u>A Commentary on the Epistle to the Romans</u>. New York: Harper & Row, 1957.

Barth, Karl. <u>Church Dogmatics</u>. Volume 4/1. <u>The Doctrine of Reconciliation</u>. Translated by G.W. Bromiley. Edinburgh: T. & T. Clark, 1956.

_____. <u>The Epistle to the Romans</u>. Sixth Edition. Translated by Edwyn C. Hoskyns. Oxford: Oxford University Press, 1933, 1968.

Barth, Markus. <u>Justification: Pauline Texts Interpreted in the Light of the Old and New Testaments</u>. Translated by A.M. Woodruff III. Grand Rapids, Michigan: William B. Eerdmans Publishing Company, 1971.

Bateson, Gregory. <u>Steps to an Ecology of Mind</u>. New York: Ballentine Books, 1972.

Becker, Ernest. <u>The Denial of Death</u>. New York: Free Press, 1973.

Bell, Daniel. "Ideology." In <u>The Harper Dictionary of Modern Thought</u>, eds. Alan Bullock and Stephen Trombley, 404-405. New York: Harper & Row, 1977.

Bente, F. Historical Introductions to the Book of Concord. St. Louis: Concordia Publishing House, 1921, 1965.

Berryman, Phillip. Liberation Theology. Philadelphia: Temple University Press, 1987.

Bertram, Robert W. "'Faith Alone Justifies': Luther on Iustitia Fidei." In Justification by Faith: Lutherans and Catholics in Dialogue VII, ed. H. George Anderson, T. Austin Murphy, and Joseph A. Burgess, 172-184. Minneapolis: Augsburg Publishing House, 1985.

_____. "Liberation by Faith: Segundo and Luther in Mutual Criticism." dialog 27:4 (Winter, 1988): 268-276.

_____. "Recent Lutheran Theologies on Justification by Faith: A Sampling." In Justification by Faith: Lutherans and Catholics in Dialogue VII, ed. H. George Anderson, T. Austin Murphy, and Joseph A. Burgess, 241-255. Minneapolis: Augsburg Publishing House, 1985.

_____. The Human Subject as the Object of Theology: Luther by Way of Barth. Ph.D. diss., University of Chicago, 1964.

Birns, Lawrence, ed. The End of Chilean Democracy: An IDOC Dossier on the Coup and Its Aftermath. New York: Seabury Press, 1974.

Boff, Leonardo. Ecclesiogenesis: The Base Communities Reinvent the Church. Translated by Robert R. Barr. Maryknoll, N.Y.: Orbis Books, 1986.

_____. Jesus Christ Liberator. Translated by Patrick Hughes. Maryknoll, N.Y.: Orbis Books, 1978.

_____. Passion of Christ, Passion of the World. Translated by Robert R. Barr. Maryknoll, N.Y.: Orbis Books, 1987.

Bornkamm, Günther. Paul: Paulus. Translated by D.M.G. Stalker. New York: Harper and Row, 1971.

Børrensen, Kari Elisabeth. Subordination et equivalence, nature et role de la femme d'aprés, Augustin et Thomas Aquin. Oslo: Universitetsforlaget, 1968. ET: Subordination and Equivalence: The Nature and Role of Woman in Augustine and Thomas Aquinas. Washington, D.C.: University Press of America, 1981.

Bouillard, Henri. Karl Barth: Parole de Dieu et existence humaine. Paris: Aubier, 1957.

Bourke, Vernon J. "Thomas Aquinas, St." In The Encyclopedia of Philosophy, Vol. 8, ed. Paul Edwards, 105-116. New York: Macmillan, 1967.

Braaten, Carl E. Justification: The Article by Which the Church Stands or Falls. Minneapolis: Augsburg/Fortress, 1990.

_____. "Liberation Theology Coming of Age." dialog 27:4 (Fall 1988): 242.

_____. The Apostolic Imperative: Nature and Aim of the Church's Mission and Ministry. Minneapolis: Augsburg Publishing House, 1985.

Brauch, Manfred T. "Perspectives on 'God's righteousness.'" In Paul and Palestinian Judaism, ed. E.P. Sanders, 523-542. Philadelphia: Fortress Press, 1977.

Bultmann, Rudolf. Theology of the New Testament. Vol. I. Translated by Kendrich Grobel. New York: Charles Scribner's Sons, 1951.

Busch, Eberhard. Karl Barth: His Life from Letters and Autobiographical Texts. Translated by John Bowden. Philadelphia: Fortress Press, 1976.

Cabestrero, Teófilo, ed. Faith: Conversations with Contemporary Theologians. Translated by Donald D. Walsh. Maryknoll, N.Y.: Orbis Books, 1980.

Caemerrer, Richard R. Preaching for the Church. St. Louis: Concordia Publishing House, 1959.

Childress, James F. and Macquarrie, John, ed. The Westminster Dictionary of Christian Ethics. Philadelphia: The Westminster Press, 1986.

Concordia Triglotta. St. Louis: Concordia Publishing House, 1921.

Cone, James H. Black Theology and Black Power. New York: Seabury Press, 1969.

_____. A Black Theology of Liberation. Philadelphia: J.B. Lippincott Company, 1970.

Cox, Harvey. Religion in the Secular City: Toward a Post-Modern Theology. New York: Simon and Schuster, 1984.

_____. The Secular City. Revised edition. New York: Macmillan Company, 1966.

_____. The Silencing of Leonardo Boff: The Vatican and the Future of World Christianity. Oak Park, IL.: Meyer-Stone Books, 1988.

Cranfield, C.E.B. The International Critical Commentary: The Epistle to the Romans. 2 Vols. Edinburgh: T. & T. Clark, 1975, 1979.

Daly, Mary. Beyond God the Father. Boston: Beacon Press, 1973.

_____. The Church and the Second Sex. New York: Harper and Row, 1968.

Dussel, Enrique. History and the Theology of Liberation: A Latin American Perspective. Translated by John Drury. Maryknoll, N.Y.: Orbis Books, 1976.

_____. "Sobre la historia de la teología en America Latina." In Liberación y cautiverio: Debates en torno al metodo de la teología en America Latina, ed. Enrique Dussel, 19-68. Mexico City: Comite Organizador, 1975.

Eagleson, John, ed. Christians and Socialism: Documentation of the Christians for Socialism Movement in Latin America. Translated by John Drury. Maryknoll, N.Y.: Orbis Books, 1975.

Ebeling, Gerhard. Luther: An Introduction to His Thought. Philadelphia: Fortress Press, 1972.

Edwards, Jr., Mark U. Luther's Last Battles: Politics and Polemics, 1531-46. Ithica: Cornell University Press, 1983.

Elert, Werner. Law and Gospel. Translated by Edward H. Schroeder. Philadelphia: Fortress Press, 1967.

"Evangelio, politica y socialismos." In Documentos del episcopado: Chile 1970-1973, 58-100. Santiago: Mundo, 1974.

Ferm, Deane William. Third World Liberation Theologies: A Reader. Maryknoll, N.Y.: Orbis Books, 1986.

_____. Third World Liberation Theologies: An Introductory Survey. Maryknoll, N.Y.: Orbis Books, 1986.

Flannery, Austin, O.P., ed. Vatican Council II: The Conciliar and Post Conciliar Documents. Vol. 1. Collegeville, MN: Liturgical Press, 1975, 1984.

Forde, Gerhard O. "The Viability of Luther Today: A North American Perspective." Word & World 7:1 (Winter 1987): 22-31.

Freud, Sigmund. Civilization and Its Discontents. Translated and edited by James Strachey. New York: W.W. Norton and Company, 1961.

Fromm, Erich. Escape from Freedom. New York: Avon Books, 1941, 1969.

García, Ismael. Justice in Latin American Theology of Liberation. Atlanta: John Knox Press, 1987.

Greinacher, Norbert. "'Liberation' from Liberation Theology? Motives and Aims of the Antagonists and Defamers of Liberation Theology." In The Church in Anguish: Has the Vatican Betrayed

Vatican II?, ed. Hans Küng and Leonard Swidler, 144-162. New York: Harper and Row, 1987.

Gritsch, Eric W. Martin--God's Court Jester: Luther in Retrospect. Philadelphia: Fortress Press, 1983.

Gritsch, Eric W. and Jenson, Robert W. Lutheranism: The Theological Movement and Its Confessional Writings. Philadelphia: Fortress Press, 1976.

Gutiérrez, Gustavo. A Theology of Liberation. Translated and edited by Sister Caridad Inda and John Eagleson. Maryknoll, N.Y.: Orbis Books, 1973.

_____. The Power of the Poor in History. Translated by Robert R. Barr. Maryknoll, N.Y.: Orbis Books, 1983.

Häring, Hermann. "Joseph Ratzinger's 'Nightmare Theology'." In The Church in Anguish: Has the Vatican Betrayed Vatican II?, ed. Hans Küng and Leonard Swidler, 75-90. New York: Harper and Row, 1987.

Heinz, Johann. Justification and Merit: Luther vs. Catholicism. Berrien Springs, MI: Andrews University Press, 1981.

Hennelly, Alfred T. "Steps to a Theology of Mind." Presentation at American Academy of Religion, Currents in Contemporary Christology, Newsletter VIII, 2 (November 1988): 24-32.

_____. Theologies in Conflict: The Challenge of Juan Luis Segundo. Maryknoll, N.Y.: Orbis Books, 1979.

_____. "The Search for a Liberating Christology." Religious Studies Review 15:1 (January 1989): 45-47.

Hertz, Karl H., ed. Two Kingdoms and One World: A Sourcebook in Christian Social Ethics. Minneapolis: Augsburg Publishing House, 1976.

Hill, David. The Gospel of Matthew. London: Marshall, Morgan and Scott, 1972.

Hofstadter, Richard. Anti-Intellectualism in American Life. New York: Vintage Books, 1963.

Hoy, Michael. "The Courage to Be Liberated." In A Crossings Celebration: Ed Schroeder and His Ministry, 53-64. St. Louis: Greenhorn Productions and HomeLee Press, 1993.

_____. "Theses for Liberating the Dialogue between Lutherans and Liberationists." Currents in Theology and Mission 13:1 (February 1986): 38-41.

Justification and Justice. Statements, Presentations, and Responses from the Conference on Justification and Justice, Mexico City,

December 7-14, 1985. Several essays reprinted in Word and World 7:1 (Winter 1987).

Käsemann, Ernst. Commentary on Romans. Translated and edited by Geoffrey W. Bromiley. Grand Rapids, MI: William B. Eerdmans Publishing Company, 1980.

_____. Perspectives on Paul. Translated by Margaret Kohl. Philadelphia: Fortress Press, 1971.

Kirchner, Hubert. Luther and the Peasants' War. Philadelphia: Fortress Press, 1972.

Kittel, Gerhard, editor. Theological Dictionary of the New Testament. 10 Vols. Grand Rapids, MI: William B. Eerdmans Publishing Co., 1964-1976.

Küng, Hans. Justification: The Doctrine of Karl Barth and a Catholic Response. Philadelphia: The Westminster Press, 1981.

_____. "Cardinal Ratzinger, Pope Wajtyla, and Fear at the Vatican: An Open Word after a Long Silence." In The Church in Anguish: Has the Vatican Betrayed Vatican II?, ed. Hans Küng and Leonard Swidler, 58-74.

Lamb, Matthew L. Solidarity with Victims: Toward a Theology of Social Transformation. New York: Crossroad Publishing Company, 1982.

LeMone, Archie. "When Traditional Theology Meets Black and Liberation Theology," Christianity and Crisis 33 (17 September 1973): 177-178.

Lindermayer, Vivian. "Liberation theology here and now: where is it going? For whom does it speak?" Christianity and Crisis 49:9 (12 June 1989): 181.

Long, Jr., Edward LeRoy. A Survey of Recent Christian Ethics. New York: Oxford University Press.

Loofs, Friedrich. "Der articulus stantis et cadentis ecclesiae," Theologische Studien und Kritiken 90 (1917): 323-420.

Luther, Martin. Luther's Works. 55 Vols. Edited by Jaroslav Pelikan and Helmut T. Lehmann. St. Louis: Concordia Publishing House; and Philadelphia: Muhlenberg Press/Fortress Press, 1955ff.

_____. "De servo arbitrio, 1525." In D. Martin Luthers Werke: Kritische Gesemtausgabe, Band XVIII, 601-787. Weimar: Hermann Böhlaus Nachfolger, 1908.

MacEoin, Gary. No Peaceful Way: Chile's Struggle for Dignity. New York: Sheed and Ward, Inc., 1974.

Machoveč, Milan. A Marxist Looks at Jesus. Philadelphia: Fortress Press, 1976.

Mannheim, Karl. Ideology and Utopia. New York: Harcourt, Brace, Jovanovich, Harvest Book, 1936.

Marx, Karl. A Contribution to the Critique of Political Economy. New York: International Publishers, 1970.

McCann, Dennis P. "Political Ideologies and Practical Theology: Is There a Difference?" Union Seminary Quarterly Review 36:4 (Summer 1981): 243-257.

McGovern, Arthur F. and Schubeck, Thomas L. "Updating Liberation Theology." America 159:2 (16 July 1988): 32-47.

McGrath, Alister E. Iustitia Dei: A History of the Christian Doctrine of Justification. 2 Vols. London: Cambridge University Press, 1986.

Míguez Bonino, José. Doing Theology in a Revolutionary Situation. Philadelphia: Fortress Press, 1975.

_____. Toward a Christian Political Ethics. Philadelphia: Fortress Press, 1983.

Minear, Paul S. The Obedience of Faith: The Purpose of Paul in the Epistle to the Romans. London: SCM Press, 1971.

Miranda, José Porfirio. Marx and the Bible: A Critique of the Philosophy of Oppression. Maryknoll, N.Y.: Orbis Books, 1974.

Moltmann, Jürgen. The Church in the Power of the Spirit. Translated by Margaret Kohl. New York: Harper and Row, 1977.

_____. The Crucified God. Translated by R. A. Wilson and John Bowden. New York: Harper & Row, 1974.

_____. "Gott in der Revolution." In Diskussion zur "Theologie der Revolution", ed. Ernst Feil and Rudolf Weth, 65-81. München: Chr. Kaiser Verlag, 1969.

_____. "An Open Letter to José Míguez Bonino." Christianity and Crisis 36:5 (29 March 1976): 57-63.

_____. Theology of Hope. Translated by James W. Leitch. New York: Harper & Row, 1967.

_____. "Toward a Political Hermeneutics of the Gospel." In New Theology, No. 6, ed. Martin E. Marty and Dean G. Peerman, 66-90. New York: The Macmillan Company, 1969.

_____. Trinity and the Kingdom: The Doctrine of God. Translated by Margaret Kohl. New York: Harper and Row,

1981.

Morse, Christopher. "Jürgen Moltmann." In A Handbook of Christian Theologians, ed. Martin E. Marty and Dean G. Peerman, 660-676. Nashville: Abingdon Press, 1984.

Nessan, Craig. "Liberation Praxis: Challenge to Lutheran Theology." dialog 25:2 (Spring 1986): 124-128.

Neuhaus, Richard John. The Naked Public Square: Religion and Democracy in America. Grand Rapids, MI: William B. Eerdmans Publishing Co., 1984.

Nichols, Aidan, O.P. The Theology of Joseph Ratzinger. Edinburgh: T. & T. Clark, 1988.

Novak, Michael. Will it Liberate? Questions About Liberation Theology. New York: Paulist Press, 1986.

Novum Testamentum Graece. Edition XXVI. Edited by Eberhard Bibelgesellschaft, 1898, 1979.

Nygren, Anders. Commentary on Romans. Philadelphia: Fortress Press, 1949.

Olafson, Frederick A. "Camus, Albert." In The Encyclopedia of Philosophy, Vol. 2, ed. Paul Edwards, 15-18. New York: Macmillan, 1967.

Pannenberg, Wolfhart. Jesus--God and Man. Philadelphia: Westminster Press, 1977.

Persaud, Winston D. "The Article of Justification and the Theology of Liberation." Currents in Theology and Mission 16:5 (October 1989): 361-371.

Preus, James S. "The Political Function of Luther's Doctrina." Concordia Theological Monthly 43:9 (October 1972): 591-599.

Rahner, Karl. Foundations of Christian Faith: An Introduction to the Idea of Christianity. Translated by William V. Dych. New York: Crossroad, 1987.

_____. Grace in Freedom. New York: Herder and Herder, 1969.

_____. Theological Investigations. Vol. 1. God, Christ, Mary and Grace. Translated by Cornelius Ernst. New York: Crossroad Publishing Company, 1982.

_____. Theological Investigations. Vol. 2. Man in the Church. Baltimore: Helicon, 1963.

Rahner, Karl, and Vorgrimler, Herbert. "Revelation." In Dictionary of Theology, 44-49. Second edition. New York: Crossroad, 1981.

Ratzinger, Joseph Cardinal, with Messori, Vittorio. The Ratzinger

Report: An Exclusive Interview on the State of the Church. Translated by Salvator Attanasio and Graham Harrison. San Francisco: Ignatius Press, 1985.

Reid, J.K.S. "The Ratzinger Report." Scottish Journal of Theology 40:1 (1987): 125-133.

Reu, J.M. The Augsburg Confession: A Collection of Sources. St. Louis: Concordia Seminary Press, 1966.

Reumann, John. "Righteousness" in the New Testament: "Justification" in the United States Lutheran-Roman Catholic Dialogue. Philadelphia: Fortress Press, 1982.

Richardson, Alan, and Bowden, John, eds. The Westminster Dictionary of Christian Theology. Philadelphia: The Westminster Press, 1983.

Roberts, Alexander, and Donaldson, James, eds. The Ante-Nicene Fathers, Vol. 1, 23-30. Grand Rapids, MI: William B. Eerdmans Publishing Co., 1987.

Rondet, H. The Grace of Christ: A Brief History of the Theology of Grace, 398-418. New York: Newman Press, 1966.

Rupp, E. Gordon and Watson, Philip S. Luther and Erasmus: Free Will and Salvation. The Library of Christian Classics. Ichthus Edition. Philadelphia: The Westminster Press, 1969.

Sanday, William and Headlam, Arthur. The International Critical Commentary: The Epistle to the Romans. Edinburgh: T. & T. Clark, 1895.

Shaull, Richard. The Reformation and Liberation Theology. Louisville: Westminster/John Knox Press, 1991.

Sobrino, Jon, S.J. Christology at the Crossroads. Translated by John Drury. Maryknoll, N.Y.: Orbis Books, 1978.

_____. The True Church and the Poor. Translated by Matthew J. O'Connell. Maryknoll, N.Y.: Orbis Books, 1984.

Steinfels, Peter. "New Liberation Faith: Social Conflict Is Muted." New York Times (27 July 1988): 2.

Stendahl, Krister. Paul Among Jews and Gentiles, and Other Essays. Philadelphia: Fortress Press, 1976.

Stupperich, Robert. "Die Rechtfertigungslehre bei Luther und Melanchthon 1530-1536." In Luther and Melanchthon in the Theology of the Reformation, ed. Vilmos Vatja, 73-88. Goettingen: Vandenhoeck and Ruprecht, 1961. Reprinted by Muhlenberg Press, Philadelphia.

Sweezy, Paul M. and Magdorff, Harry, eds. Revolution and

Counter-Revolution in Chile. New York: Monthly Review Press, 1974.

Tambasco, Anthony Joseph. Juan Luis Segundo and First-World Ethics: The Bible for Ethics. Lanham, MD: University Press of America, 1981.

Tamez, Elsa. Against Machismo. Oak Park, IL: Meyer-Stone Books, 1987.

_____. The Amnesty of Grace: Justification by Faith from a Latin American Perspective. Nashville: Abingdon Press, 1993.

Tappert, Theodore G., trans. and ed. The Book of Concord: The Confessions of the Evangelical Lutheran Church. Philadelphia: Fortress Press, 1959.

Teilhard de Chardin, Pierre. The Phenomenon of Man. Translated by Bernard Wall. New York: Harper & Row, 1957.

The Church in the Present-Day Transformation of Latin America in Light of the Council. Vol. 1. Position Papers. Bogatá, Columbia: CELAM, 1970.

The Church in the Present-Day Transformation of Latin America in Light of the Council. Vol. 2. Conclusions. Washington, D.C.: Division for Latin America--USCC, 1973.

The Interpreter's Dictionary of the Bible. 5 Vols. Nashville: Abingdon Press, 1962, 1976.

Thompson, Mark. "On Relating Justification and Justice." Word and World 7:1 (Winter 1987): 6-11.

Tillich, Paul. The Dynamics of Faith. New York: Harper and Row, 1957.

_____. "Rechtfertigung und Zweifel." Offenbarung und Glaube, Band 8, Gesammelten Werke, 85-100. Stuttgart: Evangelisches Verlagswerke, 1970.

Tracy, David. Blessed Rage for Order: The New Pluralism in Theology. New York: Seabury Press, 1975.

von Loewenich, Walter. Luther's Theology of the Cross. Translated by Herbert J.A. Bouman. Minneapolis: Augsburg Publishing House, 1976.

Wagner, C. Peter. Latin American Theology: Radical or Evangelical? Grand Rapids, MI: William B. Eerdmans Publishing Co., 1970.

Waite, Mary. A Warning to All Friends. Los Angeles: William Andrews Clark Memorial Library, University of California, 1979.

Weber, Max. The Protestant Ethic and the Spirit of Capitalism. Translated by Talcott Parsons. London: Unwin Paperbacks,

1976.

Weth, Rudolf. "'Theologie der Revolution' in Horizont von Rechtfertigung und Reich." In <u>Diskussion zur "Theologie der Revolution"</u>, ed. Ernst Feil and Rudolf Weth, 82-109. München: Chr. Kaiser Verlag, 1969.

Zimbelman, Joel. "Theology, Christology, and Ethics in the Thought of Juan Luis Segundo, S.J." Unpublished presentation at Society for Christian Ethics, Chicago, 1988.

Index

I. Author Index

Alves, Rubem, xvii
Barrett, C.K., 63, 157, 159, 160
Barth, Karl, 49, 64, 66, 67, 117, 122, 124-125
Barth, Markus, 64-65, 66, 67
Bateson, Gregory, xix, xx, 11
Bertram, Robert W., ix, xiii
Bornkamm, Günther, 62, 157
Boff, Leonardo, xvii, 39-40, 102
Braaten, Carl E., ix, xiii, xix, 97
Bultmann, Rudolph, 33, 62, 64, 68, 106
Cone, James, xvi
Cranfield, C.E.B., 61, 70-71
Daly, Mary, xvi
Dussel, Enrique, xvii, 100
Freud, Sigmund, xx
Fromm, Erich, xx
Gutiérrez, Gustavo, xvii, xviii, 91
Hennelly, Alfred T., xiii, xvii, 33
Käsemann, Ernst, 63-71, 157, 159
Luther, Martin, xiii-xxiv, 94-95, 113-141
Machoveč, Milan, xx, 11, 167
Malevez, Leopold, 144-146
Marx, Karl: xix, xx, 11-12, 167
Metz, Johann Baptist, 96
Míguez Bonino, José, xvii, 90
Miranda, José Porfirio, xvii, xix
Moltmann, Jürgen, 90-91, 93, 95, 97-99, 165
Nessan, Craig, xix
Novak, Michael, xix
Pannenberg, Wolfhart, 8-9
Rahner, Karl, 94, 118, 145-148
Ratzinger, Joseph, 21-22, 101-104, 106, 109-111, 165
Sanday, W. and Headlam, A., 61, 69
Segundo, Juan Luis: correspondence, x; life, xvii, 175-179; *See also Subject Index.*
Sobrino, Jon, xvii, 91
Stendahl, Krister, 63
Teilhard de Chardin, Pierre, xix, xx, 15-16, 21, 150-152

Tillich, Paul, 29, 119
Tracy, David, 9-10
Wagner, C. Peter, 80
Weth, Rudolf, 94-95, 124

II. Subject Index

Abraham: as example of
    anthropological faith
    (Segundo), 47-49, 159; as
    example of righteousness
    (Luther), 134-135
Allende, Salvador, 75, 77-78,
    86, 207-208
antithetical parallel, 49-53,
    120, 131-133, 135, 141,
    160-161
Augsburg Confession, 126-
    127, 134, 137
biblical theology, 32-33, 167-
    169
Bucer, Martin, 122, 136
Camus, Albert: xx; *Caligula*,
    3-5, 167
central thesis, xxiii, 2, 31
    passim
Chilean bishops, 74-89, 165
Christian Democratic Party,
    75-78
Christians For Socialism, 74,
    89, 211
christology, xxi, 40, 197
concupiscence, 42-43, 150
Congregation for the Doctrine
    of Faith, 101-102, 104-110,
    165
cooperators, human beings as,
    x, 56-61, 138-140, 141,
    153, 166

ecclesiology: Chilean bishops,
    79-84; Congregation for the
    Doctrine of Faith, 103-104;
    Segundo, 14-23, 163-166
Epistle of James, 38, 137
evangelization, xxi-xxiii
evolutionary categories, xix-
    xx, 150-153
faith: anthropological, 23-24,
    47-49, 152, 166-167;
    beginning, 26, 145, 150;
    Christian, 53-60, 168;
    definition, 3-4; and
    fundamental trust, 8-9; and
    ideologies, 1-2 passim;
    justification by, 45-49, 62-
    64, 120-123, 126-127; as
    passive, 122, 133, 141;
    referential witnesses and, 4-
    6; and religion, 8, 9-10;
    religious, 23-25; and
    righteousness of, 64-67,
    133-138; stages of, 195-196;
    work of, 67-71, 135-138
free choice (free will), 127-129
gospel: good news, xxi-xxiii,
    40-41, 168; preparation for
    the, 25
oppression, 100-102
grace, theology of: Malevez,
    144-145; problems with,
    158-169; Rahner, 145-148;

Segundo, 94, 118-119, 148-151

Hegel, 45-46

hermeneutic circle, 32-34

ideology: definition, 6; and failure, 6-7; and faith, 1-2 passim; Marxist, 11-12, 189-190; and reason, 11; and science, 11

liberation theology: black theology, xv-xvi; and Congregation, 104, 108; definition, xv, xviii; feminist theology, xvi; and political theology, 90-91, 93-100; shift in Latin American, 91-93; Third world theology, xvi-xvii

love: and faith, 20, 26; worthwhile, xxii, 26-28 passim

Lutheran theology, 173-174

Marxism: in Chile, 85-89; and Congregation, 104-106; Marxist praxis, xviii-xix; Marxist thought, 11-13, 194; masses and minorities in, 21; and capitalism, 75-78; and violence, 106

methodology, 2-13, 166-169

revelation, 19, 34-38, 151

Ricouer, Paul, 1, 33

salvation: church mission and, 16-19, 164

St. Paul: baptism, 54-55; divided being, 55-56; epistle to the *Romans*, 32, 39, 41-61; exegetical analysis, 61-71, 156-162; gospel of, 41,

61; justification by faith, 45-49; reconciliation, 49-53; stages of development, 197-198; Segundo's appeal to, 38-39, 154-156; understanding of sin, xix, 41-45, 156-158; victory over sin, 56-60

Trent, Council of, 116-117

two kingdoms 117-120, 125, 129, 141

works righteousness (Pelagianism), 26, 46, 165, 169

Vatican II, 107-108, 110-111, 118-119, 146

About the Author

Michael Hoy is currently Assistant Professor of Religion and Humanities at Capital University's Adult Degree Program in Dayton, Ohio. He has a Doctorate of Theology degree in the field of Theology and Ethics from Lutheran School of Theology at Chicago. He also holds a Master of Divinity degree from Christ Seminary-Seminex and a Master of Theology from Lutheran School of Theology at Chicago. His academic interests have focused on the relationship of Lutheran theology to the confessing movements and challenges of the contemporary age, including liberation theology. He is an ordained pastor of the Evangelical Lutheran Church in America.